TOMCAT RIO

TOMCAT RIO

A Topgun Instructor on the F-14 Tomcat
and the Heroic Naval Aviators Who Flew It

DAVE "BIO" BARANEK

Skyhorse Publishing

10 9 8 7 6 5 4 3 2 1

Library of Congress Cataloging-in-Publication Data is available on file.

Cover design by Mona Lin
Cover photo credit: Digital illustration by Dorian Dogaru

Print ISBN: 978-1-5107-4822-4
Ebook ISBN: 978-1-5107-4823-1

Printed in China.

The appearance of U.S. Department of Defense visual information does not imply or constitute endorsement.

To my beautiful wife, Laura.

BONUS FREE RESOURCES

This book comes with bonus free resources: private video interviews on my experiences flying in the Tomcat and instructing at Topgun, photos not used in the book, and more.

To gain access, register via the form on this web page https://fightson.net/bio/?utm_source=book

From time to time, you'll also receive emails sharing new articles, videos, and photos. If this is not of interest, you can easily unsubscribe.

TABLE OF CONTENTS

INTRODUCTION

Welcome to the real world of the F-14 Tomcat and the US Navy fighter squadrons that flew it! Exhilarating catapult launches…6.5-g dogfights against F-16s…reviewing the work of petty officers for a major inspection…briefing at midnight for a 2 AM launch…watching Iranian airspace, knowing I could launch a missile at a hostile target up to one hundred miles away…and later, responsibility for three hundred people…barhopping with squadronmates in Key West…watching the fireball from a 1,000-pound bomb we just dropped.

You get the idea.

This is my third book. In the other two I was in more structured environments: Naval Aviation training, junior officer in my first squadron, instructor at the now-famous Topgun school. This time I'm in an environment that I can shape to a greater extent, on the ground and in the air. New freedoms, new consequences, new risks, new adventures.

You've opened this book, you're reading this page—you must have an affinity for Naval Aviation, or for flying stories in general. So do I! The one you're holding is not just about a career. It's also a tribute to the Grumman F-14A Tomcat.

When designed and introduced, the Tomcat was the Navy's replacement for the F-4 Phantom II, which embodied the term "a legend in its own time." No one knew Tomcats would serve for more than 30 years and become legendary on their own. We were proud to fly them and confident in their effectiveness, and it is an honor to contribute to the Tomcat's legacy. But, I don't whitewash the story: I'll talk about system failures and challenges associated with keeping these jets flying.

Yes, some of these stories celebrate the Tomcat's versatility and impressive capabilities and mention my own abilities, which were the product of years of training and experience, supported by my personal commitment. But some of these stories spring from questionable decisions or less-than-optimum situations—events that made the biggest impression on my memory. Among hundreds of incident-free flights, moments like these are a part of almost any aviation experience. Naval Aviation, where an emphasis on safety has produced an incredible reduction in mishaps over the past fifty years, still presents a variety of circumstances that for an author is the gift that keeps on giving.

As I wrote this book, I thought about the many squadronmates, officer and enlisted, with whom I shared these experiences, but didn't happen to be involved in one of the stories. If you're one of those great people, I hope you'll see yourself in this book and take pride in your service to this great nation.

So get into your flight gear, strap in, and … one more thing:

Fly Navy!

CHAPTER 1

1,000-POUND MISSILE

"FOX 3!"

Trying to control the excitement in my voice, I transmit the code words. My left thumb presses a red button marked LAUNCH. And one second later a mighty AIM-54 Phoenix missile drops from the belly of the F-14 Tomcat fighter. I can almost feel the plane's relief as its half-ton, million-dollar hitchhiker roars away with its tail on fire and its radar nose sniffing out the target ahead.

I'd said those two words hundreds of times during my five years in the back seat of an F-14, flying as a RIO, a radar intercept officer. But those were training shots; nothing came off the jet. Before today, "Fox 3" meant I had targeted the adversary and could have punched the red button as a role-playing "enemy" jet streaked toward me, our two speeds adding up to a closure rate of 800 mph, maybe 1,000, maybe more. In the debriefing afterwards, the code would serve as a marker as we reconstructed the action.

Not today. This time it's totally different.

I'm flying with Jeff "Moon" Mullen, a lieutenant with three years in Tomcats, one of the junior pilots in Fighter Squadron 2 (VF-2 in Navy terms). I'm also a lieutenant, but a "mid-level" officer because it's my second tour of duty in a fleet F-14 squadron. Moon is easygoing and unassuming, but very serious about his job. This missile exercise, called "missilex," is a workout for me as RIO, but he's as focused as I am.

I'm Bio. My last name rhymes with "bionic," but that got shortened to Bio and it stuck.

We're in airspace designated for live missile launches, about 150 miles west of Los Angeles, with nothing

below but the empty Pacific Ocean. Range control makes very sure that no other aircraft strays into the airspace. No ships or boats, either.

We've arrived early and are orbiting at 300 knots until the C-130 Hercules cargo plane gets here with our target. We're shooting at a drone—unmanned, of course; it's a live missile exercise. There's a detailed schedule, and everyone is very professional—they do this all the time—but my internal clock is running about double speed as the drama builds.

Now the C-130 arrives and turns south. You know the feeling: all is running smoothly, something's about to happen—but when? We're calmly circling, circling—and suddenly the intercept controller lights the fuse: "C-130 is steady, heading one-four-zero. Bullet two-zero-five, your contact is three-one-seven at seventy-two miles. Red range. Recorders on."

I reply, "Two-zero-five coming left to three-one-zero. Red range."

The "red range" means don't launch the missile yet; the Hercules with people in it is still in the danger zone. So we start the run with a long setup of 72 nautical miles. My system is working perfectly, and as we turn northwest a symbol appears on my radar display. Its bearing and distance match the call from our controller, so I know it's the C-130. I'm building a decision matrix, and this correlation is a key element.

We're level now, at 20,000 feet. We accelerate to 450 knots—that's a mile in about twelve seconds—with a live AIM-54A Phoenix strapped to our belly. We know the deadly Phoenix can fly—and kill—from farther away than any other air-to-air missile of its day, but today's shot will be only twelve miles, so the missile will use its brain more than its legs. Our missilex is designed to check out some of the exotic moves this world-class weapon can do. Can it punch through an enemy's radar jamming? We'll see.

We're racing toward the launch point when a voice from the C-130 alerts us. "Stand by for launch. Target away!" A new symbol pops up on my display as the old symbol—the C-130—high-tails it for shore.

Back on land, omniscient in his range control center, a radar controller sees all, knows all, and calmly updates us all. "Green range," he says as the C-130 flees the scene. "Bullet two-zero-five you are cleared to arm, cleared to fire. Target bearing three-two-zero at fifty-two miles, heading one-four-five."

Now it's Moon on the intercom: "Master Arm on, Bio. AIM-54 selected. Looking good up here," he says. We haven't said much in these few minutes, but we're both on the same page. In the F-14 Tomcat, the pilot flips the master arm switch to enable a weapons launch. Master arm—what a great name for a switch!

"Two-zero-five, green range," I confirm. "Contact three-two-two at fifty." Slightly different number from the controller's call, but things changed quickly.

The target accelerated after launch, and now its speed combined with ours adds up to a closure of 1,000 knots; that's one nautical mile in less than four seconds. But it's way below us, flying as planned at only 100 feet above the water. The information on my radar confirms that I'll have to manage a three-dimensional intercept. "Moon, come right to three-four-zero," I tell him. The pilot flies the plane, but in an intercept, the RIO runs the show.

We're closing fast. At 30 miles, here it comes; the target is trying to jam my system, confusing it with a barrage of radar gibberish. I can see it on my display, and I push a button to counter it. We trained for this in simulators, and I'm glad we did, because out here there will be no do-overs. This is the real thing: real target, real Tomcat, real missile.

Well, not quite. Our missile's 135-pound warhead has been replaced with a telemetry package for today's event. This is a test shot and the engineers want all the data they can get.

"Twenty miles, start the descent," I say. Moon points the nose down ten degrees, as we practiced. It actually feels steeper than it sounds.

Things are happening fast now. I check and recheck the essentials: radar and switch settings, intercept angles and speeds and altitudes, and the letters PHA for "Phoenix, AIM-54A" glowing on the Weapon Selected display. As planned, we're in a 10-degree dive, because the target is far below us. Suddenly my red Launch button lights up; the weapons system is telling me we've closed to a valid launch distance. The button is located in a low corner of the instrument panel, but it gets my attention. At 13 miles I tell Moon to stand by. A heartbeat later I punch the button. "Fox 3!"

It takes one second for the airplane to tell the missile everything it needs to know. Then powerful explosive charges blow the missile off its rail. As it leaves the plane, I add, "Op away," a standard radio call for a missilex, to let controllers know it's on its way.

The big Phoenix falls free for a few feet, then the rocket motor fires. My brain is at hyper-speed. I recheck the displays and switches. And finally I let myself look outside. Over Moon's shoulder I see the fearsome missile roar away, trailing a vivid orange flame. It rises above our nose for a moment, then dives and speeds away.

If the human brain has a "save" folder, that brief video clip went straight into it. Those fleeting seconds are surely one of the coolest sights of my entire career! Here's my camera, brought along for just such a moment, but I didn't even try for a photo. The one in my head is enough.

Moon eases the dive, and we level off around 2,000 feet. He rolls to the right a little so we can both see the action. The target is streaming a tail of smoke to help us spot it, and the Phoenix is scribing its own smoky signature. In a few seconds the missile has dusted off the drone. I see a slow-motion eruption of flame, but that's only in my mind. In the real world it's just a close fly-by.

"Oh! That was good!" Moon yells.

"Intercept," says Range Control, calm and professional. I can almost hear him yawn. Then he vectors us to two other jets that have already shot at their targets, and we join up and go home to Miramar. Below us, the Phoenix goes for a swim, having sent its precious data and done its job well. Our target drone pops its parachute and turns on its radio beacon, to be recovered and used again. Jammer, smoke, parachute—those target drones are impressive little machines!

Back on the ground, Range Control tells us that our missile zipped past the target with a scant six feet to spare. Given a warhead and proximity fuse, scrap metal would have rained into the Pacific today.

Today? This adventure was on a sunny afternoon in March 1988. Moon and I had carefully prepared for that flight. We'd "flown" the mission at Miramar in computer-driven simulators, detailed mockups of the F-14 Tomcat's front and rear cockpits. I'd flown in real Tomcats for more than five years, so the simulators that would have thrilled any kid were, to me, well, boring. But once we started practicing the profile for our missilex, I put on my game face.

This was the Cold War era, and our forces had already seen how Soviet aircraft could send out false signals to fool a missile's radar and kick it off course. I had to learn to recognize an unusual pattern on my radar scope and route the info to the missile, while controlling the radar intercept to get us into firing position. Moon and I had to work as a team, and the payoff was that scant six feet. No boom, no flame—but hey, six feet at a thousand miles an hour! In the air, as

we confidently approached launch range, I was happy we'd run those boring simulators.

We almost got the real boom and flame that day. The day was a two-fer; we took off that morning carrying an AIM-9 Sidewinder with a live warhead to shoot down, for real this time, an unmanned QF-86 target. It was an obsolete F-86 fighter, the once-awesome Sabre jet from the 1950s, and despite its years, its shining silver finish was gorgeous.

We got into position to take the shot several times, but our cockpit display showed we were outside the launch envelope, and we didn't want to screw up. We later learned that the missilex planners wanted us to shoot outside the envelope—but they never said, "Take the shot!" So we were denied the memorable sight of an exploding fighter. We returned to Miramar to refuel, shook it off, and came out for the afternoon missilex.

What a day! It happened about a year after I came back to flying F-14 Tomcats, after two and a half years flying in the relatively simple, agile F-5 Tiger II as a Topgun instructor. It was great to be back in Tomcats, and once again be part of a fleet Tomcat squadron!

The shot that afternoon enters the books as a "lethal miss." But it enters this book as an adventure, a lesson both in the air and on the ground, a favorite file among many unforgettable entries in my cranial save folder. My time in VF-2 was full of adventures and lessons, and it set a course for the remainder of my Navy career.

Training and practice, plans and simulators, briefings and debriefings—and then the booms and the flames and the white knuckles as the make-believe becomes real. Strap yourself in and come along on the flight of a lifetime!

CHAPTER 2

BACK TO THE BIG FIGHTER (I HAVE A RADAR AGAIN!)

Being a Topgun instructor was an honor. Demanding, challenging, rewarding—but then it was over. I was a mid-level lieutenant, 28 years old, thinking, *What do I do next?*

A few instructors who left the Topgun squadron decided to go all the way and leave the Navy. They had already committed many years of their young lives in service to our country, and I respected their decisions. Sure, they ditched some massive unpleasantries—six or seven months overseas on deployments, and risking your life almost every day at your job. But they also missed some incredible experiences. Can anything beat flying jets in a fighter squadron? Not for this lieutenant. I stayed Navy. That meant returning to an F-14 squadron, which was just what I wanted.

Near the end of my Topgun tour, I was pleasantly surprised to get a letter from the skipper of Fighter Squadron 2 welcoming me to the squadron. There were ten Tomcat squadrons at Miramar, and I hadn't even thought about which one I might like to join. I knew the Navy managed hundreds of thousands of people assigned to hundreds of squadrons, ships, and other billets, and I trusted the process. Glad I did; VF-2 was a good place to be, and it felt good to be "recruited." Well, I never learned whether they asked for me, or just sent the letter after the Navy assigned me. Who cares? It was a nice touch.

I checked out of Topgun, and on February 23, 1987, checked into—not VF-2 but VF-124, the West Coast F-14 training squadron (the RAG—see Glossary). It was only a few hangars down from Topgun, so my commute

didn't change. What did change was the workload, which was much lighter during a three-month refresher course that was standard for guys with previous experience returning to the Tomcat. Like me. I'd stayed close to F-14s during my two and a half years with Topgun.

At last, some breathing room. In 1985, early in my Topgun tour, I'd married a terrific girl named Laura, and we'd bought a house. Topgun left little time for the things a new homeowner wants to do, so my flexible schedule at the RAG gave me a welcome chance to catch up. I planted a new yard. I replaced a fence. I washed my yellow '74 Corvette more often. Hey, the 'Vette fit my vision of the fighter jock image.

Before I could return to the skies in an F-14, there were two months of classes and some qualifications (quals) to renew: a "flight" in the high-altitude chamber to feel again the insidious dangers of hypoxia, a dip in the big pool for a water survival refresher. But the most memorable was Shipboard Aircraft Firefighting. Our carriers had suffered three terrible fires in the 1960s: USS *Oriskany* in 1966, USS *Forrestal* in '67, and USS *Enterprise* in '69—and the crews responded heroically. But more than two hundred crewmen died and hundreds were injured. The Navy soon realized that, in a fire, any crewman could help save the ship. So a two-day training course began, and all on board a carrier had to take it: officers, enlisted, cooks, radar operators…everyone.

I'd taken the course once before, and it was something you don't forget: the heat and roar of the orange oil-fed flames, the blinding, choking smoke that filled the training hangar. Yes, we fought fires inside a hangar. In the early classes, each fire spawned a black plume that marred the beautiful blue San Diego sky. By the time I came along in the 1980s, a medium-sized building had been erected to contain the smoke and scrub it so that only clean air was exhausted. Great for the nice blue sky, but it didn't help the folks *inside* the hangar. Including me.

The first morning introduced us to spray nozzles, fire-fighting chemicals, and the automated systems installed on carriers. Then the instructors showed us actual video from those carrier fires—a hellish horror that, believe me, got our attention. There had been major improvements in procedures and equipment in the aftermath of those fires, but when you are dealing with jet fuel, weapons, and anything else that burns, nothing makes the danger go away.

After lunch we moved outside. We warmed up (pun intended, sorry) with small fires and simple extinguishers, then moved up to bigger equipment: high-pressure water pumping through hoses as fat as your wrist and roaring out through heavy brass nozzles. Until you've actually wrestled one of those writhing snakes, you can't imagine the strength of a stream of water. We were glad they'd warned us to dress down, in clothing we wouldn't mind getting dirty or damaged. Most of us aviators wore our flight suits.

We had a great time spraying things and taming the water-serpent. But this was just the rehearsal. The second day began with more classroom time and then lunch. And then it was time for the main event: Man versus Fire!

The instructors had been savvy and professional all along, but once inside the training hangar they got more serious. The hangar floor was a diabolical clutter of metal pipes with high-pressure spray nozzles that would unleash a roaring maelstrom when the instructors ignited the spray. There were two "fire centers" that would be attacked by four teams of students wielding hoses. The walls and ceiling were black with soot. One look and you'd know what demons dwelled in here. And that floor! As you would expect, it was slippery from the water and fuel sloshing around on it every day.

We took our positions, six fire-tamers per hose. The instructors reviewed the procedures. We all said we were ready. And then the end-of-the-world inferno roared to life.

Fire has a primordial effect on the human psyche, and I was facing a huge one. But my rational brain put together the training, the powerful shaft of water lunging from the brass nozzle, and the nearness of my five teammates, and assembled it all into something I guess I could call courage. *This is training,* I kept reminding myself. Steady, steady. *This is training,* like when I rode the helo dunker in Pensacola and got waterboarded in SERE school. My team and the three others marched slowly, steadily, toward the hellfire. The water spray helped control the temperature as the oil-fed blaze radiated a broiling heat.

And then the smoke came down. That's how everyone described it: The smoke came down. The blazing oil threw up a pall of dense smoke, and those scrubbers did nothing to help us inside the hangar, so the space quickly filled from the top down. You couldn't see more than a couple of feet. The deep orange-red glare of the flames flickered through the smoke as our rational brains made us play the hose back and forth and slowly move forward. No masks, respirators, or other special equipment, just six guys and a hose.

As a lieutenant, I was the leader of my team, and I had to keep my hand on the shoulder of the nozzle man. About every thirty seconds I would tap him to go to the back of the team, and the next guy became the nozzle man. Sounds simple, until you try passing a fire hose at full bore from one man to another in the face of the fires of Hades. It's not a garden hose. That monster pulls and rears like a bronco in a rodeo!

We were attacking the fire—and winning!—when suddenly there was noise and commotion on our left. Tongues of flame lashed out where a team had been.

We saw faint flashes of sunlight as students scrambled out of the hangar through the bailout panels in the walls. We shifted left to beat back the surging fire and keep it away from a couple of guys who were trying to get to their feet on the slippery floor. In a few minutes, with an instructor's encouragement, we had the blaze contained. We were filthy with soot and soaked with spray, but the fires were out. You didn't realize how much noise they made until it was quiet again.

We hurried outside, where several classmates were reliving their adventure. It was much-needed comic relief to see wisps of smoke actually wafting from their hair and clothes. They told us what happened: One of their hose wranglers had lost his footing and fell, which took down a couple of teammates like dominoes, and they quickly lost control of their hose. They had no choice but to bail out. Luckily, no one was hurt.

"It happens," said an instructor. Then, "Next group, man your hoses!"

At the end of the day we all got paper certificates, climbed into our cars, and drove back to the real world. When I got home I had to wipe down the car seats, and Laura issued the mandatory suggestion that I leave my clothes in the garage. This was one of the things I liked about the Navy: even as an officer and F-14 RIO, I got my hands dirty.

You may think of these exercises as distractions, but while they were immensely valuable, it still wasn't flying. How long had it been since I rode a Tomcat? And when would I get back in the air in that big, brawny F-14? Now?

Not so fast. First I had to meet the same high standards of all Tomcat aircrews: an extensive written test on the aircraft's systems; another written test of seventeen emergency procedures and their sixty-nine steps, which you had to pass with 100 percent verbatim accuracy; and a safe-for-flight simulator ride that—well, if it ever happened for real it would be the most godawful flight you could imagine. Everything that could go awry did; anything that could break broke. At Topgun we were experts in F-14 tactics and weapon systems, but we rarely thought about the Tomcat's complex fuel transfer system, or the automatic wingsweep program, or dozens of other systems. So I was very pleased to find that the knowledge I had not tapped for two and a half years was still there, waiting like an old friend for a hesitant call. "You still there?"

"Yes, I'm here."

It was great to be young and doing something I truly loved. That hard-won knowledge was right there, just waiting for a refresher. Most of the RAG instructors were friends from the officers club, and some had come through Topgun as students, so I felt I was among friends. They were buddies, but they were also professionals who did their jobs to be sure I was ready to warm the RIO seat in that big fighter once again.

In April 1987, they were sure, and so was I. As I walked out to the jet with instructor pilot "Barney" Barnett, it was all very familiar. It had been more than six years since I walked along the VF-124 flight line for my first Tomcat flight, and I'd logged more than 1,200 F-14 flight hours since then. Barney was another friendly face from my years at Miramar, and I felt comfortable and confident.

It had been thirty-two months since my last F-14 flight in VF-24. Now, at last, I was again clicking the leg restraints of an F-14's ejection seat. Strapping in was like coming home. I moved the lever to close the big Plexiglas canopy. Barney started the engines, the environmental control system (ECS, our air conditioner) came on, and I started the weapon system computer. It was all very different from the F-5 that I'd been manning for the past two and a half years, down to the leg restraints; the F-5 didn't have any.

For takeoff Barney gave me the maximum afterburner experience—Zone 5!—and a few minutes later we were banking and looping above the Pacific on a crystal-clear Southern California morning. This flight was Familiarization #1, a short hop just to get me back in the jet. I had plenty of experience, seven years in Navy fighters, so the demands of FAM1 were no sweat and lots of fun. Next day, I practiced simple radar intercepts with a few cobwebs to sweep away. I was back home!

Hold it, there was another non-flying tune-up: Deep Water Survival Training, in case we ever took a dip in the open ocean after ejecting from an aircraft. We'd all had that at Pensacola, but it was a good refresher on the survival gear in the ejection seat, how to survive in cold water and tropical oceans, and everything else the Navy could cram into us in a few hours. When the instructor asked if any of us had ever ejected, my hand went up. I told the class the short version of the story. I told the world the long version in TOPGUN DAYS, Chapter Five: *Rocket Rider*. That's me: water survival poster boy.

After class, we rode a Navy utility boat to a quiet part of San Diego Bay and clambered into rafts to wait for a helicopter to pick us up. I recalled being picked up by the helicopter back in December 1981, about three minutes after my ejection. This time I waited a little longer, but I didn't have to worry about getting dragged under by my parachute, so I just enjoyed the ride.

In my first three months in the RAG I logged only five flights. No problem; I could decompress after my intense years as a Topgun instructor and enjoy some of the leave I'd accumulated. I took classes, passed tests, and proved on each flight that I still "had it"—proved to my instructors and myself.

In mid-May a RAG training detachment, called a det, shipped out to El Centro, California. I was one of about a dozen students, along with ten or so instructors, a half-dozen Tomcats, and a maintenance crew to keep them flying. Miramar squadrons went to El Centro for a variety of reasons. In VF-24, my first squadron, we'd gone on det to the sparse Navy airfield at El Centro to practice air-to-air gunnery. Though it was only 100 miles from Miramar, it might as well have been 1,000, because it got us away from the distractions of home base to focus on more training in a shorter time than at home.

This det let the RAG challenge its students to put together everything they'd learned and use it in the most realistic simulated air combat they had seen in their brief flying careers. How to fly the F-14, wield its weapons, team up with a wingman, size up an enemy, intercept him, wax him in simulated dogfights. Everything. It was simply called "Tactics."

We could argue whether learning to land on a carrier was more challenging than the Tactics phase, but in the RAG syllabus it was a draw, the twin pinnacles of challenge before students were sent to their fleet squadrons.

I was gung-ho for the Tactics det. I'd be flying with an instructor pilot in the environment I found most challenging and exciting, and I knew I'd do well. One sunny afternoon I packed my flight gear and some clothes into the Corvette and drove over the mountains into the Imperial Valley.

For me, the det was eight days and five flights. The first two were 1v1—that's one versus one, and my instructor pilots loved them because fighter pilots enjoy dogfighting. I loved them too, because, well, I also enjoyed dogfighting. But more than that, they reiterated that I was living my dream, and a thumbs-up that I had become comfortable in this demanding environment.

When I wasn't flying, I was lying…by the pool at the El Centro Officers Club. Eight days, five flights—do the math. By the end of the det I had a good tan. And in the evenings I raced the Corvette top-down along the empty roads to whichever restaurant was "designated" for dinner that night. It's what fighter jocks do.

After the 1v1 flights, my performance got more critical. The next flights included radar intercepts that led to those close-in maneuvering duels. But again, I found that my years without a radar in the Topgun F-5F were only a small problem. The Tomcat's AWG-9 radar was again my old friend, its quirks and strengths still familiar despite the intervening years. Planning, briefing, leading, and then debriefing complex flights in Topgun had given me a wealth of experience in this environment, and it applied whether I was in an F-5 or an F-14.

I didn't interact a lot with the new pilots and RIOs, the Category 1 students known as Cat 1s. We would chat by the pool and clink a beer or two in the evenings, and I'd see in them the same spirit I'd had six years before, in my first run through the RAG. But I noticed among them a RIO and a pilot who stood out from the rest. Food and Doc seemed to be at the center of the group at the club, and the top of the class in graded events. When squadrons were announced at the end of training, I saw they were going to VF-2 like me. Great news!

That three-month period in the RAG was just the refresher that I needed. My thirteen graded flights with instructors were a good transition back to the F-14, and the relaxed pace let me catch up on personal chores I hadn't had time for in the pressure cooker of a Topgun instructor's job. At last it was time to return to a fleet Tomcat squadron!

INTEL BRIEF: THE TOMCAT COMMUNITY, 1987

In 1987 the Navy's F-14 Tomcat community included twenty-two fleet-deploying squadrons (ten at Miramar, twelve at Oceana), two RAGs, and several other entities. It was a well-defined community with excellent communications.

News traveled fast in that community, and none of it faster than the shock wave of a mishap. There was a professional benefit to that, because aviators could learn from what went wrong. But there was also a personal element: You could very well know the people involved. Even more personal, the next one could involve any of us.

How often did things go awry? To consider only major mishaps, before March 1985 the average was roughly seven F-14s lost per year. In the 1980s the Navy was buying new F-14s to transition squadrons from F-4s and to replace those losses. Then, between March 1985 and February 1986, the Navy lost no F-14s in mishaps. None. This was an amazing run for any tactical aircraft, especially in those days, and even more so when you consider what a complex machine the Tomcat really was. The low mishap rate led to an abundance of Tomcats, so Navy planners used them to stand up two more F-14 squadrons, which fit perfectly into the Reagan-era, late Cold War military buildup. The happy anomaly didn't last; after 1986 the loss rate averaged around five per year. (The mishap averages came from information in an unofficial source that has proven accurate.)

During my three months in the RAG, February through May 1987, there was one F-14 crash at Miramar: The jet developed engine problems and the crew was attempting to return to the airfield, but crashed short of the runway. The pilot and RIO ejected and there were no injuries on the ground.

And those two new squadrons were disbanded after less than two years.

CHAPTER 3

JOINING THE BULLETS

"Point!"

That was Jungle, a pilot in VF-2, and the first time I heard it, I had no idea what he was talking about. We were sitting in the VF-2 ready room aboard the USS *Ranger* (CV-61), and Jungle had just seen something in the evening movie—a hot dog, a fire hydrant, something on our list of a dozen items and characters to watch for. If you spotted one and yelled "Point" first, you scored one point. No prizes, no glory, just something to do. And something for the squadron duty officer, the SDO, to do. If you had the duty that evening, you'd run the projector, change reels, and stop the show if someone yelled "Point" and you had to roll back the film to verify.

Bear called for a roll-back, but there it was, a hydrant in a busy city street scene. Point for Jungle. I would soon come to know him as a talented and colorful fighter jock, and he'll pop up again in this story.

It was great to be back in a Tomcat squadron. Even being 200 miles off the coast of Southern California, I was back in the fleet and life was good. It was June 1987. I'd checked into VF-2 on a Friday, and four days later we were at sea for training and refreshers for all pilots and RIOs in the air wing. Day flights, night flights, intercepts, carrier air defense, air refueling, and now and then a good deal such as using two hours' worth of fuel in only one hour—which would be an afterburner-rich ACM flight!

I became reacquainted with one of the most thrilling, adrenaline-pumping attention-getters known to man: landing a twenty-six-ton fighter jet on a carrier at sea.

Here's another. You just made such a landing, and before you climb out of the cockpit, a guy on the deck lays four fingers across his shoulder and points to you. Now that's a heart-stopper.

The fingers stand for four stripes, the shoulder boards of a captain, an officer one step away from admiral. And the pointing finger means there's one who wants to talk to you, lieutenant.

The lieutenant was me.

The day I got the four-finger signal was the day the carrier was supposed to vanish. Not an easy act for a floating city of steel that's longer than three football fields.

To disappear, or at least seem to, the ship turned off its radars and navigation equipment, and so did the planes. No radio chitchat, no radars. It was like time traveling to the dawn of aviation as we flew 200 miles from the ship, orbited out there for a half hour or more, and then flew back in to try to find the carrier by what mariners call dead reckoning. That means you cook your heading, your speed, your time, the wind, and a stew of other variables, and when it's time to open the oven, there's your carrier. You hope.

If the boat's not there, and if your tanks are running low, you swallow your pride and radio the magic word: *Sunrise.* The radars and navigation beacons wake up to guide you home, but you might get a new callsign, and not a good one.

If this were a real combat situation, we and the other fighters in the exercise would be out there with radars on, sweeping the sky for bogeys, a protective umbrella for the carrier with a fighter at the tip of each rib. But on this day our instructions were to leave the radars off for the entire flight. That wasn't easy; we relied on this equipment during routine ops, and it was a profound challenge to override habits that had hardened into instincts and just leave that switch alone.

I had paid strict attention in the pre-flight briefings, especially the part about carrier procedures, and was happy to feel it all coming back to me in the cockpit. My inertial navigation system, the INS, seemed okay, but the F-14's INS was known to "dump" for who-knows-why. (Nowadays GPS could do it better, but it wasn't an option for us in 1987.) And then the intensity of flight deck operations and the stunning jolt of the catapult launch were the clincher; I was once again flying Tomcats in the fleet.

Overhead the carrier, we silently located the tanker and refueled, then headed to our assigned station, bearing 310 degrees from the carrier. The pilot in the front seat was Greg Hansen, a Naval Academy graduate whose Minnesota accent got him the callsign "Hoser." He and I kept separate dead reckoning plots as we proceeded to our station: carrier heading 240 degrees at launch…refuel…head 330 degrees, 280 knots, 6 minutes…head 310 degrees, 250 knots, 35 minutes…orbit.

We were hundreds of miles off the coast of Mexico and couldn't see land. Nothing but water, sky, and clouds. No radio chatter, no simulated targets, nothing happening. It could have been boring, but our concern about navigation kept us busy.

Hoser hadn't "hit the boat" in about a month, so this refresher let him knock off the rust. Similar to the RAG det to El Centro, I quickly felt at home in the carrier flying environment as we orbited on station, chatting about the squadron and my time at Topgun—and, of course, trash-talking about our sister squadron, VF-1. This, too, is what fighter jocks do.

As planned, we spent only a few minutes out there before heading in for the Moment of Truth about our dead reckoning. Though our INS appeared stable, we kept up our manual plots, and soon Hoser said, "This should be the place." I agreed. We scanned the ocean 23,000 feet below—and saw, to no one's surprise, only waves.

"These guys are never where they say they'll be!" I snorted. But we'd just started looking and had plenty of fuel, so there was no cause for alarm. Hoser started an easy turn to fly a large circle. Even though our search was just starting, I hated the feeling of uncertainty about finding the carrier. I didn't want to be the guy who called "Sunrise!"

And I wasn't. After a few minutes, Hoser spotted the wake of a ship, followed it, and there was the beautiful sight of the *Ranger*. It was amazing how small it looked from just a few miles away, and how the dark gray flight deck blended in with the dark blue ocean, even on a clear, sunny day.

We joined up with another VF-2 Tomcat, and soon we were screaming over the ship at 600 feet and 500 knots. The other jet snap-rolled into a left turn, and when it fell back to an 8 o'clock position from us, we too hung a 6.5g left. Imagine what that feels like. A moment before, I weighed 180; in less than a second, I weighed half a ton. With hands like anvils, I began doing what RIOs do: check altitude and airspeed, call "Wings" for wingsweep mode to auto, start the landing checklist, watch our distance to the ship, do this, do that, watch the ship grow from postage stamp to Ping-Pong table to football field—and then the reassuring brick-wall jolt of the arresting cable. Home.

Man, I thought, *I have missed this!*

We did it. No radio, no radar, no hiccups. Plane captains started to chain down our jet. Then Hoser said on the ICS, "Bio, on the left, Senior Chief Dunker has a message for you."

Senior Chief Dunker was our squadron's flight deck coordinator, one of only three or four senior enlisted who had the experience, judgment, and personality to manage the VF-2 Tomcats in the incredibly dynamic flight deck environment. He had to know everything and everyone, go toe-to-toe with the carrier's personnel, and do it all in the raging din and heat of a flight deck. And now, there he stood, fingers on his shoulder, his other hand making the universal sign for "talk," then pointing at me.

Four fingers meant Navy Captain, which probably meant CAG, our air wing commander himself. CAG once meant Commander Air Group, but when "group" was changed to "wing" the CAG name stood fast, a fittingly craggy name for the commander of the eight or nine squadrons on a carrier. A moment ago I was ten feet tall; now CAG wants to talk to me. *To* me, not with me.

Our squadron CO, Commander Jim "T-Dog" Dodge, was waiting for me below deck in our ready room. "Did you turn on your radar?" he asked. I said no. "Well, a ship was monitoring the exercise and they detected your radar, Bio. They reported it and CAG went ballistic. We have to go see him right now."

How do you prove a negative? We went into a radar room where a few people were discussing the exercise. No one got lost, they said, all went well, with the exception of one F-14 radar. It's always dark in a radar room, but still I could see the expressions: You screwed up. Skipper Dodge and I got a quick recap from them, and I was asked again, and again said no. Maybe hell no.

"Well, CAG wants to talk to you."

Skipper Dodge and I found CAG in his small office, where he took a break from paperwork to, let's say, express his displeasure. CAG was a Vietnam-era pilot who had spent a few years as a prisoner of war. He'd done well since then; the Navy didn't give CAG billets to just anyone, not even ex-POWs.

He asked me if I turned on my radar. I told him the same thing I told everyone. He told me a ship detected it. There was a moment of silence. Skipper Dodge squirmed, caught between one of his officers and his boss. CAG said, "Well, get back to me," which was our cue to leave and come back with answers.

T-Dog and I went back to the radar room. We were rehashing everything for the 99th time when someone said with a sigh, "Well, lieutenant, I don't know what happened, but we got an AWG-9 radar strobe bearing two-nine-zero degrees."

A light bulb went off. "Two-nine-zero?" I blurted. "I was on station three-one-zero!" We looked at the station assignments and—hallelujah!—a VF-1 jet was assigned to 290. *That* RIO had turned on his radar, but someone had thrown me under the bus, probably because I was new to the air wing.

Skipper Dodge and I hot-footed back to CAG to clear my name. We told him. He thought a moment.

"Well," he growled, "you'd *better not* mess up like that."

He forgot to say, "Welcome to Air Wing 9." The experience stuck, I was extra careful after that close encounter with what would happen if I did mess up.

The rest of the det went well. The flight deck was a precisely orchestrated pandemonium, the flights were the usual mix of boring and challenging, and in the evening I'd relax in the ready room, a quiet haven with comfortable vinyl seats, a two-reel 16mm movie on the screen—and now and then somebody yelling "Point!"

After ten days at sea, VF-2 was back at Miramar, a month away from our six-month deployment to the Indian Ocean. Like other squadrons, VF-2 got busy grooming its jets. I got busy grooming my lawn with grass seed and installing a sprinkler system.

But there was still some very important flying to do. Hoser's imagination had been working, and he knew I liked to take pictures, so he arranged for three jets to go on, well, a "training" flight. All Tomcat squadrons flew a matrix of training and qualifications, but once in awhile there was room for a flight like this. We even had official-sounding acronyms for them. DDA was a Day Dick-Around. FACIT was F**k Around and Call It Training.

I was flying with a Topgun instructor keeping his F-14 qualification, and Hoser was in another jet with a Topgun RIO. The third jet was flown by Coney, with

Taz in his backseat. Like Hoser, Coney and Taz were lieutenants in their first fleet squadron, but had been in VF-2 long enough that they weren't nuggets; that's what we called the new guys. Coney was cool on the ground and in the air. His name was Jack Fields but friends called him Coney before he got in the Navy, and it stuck. He wasn't big, but he came across as tough. He grew up in a small town in Oregon, learned to fly as a teenager, and went through the Navy's AOCS, the Aviation Officer Candidate School.

Taz was Mike Quillin's callsign and it was short for Tasmanian Devil, an apt callsign if there ever was one. He'd gone to the Naval Academy, but he didn't fit the spit-and-polish stereotype. He was from Florida but looked like a guy who just stepped out of a Bruce Springsteen song.

In the pre-flight brief, Hoser described his photo ideas and we all discussed how to shoot them safely. One picture would be a Blue Angels-style formation, with one F-14 upright and the other inverted. Another was more challenging: My pilot and I would fly in formation with Hoser, while Coney came at us head-on and turned abruptly, like the start of a dogfight. At those speeds the timing would be split-second, but we'd seen similar photos by legendary Navy photographer Bob Lawson. If Bob could do it, well….

The weather was perfect, the jets were clean, and our preparations paid off. The flight went smoothly—and yes! We got the shots we wanted and more.

It went so well that we flew the same FACIT mission two days later. Admit it: You would, too, if you had the chance!

The next week, Hoser and I lucked into another golden opportunity. While flying cross-country around the West, we landed at remote Beale Air Force Base, miles from nowhere in Northern California. If you're an airplane freak, you know what that means. Beale AFB was the home of the super-secret, super-exotic SR-71 Blackbird spy plane, the fastest thing with wings.

I hoped we would see some Blackbirds in action. Well, we didn't. But Hoser had another idea. While the Beale Transient Line refueled our Tomcat, we strolled over to the building that housed the SR-71 squadron and casually knocked on the door. The SR-71 guys welcomed us and showed us around their office spaces. There were a few cool items on display, but nothing as fantastic as their jet. They made a note of our contact information, which would later prove useful. Soon our Tomcat was ready to go, so we climbed in for the flight back to Miramar.

FACIT, photos, the Blackbird—great stuff, but over and done. Or so we thought.

CHAPTER 4

SUPERSONIC IN THE AIR AND ON THE GROUND

When the Navy introduced the F-14 in the early 1970s, they didn't simply convert existing squadrons, they commissioned two new squadrons to fly the incredible new fighter. VF-1 and VF-2 were old numbers, dormant relics of long-ago fighter squadrons that didn't switch to new aircraft but were shut down in the 1940s. VF-1 was known as the Wolfpack; VF-2 was the Bounty Hunters, but in VF-2 we often referred to ourselves by our radio callsign: Bullet.

In the spotlight as the first F-14 squadrons, VF-1 and VF-2 soon became hot rivals. Sure, we would deploy together, and we'd go into combat together if it came to that. But in everything else we were intense competitors. Both squadrons had won awards over the years in various graded events, and the staring contest showed no letup. Nobody blinked while I was in VF-2.

VF-2 was a typical Tomcat squadron: twelve F-14A Tomcats, fifteen aircrews—that's fifteen pilots and fifteen RIOs; one of each made up one aircrew. Add to that a handful of non-aircrew for a total of about thirty-six officers. Keeping the machines and the squadron in operating condition was the work of roughly 220 enlisted men, with ranks of E-1 through E-9.

When I joined the squadron, the skipper was Commander Jim "T-Dog" Dodge, a RIO like myself. He had been an NFO in the sleek and challenging RA-5C Vigilante reconnaissance jet before moving to the F-14 when the Vigilante retired. The Executive Officer—the XO—was also a RIO, Commander Marv "Rip" Serhan, who had been assigned to the test and evaluation squadron for Navy fighters before becoming XO. The skipper

was an even-tempered guy and a born leader, and the XO was meticulous and intense. They made a good team for leading an F-14 squadron.

Aircrews don't just fly planes and watch movies in the ready room. We're kept busy and out of trouble with what are called "collateral duties." My ground job was typical for a lieutenant in his second fleet squadron; I was the Avionics/Weapons Division Officer in the maintenance department.

I didn't tell sailors what to do. They were highly trained and knew what to do to fix and maintain our Tomcats' electronics and weapons systems. They were supervised by senior petty officers and chief petty officers (CPOs), who in turn had a branch officer to help manage each workcenter. I'd been a branch officer in my first squadron. Now, returning as a division officer, I was the next higher link in the chain of command. Think of a pyramid with sailors as its foundation, then rising through tiers of CPOs and branch officers, then me, and then topped with the Maintenance Officer, XO, and CO. I was middle management for around sixty sailors.

Now that you've met some of the Bullets, what did we look like? Sorry to disappoint you, but if you met us on the street, you'd never know who was a pilot and who was a RIO. Glasses weren't even a sure bet, as not all RIOs wore them. Pilot or RIO, we came in small, medium, and large.

We also ran the full spectrum of temperament: some were funny, some were always serious, some were boring. We could be likeable or obnoxious, mature or

… let's say, still developing. Pilot or RIO, there was no stereotype.

A day at Miramar began at 0700—that's 7 AM sharp—with the most serious chorus line you ever saw. Officers, enlisted, everyone in the squadron, heads down and walking slowly in a long line across the concrete ramp like a human push-broom. This was the FOD walkdown. Foreign Object Damage is a constant threat to a jet engine, so all squadrons worked hard to prevent it. A panel fastener, a dropped tool, a pebble, a penny that escaped through a pocket hole—anything that could be sucked into a jet engine had to be spotted and removed. FOD prevention was one reason that tools and parts were strictly accounted for.

Regardless of weather, every squadron was out there at 7 AM walking their ramp. At least we were located in San Diego, where the weather was rarely bad. I knew it was important, but for me the FOD walkdown was a necessary evil, a price to pay for flying F-14s.

After the walkdown, there was plenty for the aircrews to do. It's hard to describe a typical day because they could be very different—and a "typical" day in the 1980s would be quite different in the 1990s, as we'll see later.

For a pilot or RIO, that would include briefing, flying, and debriefing two or three times a week. There always seem to be paperwork and administrative tasks, too, but most aircrews have some slack time.

So let's say it's a "typical" day. After FOD walkdown, I stay downstairs in the maintenance spaces and put in some time at my desk in the collective office for branch and division officers. Two pilots and a RIO are discussing the sports and financial sections of the morning paper. I don't join in; I have to go over some training records. I guess I take this squadron stuff seriously—no, I know I do, and for a moment I resent this casualness around the squadron. But hey, people get their breaks in different ways. And we'll soon be leaving for a six-month deployment, which is very demanding on everyone, casual or serious. So let them enjoy some

slack time; they'll soon pay for it in time away from everything they hold dear.

I get away from my paperwork, walk upstairs, and in the ready room find Hoss (a RIO) and Cowboy (a pilot) discussing some detail of the AIM-7 Sparrow missile. They have the classified manuals out, and they're drawing on the whiteboard. Very professional. I listen and learn; also very professional.

I go to the Ops office to check on our flying schedule for the next few days, then return to the ready room where Hoss and Cowboy have been joined by four more lieutenants and the session morphed into a lively conversation about the deployment that's now only a couple of weeks away. Most have never done one, so there's a lot of mystery. I've done two, so I join in.

Lieutenant Dave "Hap" Chandler, one of the new pilots, has done a tour in the Philippines, flying the adversary role in Navy A-4 Skyhawk jets. This says a lot about Hap: the exotic experience of living overseas, the huge benefit in flight hours and judgment from flying adversary for several years, and then being selected for F-14s. All positives.

Hap tells us he made many trips to Singapore—relatively convenient from the Philippines—and he's wearing the popular Seiko diver's watch. But he didn't pay the usual $200 for it; he bought a convincing copy on the street in Singapore for $20. Since we'll be in Singapore in about a month, we want to know if it was a good deal.

"Well," says Hap, "it's a perfect replica and it keeps good time. The only problem is, the date changes every day at noon instead of midnight."

We all do a double-take and then burst out laughing. Hap is embarrassed, until someone explains how to fix this "problem."

Later I would fly with Hap on one of the most harrowing training missions of my entire career, and I would know that the watch gaffe was a rare lapse in his composure.

It's hard to say that any day was "typical," and VF-2

wasn't a typical squadron. On the ground, my fellow Bullet officers covered the spectrum. But in the air, VF-2 was a consistent winner with trophies to prove it. When I joined the squadron, our jets bore a capital "E" on the fuselage. That was the Battle E, a long-standing Navy award to ships, squadrons, and other units. It stood for efficiency (it later became "effectiveness"), an award to the unit with the best scores in competitions and inspections graded by higher headquarters. In the F-14 community, one West Coast and one East Coast squadron were designated the Battle E winners each year. VF-2 won for 1986, just before I arrived.

That was a winning year for VF-2. The squadron also won its second consecutive Boola Boola Award for the highest performance in air-to-air missile shoots among West Coast F-14 squadrons. The name came from the radio code for a direct hit by a missile. (A similar award for East Coast squadrons was the Grand Slam.)

These awards were based on scored events, so every squadron had an even chance. But the Bullets had also won the Mutha Trophy, the annual West Coast award for "most colorful" Tomcat squadron. This one originated with the F-8 Crusader, a sleek fighter whose pilots were supersonic cowboys with an impressive combat record in the challenging skies over Vietnam. The RAG commanding officer alone decided who got the Mutha, so-named because the RAG was the "mother squad-

ron," or something like that. The trophy was passed to the F-14 community in 1977, and had been awarded ten times since then. Three of those were to VF-2, most recently in (you guessed it) 1986.

With more than 250 people and twelve Tomcats operating like a well-oiled machine, a fighter squadron was a busy place. Add the preparations for deployment, inquiries from CAG, and countless other pop-up concerns, and it feels like a doomsday cage wrestling match…with paperwork. As a senior lieutenant and division officer, I was up to here in all of it the minute I joined the squadron. But with eight Navy years behind me, I was ready.

Skipper Dodge led the squadron and dealt with all these demands. He was the buck-stopper, the guy ultimately responsible for the squadron, the people, the planes, from walkdown to walkdown. I remember watching him and wondering, how does one person manage all that?

He had a great team behind him. In the air and on the ground, the lieutenant commanders—Jungle, Brutus, Booger, Nasty, and the others—set the pace. Capable and dedicated junior officers—Coney, Taz, Hoser, Animal, Bear, Goober, Slush, and a dozen more—did their part, all supported by hundreds of equally motivated sailors and chiefs. You could feel the esprit de corps, and you could see it in the trophy case.

Now you know why I was excited to join the Bullets.

INTEL BRIEF: CALLSIGNS

Jungle, Booger, Sax, Munchkin, and Brutus. Not the name of a law firm in Bizarre-world, but a sampling of the lieutenant commander callsigns when I arrived at VF-2.

All carrier-based aviators have callsigns, a tradition going back decades. A callsign is a nickname, a *nom de guerre*, an alter ego. You need one when you talk on a radio and the enemy is listening. It obscures your identity, so prying ears can't identify "Lieutenant Baranek."

A callsign also provides a clear channel to a specific person. "Hap, break left!" gets the attention of one person. If the call were, "Bill, break left!" you might wonder which Bill they were talking to. An unofficial rule says that a callsign should be unique in a unit. There should only be one Cowboy, no matter how many guys come from Texas. If another aviator shows up with the same callsign, one of them has to change.

Callsigns are created in several ways. One of the most common is a play on the aviator's name. Bob Centeno was Peso, which I thought was pretty clever. Bill Shivell was Chevy. Gary Svatek was Czech.

It's also common for a callsign to say something about its owner. Munchkin was height-challenged, Bear was burly. It could be a joke, a compliment, even an embarrassment. Around the fleet several guys picked up the callsign Ripple for accidentally launching two Sidewinders during a missile shoot—that's called ripple-firing. My younger brother was a RIO. He was also a surfer, so his callsign was Shark. But that was a little too cool, and a San Diego TV station had a humorous segment with some stereotypical surfer dudes, so my brother's callsign changed to one of their names: Biff.

Maybe you have a well-known name. "Happy" Chandler was a politician and commissioner of baseball, so aviators named Chandler often had the callsign Happy or Hap. Same thing for those named Mullins or Mullen: a comic strip that started in the 1920s featured Moon Mullins, hence the callsign Moon.

I've heard that other services hold formal naming ceremonies, but the squadrons I served in just brainstormed a callsign for the new guy. I won't say "never," but it was rare when an aviator gave himself a callsign and it stuck.

There are other common sources of callsigns. One is to commemorate something that needs commemorating. Another is to use acronyms. A friend of mine was a Naval aviator many years ago, but never had a callsign. We are both Davids, so when he signed a note "The Other David," I dubbed him TOD.

My callsign was Bio. It came right out of pop culture, but I guess that's nothing new. Baranek sounds like bionic—so now you know how to pronounce it!—and everybody knew the word from the 1970s TV show, "The Six Million Dollar Man." And why say Bionic when Bio will do? It "did" for the rest of my career.

Like the leather jacket, a callsign is one more perk for joining Club Aviator.

CHAPTER 5

"WE'RE COMPLACENT!"

July 14, 1987, dawned blue and beautiful as the USS *Ranger* steamed out of San Diego with the squadrons of Air Wing 9 aboard, accompanied by the escorting ships that made up the battle group. We cruised a hundred miles off the coast of California for a couple of days of refresher flying, then headed into the wide Pacific.

An extended aircraft carrier deployment is like a force of nature, like surfing one of those giant ocean waves, the sixty-footers. You make preparations, you go out there, it's big, and you know it's coming. Nothing you do will stop it or change it. You get on it and take an exciting, unpredictable ride.

A few people don't catch the wave and are left behind. And a few pay a heavy price. Two weeks before sailing, we lost several teammates when an EA-3B Skywarrior crashed at NAS Miramar while practicing carrier landings. The A-3 had no ejection seats, so all three crewmembers rode it to the ground on an empty part of the airfield. The mishap happened around 10 PM on a Friday night, so the public was barely aware that three people had died. There was just a small article in the local paper.

Then, the day after we left San Diego, a VF-1 Tomcat crashed during a routine training flight. Both pilot and RIO ejected and were fished out of the sea, and only the empty Tomcat was lost in a mighty splash.

Sure, we knew these events were part of life in aviation, especially carrier aviation. We tried to learn from what happened, and we did our jobs. Airplanes could be replaced but the crewmen were our shipmates, our friends. When we lost people it hit us hard.

This was my third extended deployment, and I'd had three years of shore duty since my last one. Laura and I had married and bought a house, so getting out of town was more complicated and emotionally harder than when I was an unattached bachelor. But leaving a precious normal life behind was part of being Navy, like gray paint and wilted lettuce.

Why do big airports have several runways angled in different directions? When a plane speeds down a runway at 100 knots, head-on into a 20-knot wind, its wings are getting 120 knots worth of lift, so it takes off in a shorter run. The same effect helps it to land. With runways at several angles, planes use the one best aligned with the wind.

A carrier doesn't need all those runways. It simply turns to head into the wind. At full speed, it can add about 30 knots to the headwind. With catapults for takeoff and arresting cables for landing, you can see why a thirty-five-ton jet can operate off a floating airport that would be too small for even a light plane ashore.

The downside is that turning into the wind takes the ship off course and adds to the time en route. By not flying, the carrier battle group could steer best course around the clock and reach Hawaii in four days. So we didn't fly. Without that activity, the days dragged on for us all. VF-2 maintenance worked on the jets, and the officers held training meetings. The senior officers announced new standard aircrews, the pilot-RIO pairings for most of our flights. My new pilot was Hooter.

What a team we made! Hooter had joined VF-2 just a month before me, so we were both new guys in a squadron that seemed pretty close-knit. He wasn't big or tall, and he didn't particularly look like a fighter pilot, but a fighter pilot he was. His real name was Jon Schreiber, but I never called him Jon. His first fleet tour had been with an F-4 Phantom squadron, where he'd logged 1,000 flight hours in one of the last US Navy squadrons to fly the legendary fighter. He'd done a tour as an instructor pilot, then transitioned to F-14s and joined VF-2. He was a fighter pilot with the heart of a poet and the wit of a…well, a witty fighter pilot.

One of our first flights together was an air defense exercise northeast of Oahu. We had a catch-all term for such flights: CAP, for combat air patrol. We'd flown little in a week, so we expected a ho-hum flight—uneventful but good training for carrier ops, aerial refueling, command and control, and other skills that required frequent refreshing. We might be tested by an adversary from one of the bases in Hawaii, but it seemed unlikely.

We manned up on a balmy, breezy afternoon, perfect for flying. Hooter and I were well matched in experience: both had a previous squadron tour with hundreds of carrier flights and more than 1,000 flight hours. We quickly became a team, comfortable again in the demanding carrier environment. Pre-flight, man-up, start, and launch all went smoothly. After the cat shot we climbed overhead the carrier and joined on the A-6 tanker. It was a practice plug; they didn't give us any more go juice. Then we aimed our jet 290 degrees, climbed to 23,000 feet, and cruised to our assigned station at about 230 knots to make the most of our fuel.

If you love the sight of those popcorn clouds from the beach, you should see them from up close. Fly among them, and it's like cruising among jumbo dollops of whipped cream. We enjoyed their company as we flew along guided by the inertial navigation system. Our ANS-92 INS was state-of-the-art when the F-14 was designed in the late 1960s, and was widely used by carrier-based jets, but I was always suspicious of it. Still, it was part of our weapons system and a valuable tool for navigation. Our system looked stable that day, so

we used it to get to our station while I set up our radar for long-range surveillance.

Our INS directed us over the lush island of Kauai, backlit by the late afternoon sun. That's odd; we thought we'd be stationed over the ocean. Well, the nav system looked good, so we proceeded. I had the radar scanning our sector, and pretty soon we saw a target approaching about sixty miles away. Great! This would be more exciting than we expected.

We ran a simple radar intercept and—oops!—it was a DC-9 airliner. We made sure we didn't get too close, but we could see it was a colorful Hawaiian Airlines jet. I didn't know where it was coming from, but it wasn't part of our exercise, so we hightailed it back to our station.

As soon as we reset, the radar showed another target. Surely this one would be a Navy adversary aircraft testing us, I thought, as we ran another intercept, which ended in another airliner.

Question marks sprouted over my head. Then, up front, Hooter realized yet another oops. "I forgot to synch the compass," he said. Pilots usually did that right after takeoff as they flew away from the enormous metal mass of the carrier. Don't ask me to explain magnetic fields and their effect on our swing-wing jet fighter's compass, I just know that when Hooter pushed the Synch button our displays shifted by 20 degrees. We were 60 miles south of our station! The INS was fine, as things turned out.

Hoping nobody was looking, we quietly eased north to where we should be. The rest of the flight was uneventful. The bad news was that no radar controller had called to check on why we were so far off. The good news was that no one ever asked why we were flying over Kauai. Good or bad, the flight made an impression.

The next day Hooter and I got the usual briefing and walked out on the flight deck for another afternoon flight. The sky was overcast and the mission was again routine. A brisk breeze cooled us in our flight gear, but I could still smell the big ship's peculiar odor—the oily steam from the catapults, the jet fuel, the complex aroma of aviation. Even out here on the open ocean, the carrier had its own distinctive scent.

We did the usual preflight. Starting at the jet's boarding ladder (left side), Hooter moved forward along the nose and then down the right side of the jet. I moved aft from the ladder and checked the left side. We opened panels, checked gauges, examined fasteners, kicked tires, and jiggled missiles and fins to make sure they were firmly attached. It's all in the flight manual, plus our personal experience and anecdotal lessons from other aviators. Our Tomcat was parked at the edge of the deck with its tail out over the water, so we couldn't walk around behind it, but we looked closely at the engine exhaust nozzles, tailhook, and other moving parts. Then we switched sides, met at the ladder, and climbed up to check the top of the aircraft and our ejection seats. The standard preflight covered more than one hundred items, and we took every one of them seriously.

Around us, ten other aircrews were preflighting their jets in the uncanny calm of a flight deck before engine starts. Then we all climbed into our cockpits as the Air Boss in the control tower made his customary announcement over the incredibly loud 5MC announcing system:

On the flight deck, aircrews are manning for the 1700 launch. All unnecessary personnel clear the flight deck. Remaining personnel get into the proper flight deck uniform: helmets on and buckled, life vests on and fastened, goggles down, sleeves rolled down. Check chocks and chains, loose gear and FOD around the go aircraft. It's time to start 'em up. START 'EM UP!

He barked his words like a machine gun. Of course, he barked this spiel six or seven times a day—before every launch—so it was one of those things that's more than

memorized. And like a starter's pistol, it got everyone's attention every time.

The flight deck came alive. The quiet intensity of preflight dissolved in the roar of diesel engines as the low-slung "start carts" quickly moved into position, turbines whining as they spooled into action to start the engines. We needed the thick air hose from these carts and a heavy electrical cable plugged into our jet to make it happen. I often sat in the cockpit thinking, "This is embarrassing!" The Navy's smaller F/A-18 and most US Air Force fighters of the day had self-start. And here's the big, sexy, swing-wing F-14 Tomcat that can't even start itself. Well, at least it wasn't alone. The A-6 Intruder and many other carrier aircraft of the 1980s couldn't start their engines without a plug-in and a shot of high-pressure air from the start cart.

There's a good reason for that. A carrier plane is a burly beast, built for stresses and strains that a land-based plane doesn't have to handle. Less weight means less stress, so leave the start-up stuff on the ship. It made sense, but I didn't have to like it.

The noise and bustle energized the plane captains, aircraft directors, and other flight deck personnel. Starting engines meant the launch would begin in about twenty minutes—twenty very intense minutes of final checks and taxiing twenty-five- and thirty-three-ton aircraft around on a rolling deck with a lot of things to bump into, and a strong, steady wind. If that sounds dangerous, exhausting, nerve-racking, well yes, it would be to some. Not these guys. Believe me, virtually every man on the deck loved the activity and excitement and was proud to be part of it.

Hooter and I strapped in and checked our cockpit switches. Our plane captain (PC) pushed a button on the side of the jet to activate electrical power, and we went through our familiar start procedures. Good ICS check, and Hooter was clear of the canopy, so I lowered the Plexiglas clamshell. The PC coordinated with Hooter to start the engines, then loosed the start cart to scoot over to our wingman and start his jet.

The closed canopy muffled the clamor around us, and we focused on our post-start procedures. I fired up the INS and watched it wake up while I monitored other start-up checks of the AWG-9 and our missiles. Hooter extended the refueling probe, just one of the checks he and the plane captain did together.

We both kept scanning the people around us for signals. We couldn't yell or pass notes, so we talked with our hands. Hooter gave the plane captain a thumbs-up. The PC relayed it to a flight deck director, who gave the break-down signal: one hand brushing off the other forearm, then switching hand and arm. The director held up a clenched fist; that told Hooter to hold the brakes while the PC literally ran to various parts of the plane and released the heavy tie-down chains. There were six of them, and he threw them onto his shoulders as he released them one-by-one. Finally the director saluted Hooter, and with a sweeping gesture handed us off to another yellow-shirted director.

Sounds complex, and it was, but everyone in this intricate choreography knew every step by heart and strove for perfect execution every time. Perfect, because these large machines were moving among other large machines and people, and there was no tolerance for error. Contact would cause damage, and it was very rare. Perfection was the norm. It is not an exaggeration to say that everyone on the flight deck was comfortable operating at this level.

Guided by our director, Hooter eased us out of our parking space as I started the take-off checklist. Suddenly everything froze as a figure dashed to our side, pumping an emphatic thumbs down.

"Bio, look at that guy," said Hooter calmly. "He's saying we're down. Got any idea what that's about?"

"Nope," I answered. "Let me check with the Boss." The Air Boss was the officer in charge of everything that flew and everyone involved with flying, on the flight deck and in the airspace around the ship.

A thought occurred to me. Hmm … before I can call the Boss I have to turn my radio volume up from

zero. I should've checked it as soon as we strapped in … a rookie mistake that would've been embarrassing even back in Pensacola. A bit red-faced, I mentioned it to Hooter.

"Boss, two-zero-six," I radioed. "We just got a signal our aircraft is down, but we're up and ready."

"Two-oh-six," the Air Boss replied, "I've been trying to call you. Your control frequency has been changed to button ten instead of button nine. Is your jet up?"

"Boss, two-oh-six is up. Copy button ten." Wow, a minor administrative change had spotlighted my error and almost disrupted the launch.

Hooter and I got our heads back in the game. He taxied us to the catapult, and seconds later we were flung into the air, going from zero to more than 150 knots in two seconds. A few more seconds and we were flying level, 600 feet above the blue-gray ocean, and accelerating.

Hooter had time to process the events of the last few minutes and last few days. Suddenly he blurted out, "Bio, we're complacent!"

To anyone in Naval Aviation, that was a powerful codeword, a red flag in my face. The Naval Safety Center had done a study comparing accident rates to the number of flight hours, and they found that aircrews became safer as their experience built—up to a point. Then there was a sharp increase in mishaps. The analysts asked why, and the answer was there in the data: complacency. You get good, then you start thinking you're good, then you get careless. Complacent. Hooter was right; that was us.

The good news was that once aviators passed this stage they again became safer. Hooter saw the light, and his wake-up call got my attention and stayed with me for the rest of my flying career.

We made it through that flight with no incidents, and it felt like we'd dodged a bullet. Flying was risky enough, and our new awareness helped us battle one more demon: complacency.

The *Ranger* operated near Hawaii for a few days,

but bypassed Pearl Harbor and headed as planned into the western Pacific Ocean, where Soviet surveillance aircraft could be expected almost any time, day or night.

When sailing from Hawaii to the Philippines, aircraft carriers always maintained an "alert" posture. During daylight hours, if no planes were airborne on training flights, each F-14 squadron kept one Tomcat on Alert 5: aircrew in the cockpit, strapped in; ground crew standing by; power cord and start cart plugged in; live weapons aboard; and a clear path to the catapult. The F-14s could be off the deck within five minutes.

Pilot and RIO would usually sit there for two hours. So the occasional launch was exciting, and a test of everything we had learned about our aircraft, carrier procedures, and crew coordination. When the Air Boss hollered "Launch the Alert 5 fighters!" everyone sprang into action, with two crucial goals: (1) be airborne in five minutes, and (2) beat the other squadron.

Usually, a support package was also on alert: E-2 Hawkeye airborne radar, A-6 Intruder tanker, and SH-3 Sea King helicopter. They had more time than the fighters—off the deck in fifteen minutes, maybe thirty.

At night the posture was Alert 15; five minutes became fifteen for takeoff. Each F-14 squadron had an aircraft "set" on the flight deck, but the aircrew could relax in the ready room as long as they were in flight gear. That was more comfortable, so crews stood Alert 15 for four hours instead of two. And that's where Hooter and I were assigned. The trip from Hawaiian waters to the Philippines took thirteen days; he and I stood Alert 15 at night eight times on the way.

One night we suited up, got our jet and ourselves ready to go, and settled into the ready room for a few relaxing hours. But then the flight deck was rearranged. They moved our jet. That made it unready for launch, so we had to get up and do it all again. Glitches and airplane moves punctuated our four-hour night alerts, but we never launched. Hooter and I both agreed it wasn't so bad and we didn't complain. It was a chance to be team players.

A small decision also made my overnight alerts easier. In the days before deploying, I had decided that the standard Navy flashlight wasn't good enough. Not enough light. Now I strode the nighttime deck with the best bulbs and batteries off the shelves of K-Mart. Even with the mandatory red filter, I finally had a useful light.

It's the little things.

To keep our edge the carrier practiced its disappearing act, this time in the wide Pacific instead of a few hundred miles from the California coast. Air is air, but when it's this far from home, you're like a new swimmer: comfortable in the shallow end but not the deep end. We were definitely in the deep end.

On normal training flights our TACAN always told us where the carrier lay. It was a radio-based instrument; you dialed a station and it instantly told you the bearing and range. Familiar, reliable, comforting—but wait. It sends out radio signals. That means an enemy could also use the signals. So we shut it down for these exercises, along with all the other radios and radars on the ships. We were allowed to radio other planes in the exercise in secure mode, and a few hundred miles from the carrier we could turn on our radars. No chats with CAG this time!

In that kind of silence, Hooter and I launched, refueled overhead, and sped to our station. It was a beautiful day, but we were preoccupied with manually tracking our heading, speed, and time. I did it on a navigation chart unlike any I'd ever used. It showed about a quarter of the Pacific—a GNC-7 chart, as I recall. How I wish I'd kept it!

I drew a small 'x' on it for our launch position, then another and another as we flew. My careful plot agreed with the INS, so all was well. But the Pacific Ocean is one helluva pond, so hundreds of miles made a pretty short line of x's on the chart, and that made any errors harder to spot.

Safety lessons in aviation are usually written in blood. Somebody screws up, and you learn not to do what he did. Just eighteen months earlier, an F-14 was flying this same exercise in this same area, but the crew hadn't kept a good line of x's and realized too late that their INS had failed. They didn't want to admit that they were lost, and when they finally did, the homing directions they got were faulty—bad info when they needed it least. They ran out of fuel, ejected, and spent the night in tiny life rafts. Incredibly, a search plane spotted them in that vast ocean the next day. No blood this time, but the Navy lost a Tomcat and the RIO lost his wings.

Shortly after it happened, I got a detailed report from a highly reliable source: my kid brother. He was a RIO in that same squadron and was flying in the same exercise! I was one of five children, and this guy, a year younger than me, loved aviation as much as I did. I would sometimes hear him on the radio at Miramar, and we often caught up at the O-club. Over the years, it's been great to go "hangar flying" with a bro.

Those little rubber rafts bobbed about in my stream of consciousness as I plotted a meticulous track back to the carrier's planned position. Somebody must have thought it was a great joke to not be where they said they would be, but we found it anyway.

A few days later the *Ranger* pulled into the US Navy facility in the Philippines, a sprawling complex with an airfield and carrier pier at Cubi Point and a naval station next door at Subic Bay. We were one month into a planned six-month deployment, and this was just a two-day stop—time enough, though, to get off the ship and grab a beer and some different food on ground that didn't move.

As I strolled through the lobby of the O-club, the TV showed Dan Rather doing the CBS Evening News. I froze in mid-stroll as he said something like, "U.S. Navy F-14 Tomcat fighters in the Strait of Hormuz launched missiles at Iranian fighters yesterday in a confrontation that is indicative of the tensions in the region. No aircraft were reported lost by either side."

Strait of Hormuz? That's where we were headed!

CHAPTER 6

OPERATION EARNEST WILL

The news from Hormuz spread like wildfire, but our info was sketchy. We eventually learned that a suspected Iranian fighter was approaching a US surveillance aircraft, and a pair of F-14s from VF-21 on the USS Constellation (CV-64) had been vectored on it with clearance to fire. Each jet launched an AIM-7 Sparrow missile at medium range. But it was a very hazy day and the flight lead realized they did not have good SA, so he chose to abort the intercept. The F-14s made a hard 180-degree turn, which broke their radars' lock-on with the missiles. So it was an exciting event, but it could have been an international incident.[1]

Being cleared to fire—to launch weapons—was incredible. Tomcats had flown thousands of CAP flights and encountered hundreds of hostile or potentially hostile aircraft—Libyan mostly, sometimes others—but clearance to fire was exceptionally rare. So things looked to be a lot hotter around Iran than when I was there three years before, with VF-24.

A secret thought crossed my mind. This might be my chance to get a kill, to shoot down an enemy aircraft in combat. I suspect my squadronmates felt the same, but nobody went wild-eyed at the prospect. We knew combat would be dangerous and complex, but we'd been well trained, and we were flying fighter planes, after all. Maybe this would be the moment of truth.

The *Ranger* left the Philippines, paused in Singapore, and steamed into the Indian Ocean. The VF-21 missile

episode had gotten everyone's attention. We'd been on deployment more than a month and we were comfortable with blue-water operations, flying with no land airfield to divert to. In a week the *Ranger* Battle Group would be on station in the North Arabian Sea, near Iran in the northwest corner of the Indian Ocean. And we'd be ready for anything.

We called the area "Gonzo Station." The term apparently originated several years prior as an acronym for Gulf of Oman Naval Zone of Operations. To me, Gonzo had just the right amount of irreverence.

Hooter and I were the newest members of VF-2. All other pilots and RIOs had been in the squadron at least several months longer, and had completed the pre-deployment training program. But we were ready, too. And we were constantly vigilant for complacency.

The *Constellation*'s flash of excitement had come near the end of her patrol in the North Arabian Sea, and as the two carriers passed each other in the Indian Ocean we paused half a day for the customary "turnover." Choppers flew *Ranger* people to the *Constellation* for notes, charts, debriefs, and advice.

The turnover was valuable. Iraq and Iran had been at war since 1980. Attacks on oil tankers had intensified, often involving other countries' tankers. That threatened a key oil supply route, so in May 1987 President Reagan approved Earnest Will, a program requested by Kuwait to re-register Kuwaiti tankers as American ships, making them eligible for US Navy protection. That was now our battle group.

Something else came aboard in the turnover:

---

1 For a more detailed account of this incident and the bigger picture of US operations in the region, read the book *America's First Clash with Iran: The Tanker War, 1987-88*, by Lee Allen Zatarain.

several dozen brand-new AIM-54C Phoenix missiles. The 54A was a world-beater—long range, large warhead, sophisticated guidance—but in the C-model the mighty Phoenix had gone digital. Glitches were corrected, drawbacks were erased, and the tracking logic brought one word to mind: tenacious. The *Constellation* was probably the first carrier to deploy with the new Phoenix, which would make the *Ranger* second.

We knew we weren't sailing into a smoking-hot combat zone, but it was at least a warm spot, so the ship was ready for anything. Iran used "swarm tactics," sending small boats in suicide attacks on larger vessels, so the *Ranger* mounted .50-caliber machine guns at vantage points, set large orange spheres afloat, and took target practice. The heavy *pom-pom-pom-pom* seemed out of place beside the jets and missiles on the flight deck and the carrier's own self-defense missiles and Gatling gun. But the .50 cals played a role in the layered defense: a low-tech weapon against a low-tech threat.

Military courtesy says you should stand at attention when a superior officer enters the room. When it's an admiral, you don't just stand; you *jump* to attention. When Rear Admiral Anthony Less strode into our ready room, we jumped. He was the commander of the battle group, and he visited every squadron ready room to discuss the international situation, the US Navy's role, and the rules of engagement. In my first two deployments, the battle group commanders didn't do that, so we knew things were more serious this time. He didn't just get us standing at attention; he got our attention.

Admiral Less was a 2-star, an attack pilot with hundreds of combat missions in Vietnam and a tour as CO of the Blue Angels, so he had boatloads of credibility. He quickly told us to take our seats. He reminded us to be professional and restrained, but he also said we didn't need to accept unnecessary risk. He reassured us of his support and his confidence in our abilities and training.

Rules of engagement: that's the term for what you can and can't do in combat. From the VF-21 dust-up

we already knew that launching live missiles was a "can do." If we're shot at, shoot back, like aircrews did off Libya in 1981. But if an enemy ship or plane showed what's called "hostile intent," we could place a finger on the trigger but had to warn them first.

Someone had a great idea: laminate the text of a warning on the frame of our radar scopes:

> *Iranian/unidentified aircraft on course ___, speed ___, altitude ___. You are approaching US Navy aircraft. You are standing into danger. Alter your course immediately to ___ to remain clear.*

We would fill in the blanks to fit the situation. And if they didn't understand English, they would surely understand a Phoenix coming at them.

In VF-2's ready room we taped together navigation charts of Iran and hung the big map on the wall. This was great, but I wanted more. I pored over the highly classified contingency plans, which would be square one for actual combat ops. I got a chart and plotted the routes and locations in the plans. Then I cut a triangle of clear plastic to simulate F-14 radar coverage, and marked it with ranges in the scale of the chart. Low tech, but it helped me feel prepared.

We arrived in the North Arabian Sea on August 29, 1987. The *Ranger*'s skipper addressed the entire ship on the 1MC public address system, not the 5MC that served just the flight deck. He outlined how the carrier and air wing would support Earnest Will. When oil tankers assembled to transit the Strait of Hormuz, ships from our battle group would escort them. A-6 Intruder bombers and their cousins, the EA-6B Prowlers with their electronic eyes, would be aloft for the entire transit, and four to six F-14s would be up there ready to fight. The high-risk part of a transit would last about eighteen hours, but for the whole trip the squadrons would be flying air cover for about three days, twenty-four hours a day.

Three days of intense flying! I loved it.

For me, it began with a 6 PM briefing on a Saturday. The clock and calendar didn't mean much; what mattered was the briefing info on the TV screens in ready rooms throughout the ship. Aircrews listened intently. The attack guys scribbled notes about which Iranian Silkworm missile sites were probably active. The fighter guys kept tabs on the fighter airfields in southern Iran. Then each squadron in the air wing held its own briefing for the details.

But the ready rooms were nearly empty. Normally six to ten guys would be hanging around, quietly waiting for a briefing to finish before resuming their conversation. The twenty-four-hour schedule thinned the crowd to just the aircrews and the duty officer. The briefer seemed more serious, too, and in less than thirty minutes his job was done.

Hooter and I relaxed a bit, downed a soda, made a pit stop, then suited up. The sun was coming in for a landing as we walked out onto the flight deck. We checked our robust missile load: three Sidewinders, two Sparrows, and a Phoenix, plus a full load of more than six hundred 20mm rounds for the gun. We knew from the maintenance log that they'd be there, but it was cool to see all the weapons loaded.

On start-up, I fed Iran's coastal airfields into the AWG-9. Then I tricked it into depicting a crude outline of the coast. RIOs did things like that in days before moving map displays.

The sun was in the hangar when the cat shot hurled us into the deepening twilight. We joined up with our lead Tomcat and a KA-6 tanker 16,000 feet above the carrier. If this were a training flight, we'd do a dry practice plug, but this evening we topped off to maintain a combat fuel package. This was the real world; we were flying a BARCAP, a Barrier CAP in support of high-visibility ops on the doorstep of a belligerent threat.

Our two Tomcats headed west into the Gulf of Oman. Voices crowded our radios—radar controllers from the *Ranger* and an E-2 Hawkeye, and maybe ten other warbirds gliding to their assigned stations. There was another move that didn't happen in training: The guys we were relieving didn't leave until we were there. Making it seamless also made it complicated, another indication that this was a serious mission.

In twenty minutes we were there. I aimed the radar toward the threat, and Hooter flew a two-minute racetrack pattern while it scanned the area. Then he reversed for two minutes to reposition. I kept busy for an hour with various radar modes and scan volumes. Make a change, watch for a few sweeps, make another change. Tedious, but typical for a Tomcat on deployment.

It was a moonless night and clouds hid the lights of both Iran and Oman, each about 100 miles away. There were no lights from ships below us, either. Ho-hum. We could have been sitting in the simulator back at Miramar!

Instead I was sitting up here, flying 22,000 feet above a latitude and longitude in the water. It was my first mission supporting Earnest Will, a real-world oil tanker escort mission approved by the President, a carbon copy of the one where our VF-21 brothers got a hot vector and launched missiles only a month before—and I was, dare I say it, bored.

So was Hooter. "Bio," he said on the intercom, "dial up the TACAN for the frigate that's supposed to be down there."

I switched to the frigate's channel and, to my surprise, its location was almost below us. Hooter rolled us into a steep bank, we turned off the cockpit lights, and there it was, a wan glimmer in the utter blackness that looked like one of those candle-shaped night lights.

"Is that it?" said Hooter. "That faint speck?"

"Must be. It matches the TACAN."

"Wow, I'm glad I'm not down there!"

Exciting, right? Well, it didn't get any peppier for the rest of the mission—until the carrier landing, in the dark, on a moving runway, with live weapons aboard, and other planes landing behind us, and then the jarring slam onto the deck, and the eye-popping yank of the arresting cable that shows you how that dog on the Tom and Jerry cartoons feels when he runs to the end of his leash.

Was it over? Not yet; now the Tomcat had to move very precisely, with Hooter doing some delicate taxiing around the crowded and bustling deck, sometimes with our nosewheel at the very edge of the deck and our nose jutting over the black ocean and us sitting almost atop that nose. He was doing the flying and landing and driving, but I was, shall we say, heavily invested.

Once we shut down and climbed out, the contrast was profound. We had survived again. We went below, reported a few glitches to Maintenance, and vectored ourselves to the wardroom for some midnight pizza. We'd logged 3.1 flight hours.

VF-2's ready room on the *Ranger* was only a few steps from the "dirty-shirt" wardroom, where aviators ate most often because flight suits were welcome. Several decks down, in the middle of the huge carrier, the ship drivers ate in the "clean-shirt" wardroom, where an officer had to be in khakis. The formality seemed to me like something out of the 1800s, but being close to the dirty-shirt made it something we could ignore.

We debriefed, swapped jokes, complained about the paperwork we weren't doing, and then got some coffee. In the Navy, where left and right are port and starboard and a drinking fountain is a scuttlebutt, coffee is usually called, oddly enough, coffee. But coffee with pizza? That's odd enough, too, but for our next Earnest Will flight, Hooter and I briefed at 1 AM—just a few hours after that landing. Whatever you call coffee, we needed it.

A night cat shot is an act of faith, so jarring for that critical second or two that each time we climbed away I thought, *Well, I guess I survived another one.* As we climbed after our cat shot into the 3 AM blackness, instead of an overhead rendezvous we were vectored northwest to refuel from an Air Force KC-10 tanker that was supporting Earnest Will, and it was the centerpiece of a surreal scene. The clouds had cleared and I could see lights on the distant shore of Oman. But the brightest object was the KC-10, which looked like it was only five miles away. It was actually more than 50, lit up like an all-night gas station on a dark stretch of highway—which, except for the asphalt, it was. Hooter finessed our refueling probe into the basket at the end of the tanker's dangling hose. We topped off and proceeded to our station, thankful for the energy from the fuel, the pizza, and the coffee.

As before, it was a chance to practice professionalism—and watch the clock until our relief arrived. We landed just before sunrise, 3.4 flight hours later. Two flights and 6.5 hours, not bad for one night. The VF-2 ready room was still a ghost town, so I had breakfast and slept all day until my next event, the alert at 7:30 PM.

The air wing flew for thirty-six hours to support this event. Sometimes Earnest Will required forty-eight hours or more of continuous flight ops, sometimes only one day. A single aircraft carrier and air wing are set up best to fly for twelve hours, rest, fly for twelve more hours, rest—and they typically operate like that for a week with no sweat. But round-the-clock ops can quickly overwhelm all the moving parts. So we would support a tanker transit, then sail south for a day or two without flight ops to catch up on maintenance and sleep.

Earnest Will sounds like a guy's nickname. Now that you've met him, you've got an idea of what it was like to support him. He was pretty predictable. But not always.

INTEL BRIEF: "MONKEY"

Despite all the training and briefing, even a naval aviator can sometimes lose the bubble. You'd hear a quick radio call, something like, "Rider zero four come up base." Translation: "Call me back on the squadron's radio frequency." Sometimes the caller would try to hide behind a fake callsign, but after months of working with the same people, you'd usually know who it was.

We all carried a kneeboard card with each squadron's base frequency, so if you were bored you could dial up another squadron's base freq and eavesdrop. You might hear something like, "I don't remember my assigned control frequency. What did they brief?"

Kind of embarrassing.

Well, VF-2 had a codeword that only Bullets knew: Monkey. We also used an unassigned frequency that we kept strictly to ourselves. So you're flying a mission, and you're on the frequency assigned to the mission, and a voice casually drops a single word: "Monkey."

If you're not in VF-2, maybe you heard it wrong. But if you're a VF-2 Bullet, you switch to our "secret" frequency and the conversation goes something like this:

"Nasty, this is Bear. We were headed to three-four-charlie, but the E-2 is sending us to three-two-delta. My RIO and I want to verify."

"Yeah Bear, that was changed late in the brief. You guys must've missed it."

"Thanks." Click.

I ask you: How cool is that?

CHAPTER 7

FLYING THE STRAIT

In a chess game, black is black and white is white and never the twain shall meet. But on the global chessboard, the white knight can go black overnight. Less than ten years before, Iran had been our friend, aligned both politically and militarily with the United States. In fact, Iran was our only overseas customer for the state-of-the-art F-14, the AIM-54, and some other advanced American weapons. With the Tomcat and Phoenix in her holsters, Iran stood tall as a regional bulwark against the Soviet Union and a balance to neighboring Iraq, which was aligned with the Soviets.

Not anymore. With the fall of the Shah in 1979 a staunch anti-American regime came to power in Iran. Suddenly it was a whole new chess game. And a whole new set of rules, made crystal clear by the storming of the US embassy in Tehran in November 1979. For 444 days, fifty-two Americans were held hostage, in open contempt of the sanctity of embassies long observed by civilized nations. From that day forward, Iran blustered and threatened the United States and the oil that transits the Strait of Hormuz.

This wasn't distant geopolitics. It was close range and relevant to USS *Ranger*, VF-2, and me. Iran and Iraq had already attacked oil tankers, sparking fears that Iran would try to close the Strait of Hormuz. They couldn't fence it off physically; the strait is far too wide for that. But we'd already seen that the threat of attacks could disrupt tanker traffic. That's why the US Navy was here, with ships to escort oil tankers that were now flying the Stars and Stripes.

First things first. US strategists needed up-to-date intelligence—intel, for short—on Iranian military installations along the Strait of Hormuz. To get it, they sent an EP-3 through the strait. A variant of the large P-3 Orion patrol plane, the EP-3 is crammed with sophisticated electronics and other intelligence-gathering equipment, with a crew of more than twenty to man the scopes and switches. It's a versatile and capable beast, but this EP-3 would be vulnerable to Iranian harassment. It would need an escort.

That's where we came in. Our air wing would provide two F-14s as air-to-air fighters, in case Iranian fighters menaced the EP-3. The package also included a third F-14 carrying a TARPS[2] reconnaissance pod to supplement the EP-3's abilities. And to cover all the bases, an EA-6B Prowler electronic warfare plane and two A-6 Intruder bombers tagged along for this thrill ride—which it would quickly become if Iranian ships or missile sites launched weapons at us. In case you're wondering, all these aircraft carried live weapons.

I would be flying in one of the escorting F-14s. My pilot was our Deputy Air Wing Commander, Captain Bill Bertsch; he'd been XO and CO of VF-24 when I was there. He was now known as D-CAG, or just Deputy.

A few days before the event, I was in the carrier's intelligence spaces helping to plan the mission. An A-6 Intruder pilot was there working on something, and he asked me, "Whatcha doin'?" I told him about the escort mission and we talked about the fuel specs for the F-14

---

2 TARPS = Tactical Airborne Reconnaissance Pod System, a large pod stuffed with two visual-light cameras and an infrared system, designed for the F-14. More details later.

and the A-6. He verified the numbers I was using for planning. After a minute, we introduced each other.

"I'm Denny Seipel," he said. "I go by 'Seadog.'"

He was a lieutenant commander, had a lot of flying experience, and it was obvious that he enjoyed Naval Aviation. We talked a little about the A-6, which he loved. His experience was matched by his enthusiasm, and he seemed to enjoy mentoring a fighter puke— that's what the attack guys called the fighter guys. Of course, we called them attack pukes.

Seadog. Perfect callsign. And a good man to talk with when planning a mission. I thought, *Next time I plan a strike involving A-6s, I'm calling this guy!*

In those days, the eyes of the world were on the Strait of Hormuz. Flying through it, in Iran's backyard, was like playing with a beehive. You could get stung. But part of the Navy's mission has always been to maintain freedom of the seas. It was our turn to step up.

And now it was time: September 9, 1987. The brief started at 8 AM. I sat next to Captain Bertsch, but it wasn't old home day. We'd been in the air wing together for several months, and we'd already chatted, but now the stress level was high. He was very serious; we all were, as we focused on the mission.

The intelligence briefer covered the threats to surface ships, whether oil tankers or their Navy escorts:

- The Silkworm missile, a relatively modest weapon launched from shore installations. The Iranians shifted missiles between several prepared sites, and one of the primary intelligence goals of the flight was to see which Silkworm sites were occupied.
- Mines laid across shipping lanes. Simple, but still effective: an oil tanker had struck a mine just a few weeks before, during the very first Earnest Will event.
- Iranian navy vessels, ranging in size from missile-armed frigates to small boats for swarm attacks.

These were real threats to ships, but not to me as I pondered the upcoming flight. But then the briefing turned to weapons that sure did threaten my mission, and my hide:

- The Iranian air force, flying those F-14s we sold them, plus F-4 Phantoms, and F-5E/F Tiger IIs like the ones I'd flown as a Topgun instructor.
- Surface-to-air missiles, including the very capable Hawk missile. Iran had recently received new parts for their Hawks as a result of the Iran-Contra Affair. We could expect to be dodging those Hawks on any of our air strikes. Again, abstract headlines became all-too-real briefing items for deployed Navy squadrons.
- Hundreds of anti-aircraft guns, of course, around any areas of interest.

Some of Iran's weaponry was pretty unsophisticated, but the fanatical determination of the people wielding it could become a factor. Scoffers who dismissed the Iranian military were forgetting that those we faced in 1987 had survived years of war with Iraq. I'm going over the threat brief in a bit of detail because it was relevant for our entire deployment.

The event brief finally ended, we grabbed a quick lunch, and then got into our flight gear. CAPT Bertsch and I stepped out of the chilly innards of the carrier and into the midday heat of the flight deck. We walked in silence to our jet. One Phoenix, two Sparrows, and three Sidewinders greeted us—a versatile missile load. My nerves were like piano strings, but for the deck crew it was ops normal. It was, after all, an escort mission, not an attack. But that could change in a flash.

As we manned up and started our jet, the clock seemed to speed up. We ran through our normal procedures, but I kept thinking ahead. Join up with the EP-3 … fly the high-visibility mission … keep track of—and then my TID went black. That is, or was, my primary display! I'd dealt with such glitches before, and sometimes it was my mistake; did I screw up? I checked the switches. Nope, everything's as it should be. When all else failed, I had to admit to D-CAG, "Deputy, my TID is blank."

The stress in his voice was clear. "Are we up or down, Bio?"

My brain kicked into afterburner. What work-arounds can I resort to? How badly do I *not* want to be the cause of us missing this flight? It took half a second to decide. "We're good to go," I replied.

I now owned our mission's success. Or failure.

With the TID gone, I'd lost the source of a good deal of my SA, even though our radar and weapons were fully functional. I figured the odds were small that we would launch weapons on this flight, and I knew I could John Wayne it if I had to. I did have to ask D-CAG when the INS completed its alignment (he could see it on his repeat display), but after that I didn't ask questions. With only the small DDD and its raw radar display, I was sure that I could still do my job. I was thankful that I'd made a habit of tinkering with my radar during the many boring hours I'd spent on CAP.

We taxied to the cat, launched, and refueled from a KC-10. The escort package left the tanker as a group. With radar control from the E-2 Hawkeye, we joined the EP-3 and headed northwest into the Strait of Hormuz.

Consider the scale of this event. The start of the route was about 200 nautical miles from our launch point, and the route stretched another 250 nautical miles; that's 450 one way. Then we'd have to go home. That's another 450, for a total flight of more than 900 nautical miles. Think New York to Kansas City.

The EP-3 was the lead aircraft, and it guided us to each of the waypoints on our path. We'd been briefed that every ship and aircraft transiting the strait had to conform to strict rules and precisely follow the route it had declared. I had no idea who might enforce this, but no one wanted to go on record as the guy who caused a protest against the United States for not following international protocols.

The air was almost translucent with a dusty brown haze. We could barely see Qeshm Island, a large mass just off the Iranian coast, even though we were passing by it less than 20 miles away. The propeller-driven EP-3 set the pace, cruising around 300 knots up here at 26,000 feet, which also worked for the jet-powered escorts.

Without my main screen, I was half blind. As our ungainly formation rounded the tight curve of the strait centerline and headed southwest, my DDD showed a contact closing at a pretty good clip. I didn't take a radar lock to determine range, but blurted to D-CAG, "Closing contact at eleven o'clock, slightly high!"

"That's an Airbus, Bio. It's less than 20 miles away. Look."

I looked. I watched the airliner cruise past us. And I vowed to take a breath and get a little SA the next time I had a contact. But no one else dared to venture into my radar bubble that day.

That could have been a textbook situation to use one of the F-14's more unusual sensors, the television camera set (TCS), except the image displayed on the TID and mine was dead. You won't hear me mention the TCS again because, while it sometimes provided cool video pictures, I just didn't use it much tactically.

Our route roughly traced the centerline of the strait, and about 40 minutes into our transit we reached the turn-around area. The EP-3 made a 90-degree right turn, followed by a left 270, and headed back through the strait with six jets on his wings like geese flying south for the winter. Thirty-five uneventful minutes later we completed our transit route, and soon landed after a flight of 3.8 hours. No drama; this was just another mission. As if to underscore that, shortly after landing I briefed as the spare for another flight. It was standard practice to have a spare jet ready in case one of the go jets had a problem.

The EP-3 mission was routine, and successful. Despite the haze, we brought home some useful photo intel on military installations along the Iranian coast—grainy images that showed weapons at some sites and other sites empty—plus the electronic intelligence the EP-3 sniffed out.

The ship then took a three-day break from flying, moving south into the Arabian Sea, away from the Iranian threat. Then we steamed back into the North Arabian Sea for four days of flying. The *Ranger* Battle Group did this about ten times during the thirteen weeks we were in the Indian Ocean: surface ships escorting tankers, aircraft on station ready to provide cover or a strike response.

After that four-day stretch we had a no-fly day. Then we were flying again. And then something bad happened.

Friday, September 18, was a normal flying day. After dinner I was in the intelligence center, looking at maps and preparing for an upcoming flight. The ship rumbled as planes were launched for night flights. You could feel a *thump* reverberate through the giant carrier as each catapult hit the water brake at the end of its track. We all got used to that, and we all had the same thought: *Good luck, guys.*

A few minutes later the planes from the previous event started to land. They'd been in holding patterns about 20 miles from the ship, stacked at 16,000 feet and higher. In a room next to the intel center, radar controllers monitored the process and talked with the fliers. Timed within seconds, each pilot would fly to an assigned point and begin a steep descent. At 5,000 feet the pilot would pull up to a shallower descent.

Suddenly a commotion stirred in the intel center. People were talking in strained voices. Something bad had happened. They were saying an aircraft had vanished from the radar. People hurried into the room, people hurried out. Like everyone else, I prayed that it was a simple equipment malfunction. Something harmless. But my gut feeling said it wasn't.

Then they were saying the missing aircraft was an A-6. There had been no final radio transmission and no one was receiving an emergency radio beacon, an automatic feature of our ejection seats. Our worst fears were materializing.

Aircraft and aircrews are tracked very carefully,

and soon more information came out: the pilot was Lieutenant Commander Seipel and the Bombardier/Navigator (B/N) was Lieutenant Healy.

Seadog! How could that be? He seemed not only bulletproof, but blessed—one of those guys who was already a legend and would live forever. And we knew young Steve Healy as a solid, capable B/N. Two of the best were in that jet.

The ship responded quickly when the A-6 disappeared from radar. A helicopter roared away to its last known position. In the intel center we heard that the chopper crew swept the sea with a spotlight and saw evidence of an impact and some small pieces of debris. No survivors. Our fellow warriors were gone.

It was that simple. It could not be undone. We would never know what took the lives of these experienced aviators. A malfunction at the worst possible time? A desperate struggle? A momentary distraction? We would never know.

The shock waves spread quickly through the air wing. The event that had just launched was recalled, and flight ops the next day were cancelled. Two days later, September 20, there was a moving memorial service on the flight deck. We all wore our white uniforms in the brilliant tropical sun. The carrier slowed almost to a stop and went with the breeze, so the flight deck was calm and quiet, a stunning contrast to the usual sensory assault. After brief tributes and prayers, the service ended. All squadrons spent the afternoon in "safety standdowns," discussing what little we knew of this tragedy, mulling over the safety lessons it might hold, and just talking it out.

But we were here to fulfill a commitment. On September 21 we were flying again. That's the way it was. And still is. Our lost shipmates live on in our memories.

On the flight deck, aircrews are manning for the 0600 launch. All unnecessary personnel clear the flight deck. Remaining personnel get into the proper flight deck uniform….

This is the RIO's office, the rear cockpit of an **F-14A** Tomcat. The square scope at top is the DDD, the raw radar. The round one below it is the TID that displays info in symbols. The "stick" doesn't fly the plane, it controls the radar. The red button at lower left is the missile launch button. *Credit: Tom "Tumor" Twomey*

Laura and me heading for my "hail," the traditional welcome aboard to VF-2 in June, 1987. That's the 1974 Corvette that served me so well.

F-14A Tomcat of Fighter Squadron 2 (VF-2) "Bounty Hunters" cruises above beautiful San Diego.

Perfect timing during a photo-ex! Add the speeds of these two VF-2 Tomcats, and their closing speed would be near supersonic.

The infamous mirror pass described in Chapter 3. In Chapter 12 it got a little more attention than we wanted.

Hoser relaxes in the VF-2 ready room aboard the *Ranger* during the 1987 deployment. Squadron members taped together detailed charts of Iran and the Persian Gulf to keep us oriented and prepare for contingency ops.

This was the warning we were to read to an unknown aircraft before launching missiles. Imagine trying to read this in a volatile situation.

A Tomcat gets a fill-up from a USAF KC-10 Extender. We refueled almost every flight, and I was impressed by how big these tankers were.

Look closely and you'll see one Phoenix, two Sparrows, and three Sidewinders on this Tomcat banking and descending during return to the *Ranger* on a hazy day. This was a common loadout during our 1987 deployment.

Plugged in! This is how a refueling looked from the RIO's back seat, with Pager in the driver's seat using all his skill to ease the probe into the basket.

Bullets join-up on Pager for the return to the carrier at the end of our long flight. Tailhooks already lowered, and we are dumping fuel to get to landing weight.

Sitting in the Alert 5 on the flight deck of the USS *Ranger* in 1987. I agree with you, those are the coolest sunglasses I've ever seen.

Reunion! Laura and me moments after the VF-2 fly-in at the end of the 1987 deployment. No wonder we're smiling! *Credit: Jim Ray*

Sitting by the runway during a two-day visit to Beale AFB in February 1988, I had a great view of the Blackbird's takeoff, spectacular in sight and sound. This jet had a temporary design on the tail, drawn in chalk.

VF-2 missile-shooters at Miramar's weapon loading area in March 1988. Left to right: Rip, Moon, Sax, me, Goober, and Hoser.

When we practiced air-to-air gunnery, we shot at a banner like this. A pilot counts holes after the banner was recovered. You can see one near his left hand, outside the orange circle.

The Tomcat's impressive afterburners, captured one evening off the coast of Mexico. You can even count the "shock diamonds" in the spectacular plumes. The Internet can tell you how they're formed. I'd rather just admire and shoot photos.

Peso and Bing in an F-14 loom large beside Beef in an F-16N, a challenging adversary in air-to-air combat training, as they fly home after an ACM mission over the Pacific off San Diego.

In the spirit of FFARP, VF-2 pilots and RIOs used watercolor paints to camouflage aircraft in June 1988. The blue tube on the rail is a Sidewinder simulator. We called it a "blue tube." The orange tube sends info to the TACTS system; we called it a TACTS pod.

Lumpy and me manning up our camouflaged jet in the brilliant afternoon sun at El Centro. I thought the camo paint made the F-14 look even cooler.

Flying in formation with a jet from our sister squadron, VF-1, during a FFARP sortie. They didn't camouflage their jets for the program.

Fox 3! Two Tomcats have sneaked up on two bandits and launched Phoenix missiles for the kill. Well, this is what it would've looked like if a situation described in Chapter 14 were real. *Credit: Digital illustration by Dorian Dogaru*

The Navy introduced low-visibility gray paint for all tactical aircraft in the 1980s. The transition was gradual, as shown by these two VF-2 jets. The new paint made the big jet harder to see outside of about five miles.

VF-2 personnel and one of our Tomcats gather for a dramatic portrait under the flag we trained to defend. Enlisted are uniformed in light blue, chief petty officers and maintenance officers in khaki, and aircrews in green flight suits. The full squadron would be a dozen Tomcats and twice as many sailors. *Credit: U.S. Navy photo*

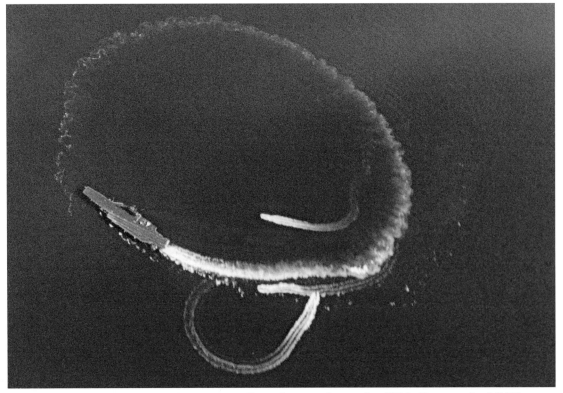

US Navy speedboats simulate a small-craft attack on the USS *Ranger* in 1988. Moments later, Tomcats simulated strafing them to prepare for whatever may happen in the upcoming deployment to the Persian Gulf.

Afterburners in full roar, Bullet 202 aims for the stratosphere above the South China Sea. This is the shot described in Chapter 19. Long before digital, the ASA 800 film actually adds a dramatic grainy effect.

The moment of truth: a VF-2 Tomcat slams onto the deck of the *Ranger*. The black smudge above the tail is the wingman, starting his turn to final approach.

Under dramatic clouds, a VF-2 Tomcat is taxied to the catapult aboard the USS *Ranger*. This required incredible precision and teamwork—every time.

A high overcast provided even lighting for this shot of Bullet 201 hawking the deck, moments before descending for a carrier landing.

CHAPTER 8

GOING OFF THE LINE

We spent thirteen weeks in the Indian Ocean. My logbook remembers the numbers: forty-five flights, about one every other day; 110 hours in the air, about 2.5 per flight. Off the top of my head I'd say about 90 percent of the carrier landings were at night. My logbook remembers it differently: twenty-one night carrier landings. About 47 percent. Logbooks don't have white knuckles.

Why was my recollection so far off? My only explanation is that night landings make a big impression on aviators. Our logbooks keep us honest.

Those Earnest Will escort missions required round-the-clock ops that stressed both machinery and people, so we really needed those no-fly days after each mission. To stay out of the bad guys' crosshairs, the carrier steamed 300 miles south of our normal station, farther into the Arabian Sea, to an area east of Oman. Sometimes the ship dropped anchor, other times we slowly steamed through the sea. We kept fighters on alert around the clock, and were always escorted by ships with air defense capabilities. But without normal flight ops we had a chance to catch up on repairs, maintenance, rest, meetings, and of course, paperwork. There was always paperwork.

To do my job as Avionics/Weapons (Av/Weps) Division Officer I visited workcenters scattered around the ship. We called them "shops": the AE shop for Aviation Electricians Mates, the AO shop for Aviation Ordnancemen (Ordies), and so on. Each was the workplace for four to ten people at a time, working days and nights, 12 on/12 off. For sailors in F-14 squadrons on deployment, that was normal. But the blunt reality was more like 16 on/8 off.

Each shop was cluttered with tools, test equipment, manuals, supplies—and the occasional guitar case, or maybe a surfboard, or who-knows-what that wouldn't fit in some sailor's personal space. The *Ranger* had been in Navy service for thirty years, and these spaces had seen a lot of sweat, tools, and camaraderie.

The shops were alive, charged with energy, vibrant with young men 18 to 25, with a few "old guys" in their 30s as supervisors. You'd dodge out of their way as they scurried up a ladder (Navy term for stairs) to the flight deck to support a launch or make a quick repair. You'd see them plopped into a chair after hustling up and down with heavy toolboxes and those black boxes that were essential to our jets. These guys had the same commitment to the Navy and the squadron as the aviators, the same pride in making the Tomcat a war machine. They worked hard, and there was rarely a malcontent among them. Those workplaces were clubhouses, fraternities, study halls … "home" for six months for these sailors. Show me an office with that kind of spirit!

I joined the Navy to fly jets. I hadn't thought about what aviators did when they were on the ground. But in my first squadron I learned that the ground job—called "collateral duties"—was a rewarding flip side to the flying experience. And so it was aboard the carrier. I made it a point to visit the five shops in the division at least every other day when we were busy, and every day when we didn't fly. It was part of my job as division officer, and I truly valued the camaraderie. The men of Av/Weps always treated me with respect, and I always tried to deserve it.

I did say men. In the 1980s the Navy allowed only men to serve in combat units such as fighter squadrons and aircraft carriers. Later, during my final squadron tour in the 1990s, women were included in many combat units, and that same energy, camaraderie, and commitment still energized the ships.

A division officer's duties always included some paperwork—requests for specialized training, follow-on orders, etc.—and it had to be in the proper format and endorsed on up the chain of command. The trickiest were the fitness reports, the annual evaluations of each person's performance, because whatever you wrote could make or break a career.

On top of all that, I was shuffling cards, hundreds of them from every RIO in every F-14 cockpit on every flight that left the carrier deck. It was the XO's idea to see how reliable those new AIM-54C Phoenix missiles really were. Every RIO would run a series of built-in tests (BITs) of the radar and missiles on every flight and jot the results on a card. No faults? Check the square. Something amiss? Jot down the three-digit code for it.

The cards were nothing new; the Aviation Fire Control Technicians (called AQs, for some reason) used them to troubleshoot long before I came along. But for this deployment I tracked every card for codes related to the AIM-54C. After a few weeks of collecting the data, it was apparent that the new missile was very reliable, but I continued to collect the data anyway. I had the time.

I also worked with the Ordies, who managed the missiles, to track the flight time of each missile. Yes, the Navy keeps flight times for its missiles.

Remember, one item in the list of things we caught up on was "meetings." Many no-fly days included either an all-officer meeting (AOM), an all-aircrew meeting (AAM), or both. For AOMs, VF-2 officers would discuss squadron business in the ready room for an hour or two—the rules for submitting award nominations, or maybe the latest rumor about port visits. AAMs might include a training lecture on an aircraft system, or tactics, or other flying-related topics. They were a necessary evil, because there always seemed to be plenty of things we needed to talk about. The meetings ended with "pop-ups," a chance for anyone to talk.

All squadrons had these meetings, and in such numbers that they were a running joke. Aviators made a note of every hundred landings we made on a carrier; when I notched a hundred landings on the *Ranger* I became a "*Ranger* Centurion." Sure enough, some junior officers played off this and, after enduring enough meetings, sewed "AOM Centurion" patches on their jackets.

The Bullets were lucky; our ready room was just a short stroll from the wardroom, where a soft ice cream machine ran non-stop. It was always vanilla. You'd plop some in a mug, then fill it with coffee in the ready room. It would get you through the yawningest of meetings, and put a childlike smile on the face of any 25-year-old fighter pilot—or this 29-year-old RIO.

Yearning for some ice cream now? This will kill your appetite. We rarely called it ice cream; to us, it was "auto-dog." Watch how the soft ice cream comes out of the machine, and you'll know why. Hey, it's a common term; I didn't make it up. And I did warn you awhile back about sailor lingo. So throw away your unused cone and let's get flying again.

CHAPTER 9

FNG

We were climbing through blackness to 23,000 feet. It was my kind of night: clear, with lights on the coast of Oman and the United Arab Emirates—UAE—giving us a very comforting horizon reference one hundred miles away. We joined up with our well-lit KC-10 tanker and eased into position to refuel.

It took great skill and concentration for a Navy fighter pilot to get the plane's refueling probe into the drogue, the receiving "basket" that trailed from the tanker on a 60-foot hose. When the tanker refueled a U.S. Air Force plane, a guy on the tanker "flew" the probe into a receiver. Not us. When the Navy pulled up, they deployed the drogue and the pilot flew the probe onto the basket. And if we did it wrong the hose and basket could damage our jet, and Air Force tankers were famous for having a stiffer hose than our air wing's A-6 and S-3 tankers. (A situation that would be improved years later.)

My pilot was Pager, a new Tomcat pilot fresh from the RAG who had been in VF-2 less than a week. Pager was an FNG (f***ing new guy). That meant he still had a lot to learn. And I'm there in the back seat, wishing I had chatted a bit more with Hooter and the other pilots about air-to-air refueling, so I could coach the FNG in the front seat about how to plug that basket.

Pager deftly positioned us under the enormous KC-10 and I looked up to see the familiar pattern of lights. We were stabilized right where we should be, 60 feet from its underbelly—but to me it felt like 10 feet. Maybe less. Pager held us steady, inching us toward the basket while I gave him the standard RIO commentary, as if he really needed it: "Up…right…right…We're in!"

Pilots would say they held the stick so tight they were squeezing the black out of the plastic. If Pager felt that way, he didn't show it. Two minutes later our tanks were full. We backed out of the basket, paused on the tanker's right wing, and then peeled away to head for our assigned spot in the sky.

Pager joined us in mid-September, a couple of months into the deployment. The ship and air wing were well settled into the deployment routine. A bulky C-2 Greyhound transport thumped onto the deck every couple of days with a load of mail, spare parts, and usually some passengers. Busing people to and from an aircraft carrier in the Indian Ocean wasn't easy, so the Navy kept it to a minimum, but with more than 6,000 people in the battle group, some passenger traffic was inevitable.

So one day an enthusiastic young F-14 pilot stepped out of the C-2, dodged the pallets of parts and mailbags, and asked the nearest sailor, "Can you tell me where the VF-2 ready room is?"

That was Lieutenant Tom Page, a Naval Academy graduate with the callsign Pager. He could've been a male model—well, couldn't we all?—and had done so well in the RAG that they were comfortable sending him to the front lines. Thinking back to my own arrival in VF-24 at Miramar, I can only imagine the shock of flying halfway around the world to join a squadron on deployment in an international hotspot. But this guy had the right attitude and a lot of confidence.

Good thing he did. Pager had barely stowed his gear when they threw him into the deep end of the pool: a day flight supporting Earnest Will, then another that night, then next day an alert. That meant sitting in the ready room in flight gear for two hours, then baking in a hot airplane, with little chance of doing anything but sit.

If there's such a thing as beginner's luck, Pager had it. He launched on his first alert! And what a launch it was. Blasting off the waist catapult in full afterburner, he snap-rolled into a 90-degree angle of bank and stood the Tomcat on its wing as it roared across the bow of the ship at flight deck level. Clear of the bow, he rolled wings-level on his assigned intercept vector and pulled up into his climb.

Down here on the deck, we loved his impressive performance and enthusiasm. Some said they could look straight into the cockpit and see the tops of his boots! Who could fail to enjoy that breathtaking airshow?

Well, two could: the Captain of the ship and CAG. When Pager landed, he likely got the same sign language I'd gotten several months before: fingers on shoulder, talking gesture, point to Pager. "CAG … talk … you."

Once again, Skipper Dodge ran interference for one of his new officers. Pager vowed that he'd simply misinterpreted the instructions for an alert launch. The pilot was supposed to turn to his intercept heading immediately, and that was about as "immediate" as he could get. The "FNG defense" was the kind of excuse you can use only once.

When the smoke cleared, I was assigned as Pager's RIO. The Skipper and Ops O decided that I'd been back in the Tomcat long enough to fly with a new pilot. So long, Hooter, and thank you for alerting me to the danger of complacency! As I had been in VF-24, I was once again the seasoned RIO, showing a new pilot the ropes.

That refueling off Oman and the UAE was my seventh Earnest Will mission and my first flight with Pager. The brief started fifteen minutes after midnight, but on these ops, night or day was irrelevant; we shifted our eating and sleeping to match the flight schedule. After the brief, we got into our flight gear and walked out onto the warm and quiet flight deck at 2 AM.

Hundreds of times in my career I've stepped out onto the flight deck of a carrier. The enduring impression is howling jet engines, thrashing propellers, people scurrying, catapults flinging airplanes off the bow, and a steady 30-knot gale that I'd have to lean into while it tried to blow me into the sea. But the reality was that we usually manned up between launches and recoveries, and I was always taken aback by how quiet a flight deck could be.

We carried our helmets instead of wearing them. We talked at a conversational level as we greeted our plane captain and the other guys at the jet. We made small talk while we hung our helmets on latches at the boarding ladder. Pager and I preflighted the plane and payload: a live Phoenix missile nestled on its launch rail on the Tomcat's belly, a Sparrow behind it and another one on a wing pylon, and just in case, two Sidewinders.

Time for our appointment with that KC-10. Helmets on. Climb in. Fasten the shoulder straps and lap belt. Finish the cockpit preflight and start 'er up. Taxi the big Tomcat to the catapult. Roger the weight board. Hook up. Salute the shooter to tell him we're ready. Just like in the movies.

No theater could survive the next scene. Livid cones of fire shooting 30 feet out of the Tomcat's tail in an Armageddon of roar and fury. Our heads and bodies pushed into our seatbacks as if we were sat on by a sumo. The carrier pulled out from under us like a rug. Gas station, here we come.

After that pulse-pounding intro, the flight was uneventful. Everything worked well as we flew a racetrack pattern and monitored the Iranian coast. Later we tanked again, spent another hour on station, and then returned to the ship in the dark. No airshow this time; Pager flew a nice textbook pass to landing, and 3.8 hours went into our logbooks. A typical mission.

Ho-hum? No way. "Flew a nice pass" sounds pretty casual, but a well-known recruiting film from the 1970s said that a pilot's fastest heartbeats on a combat flight were during the night carrier landing at the end of it.

This wasn't just our job, it was our life. We dealt with the thrill, the danger, the excitement, the boredom, the spectacle, all of it and more. And we wouldn't have traded places with anyone.

We landed just before 6 AM. After a brief debrief, we recapped what we'd learned over breakfast with our flight lead, Hoser, and his RIO, Goober. Pager was a sponge. He had real talent and was soaking up all he could learn.

Hoser kept an eye on the clock. He was an LSO, a Landing Signal Officer, so at the right tick he went up to the LSO platform on the flight deck, near the arresting cables, to watch a recovery. Pager tagged along to watch flight ops from a front row seat (although there were no seats on the LSO platform).

Goober and I decided to see what was on TV. The *Ranger* had two channels that showed movies nonstop. Bad movies, mostly. But when you've been working all night, even a bad movie is tolerable. We lasted half an hour. Then I hit the sack and slept most of the day.

And then things got interesting. Our flying during these weeks was about half and half, day and night. On night flights the carrier approach was very carefully controlled by radar. A daytime approach was more dynamic, with a complex set of rules and patterns for safety, but a lot more leeway to make your own decisions. The Navy trains pilots in day carrier landings beginning in training squadrons and continuing in the RAG, but Pager had missed some of that by joining us when he did. So, courtesy of my FNG pilot, he and I got extra daytime flights. And those flights were scheduled for ACM. Dogfighting!

I'd flown only two real ACM flights in the two months we'd been on cruise. Now and then we'd whip the Tomcat into a hard turn as part of an intercept, but there were rules about actual dogfighting and we just didn't break them. For awhile, we were prohibited from fighting 1v1 against other Tomcats because there'd been a mishap. Rules like that wouldn't last long, but there were plenty of others that would.

So there we were in powerful, maneuverable Tomcats, constrained by rules and reality. Besides the rules, one of the realities was fuel: real ACM required afterburner, which consumed fuel quickly and would require aerial refueling to get through the scheduled flight time. The carrier rarely scheduled tanking that would support ACM. But sometimes it did.

And so, on a sunny afternoon 20,000 feet above the Indian Ocean, Pager and I were heading west away from the ship. Our flight lead, Brutus and his RIO, were circling behind us to put some distance between us. We'd been slotted between 40 and 60 miles west of the carrier. Our callsigns were changed every day, and today we drew a decent one: Arrow. The words were random and didn't mean anything, but still, who wants to fly as "Dump truck" or "Flower pot"?

Our radar controller on the *Ranger* radioed the magic words: "I show 20 miles of separation."

"Arrow zero-one turning in," Brutus' RIO replied. "Fight's on."

We were ready. I replied, "Zero-two, fight's on."

Pager went to MIL power and rolled left, pulling back on the stick into a hard turn. My g-suit inflated, its air pouches squeezing my legs and torso to keep the centrifugal force from sucking the blood down from my brain where it just might be needed to keep me conscious. But at 6 g, with everything weighing six times what it would on the bathroom scales, I could feel the dizzying effects. So I added my own squeezing, tightening my stomach and leg muscles to prevent gray-out. It had been a long time since my daily high-g flights at Topgun.

"Let's steady up one-two-zero," I told Pager over the ICS. "We'll build some target aspect. I'm in pulse search."

"Roger," he confirmed.

The intercept controller chimed in. "Zero-one, your target is 255 at 22 miles, inbound."

"Single contact," I told Pager. "30 left, 22 miles. Come left to zero-nine-zero."

We accelerated through 350 knots as the distance closed. I got a radar lock and told Pager, "Brutus is level at 23 thousand, accelerating through 400. Come left to zero-eight-zero."

With ten miles between us, Brutus radioed, "Speck in the diamond."

"Tally," Pager responded. We'd seen each other.

At three miles Brutus called, "Left to left," to make sure we all knew how we would pass.

Pager replied, "Roger," and twelve seconds later Brutus' Tomcat flashed past our left side and immediately zoomed into the vertical. We could see his wings swept all the way back—he was hauling butt!

Pager yanked into a hard left turn and lit the burners. I twisted around to keep sight of Brutus' rapidly shrinking Tomcat. As our "enemy" traded airspeed for altitude, I could see his variable wings pivoting forward for the greater lift he would need for what he did next. He pulled his Tomcat on its back for a shot at us.

Pager hadn't forgotten his training. He rolled wings-level and started a climb toward Brutus. That blunted the attack. For the moment.

Brutus was showing us that he could still dogfight. Like Jungle, Brutus was a lieutenant commander doing his second tour in VF-2. Those guys set the pace in the squadron. And up here, too. He was aggressive and skillful as he honked his Tomcat around the tropical sky. The engagement soon became a rolling scissors, then a tight spiral, each Tomcat trading altitude to keep up airspeed for maneuvering. It was a stalemate, and after a few turns Brutus called, "Knock it off."

I replied, "Knock it off," then added a gas gauge report. "Pager state twelve point eight."

"Brutus thirteen-two."

It was great to be back in ACM, with the horizon tilting and clouds sweeping by as we rolled, climbed, and dived, with pilot and RIO in lockstep and wringing from the Tomcat all that it could give.

On the ICS, Pager said it best: "Man, that was fun!"

We'd burned several thousand pounds of precious jet fuel, but we had enough for two more runs with MIL power only. Then it was time to go home, setting the throttle to max conserve so we'd have enough fuel to get there. We lowered our tailhooks and pointed our noses toward the *Ranger*. Brutus led us to low holding, where we circled and watched the next event launch. Then both Tomcats swept our wings aft, and we flew over the ship at 600 feet and 500 knots. Brutus gave Pager the "kiss off" signal, rolled left, and with a pull on the stick was gone. Then it was our turn.

I'd done the carrier break hundreds of times, but this time I was flying with a new pilot. I wished I'd done a tour as a RAG instructor like so many of my RIO brothers. They had to know the business inside out and be ready to coach a pilot through the tough stuff that is part of the routine.

But it turned out like the tanking on the KC-10 that night. If Pager was squeezing the black out of the plastic, it didn't show. I was at full alert, but that's always good. And maybe I made a few comments, like "Come right, we're a little too close abeam."

With or without my kibitzing, Pager nailed it. He turned onto final approach, flew the ball like a champ, and slammed us onto the deck with no drama. Well, no more drama than setting a 51,800-pound airplane flying at 134 knots into an area the size of a basketball court that is rolling and bouncing through the ocean at 20 knots, and then bringing it to a stop in less than two seconds. No more than that.

Pager and I flew daytime ACM flights against several of VF-2's lieutenant commander pilots—Jungle, Hooter, Sax, Booger—and some of the lieutenants. He quickly earned a reputation as a good stick. The LSOs watched him carefully, too. They judged his approaches, his ball-flying, and his landings, and he was always open to their critiques. His RAG instructors made a sure bet when they sent Pager to the fleet.

CHAPTER 10

THE SECOND HALF—IT'S NOT OVER TILL IT'S OVER

When I was 10, I went plane crazy. My favorite was the Vought F-8 Crusader, a single-seat US Navy fighter that first flew in the 1950s. It set speed records, everyone who flew the big beast loved it, and I dreamed of being one of them. But my timing was off. First I had to spend a decade growing up. And then my eyesight started to blur. There was no way I could pilot the Crusader I loved. On the rebound I fell in love with the F-14, but you know how it is with your first love. The F-8 Crusader was always my sentimental favorite.

So one October day was a big one for me because I got a chance to fight against the F-8. The last Crusader fighters had retired from the US Navy in 1976[3], but they were perfect for the smaller carriers of the French Navy, where they were updated and flown until 1999! And here was the French carrier *Clemenceau* with Crusaders on her deck, prowling the Gulf for several weeks before the *Ranger* arrived.

We knew our Navy had racked up an impressive combat kill record with the agile F-8 in Vietnam. The Tomcat's designers had learned a lot from them. So we didn't expect the smaller and older F-8 to be a match for our Tomcats. But we knew French pilots were skilled and aggressive, so we took them seriously—as we would any adversary, for practice or for real.

Aircraft from the two carriers had squared off in a number of training events. Hooter and I had fought French Super Etendard attack jets in September, and

most Bullets had fought one or both of the French jets, but this would be my first look at the F-8.

The event was a 2v2, and Pager and I were the wingman because he was the junior pilot. The scenario allowed for forward-quarter missile shots but no kill removal, because we all wanted to engage—to dogfight!

At the merge both Tomcats had both Crusaders in sight. "Tally two," said our lead pilot. "I'll take the lead."

"Tally two, I have the wingman," Pager replied.

The menacing shapes flashed past us. I thought their dark blue-gray paint looked cool as they deftly neutralized our intercept and split up, one zooming vertical and the other snapping into a turn. *Tres bien, mes amis,* but we had good knots, used our superior turn rate and every other advantage, and soon called kill shots.

We killed again on two more runs. Did I feel bad as a Tomcat RIO "shooting down" my boyhood aspiration? Not at all. My only regret is that I didn't ask them to join up for a moment and take a nice photo.

Ranger and *Clemenceau* learned a lot from each other with many training events, but once in a while it was like fitting a Peugeot fender onto a Ford. Late one evening I was in a group of aircraft returning from a mission as another group took over. Think "shift change in the Gulf of Oman." Suddenly our radio blurted an urgent call from a *Ranger* controller. We all looked—and did the classic double-take at a flock of aircraft lights at our altitude and closing. I'd never seen the French operating like that, but we didn't hang

---

3 A reconnaissance version, the RF-8, flew with the US Navy Reserve until 1987.

around for an explanation. We ducked out of that altitude and watched them zoom by where we used to be.

The flying was great that October. And on the 9th, things down there on the ship got interesting, too. It was Beer Day! Yes, alcohol is prohibited on US Navy ships. But when you've been at sea for awhile, the Navy knows you could use a morale booster. So after forty-five days you can knock back two cold ones as a thank-you for your hard work and sacrifice. It's not as much fun as a port call, but it helps.

We were forty-four days out of Singapore. Nobody would be flying tomorrow. A cookout on the flight deck was set for the crew. 'Twas the night before Beer Day, and all through the ship—

All through the ship boomed the voice of *Ranger's* commanding officer. He sounded unusually serious as he said something like this:

> *This is the captain speaking. We have just learned that Iranian speedboats fired at an unarmed US helicopter patrolling in the Persian Gulf this evening. US Army helicopters responded and returned fire, sinking several Iranian boats. There were no American casualties, but we don't know if this signals a new level of Iranian activity. We must remain ready to respond to any action, so I'm going to cancel Beer Day tomorrow. Don't worry, the beer is in the refrigerator getting colder and we will reschedule as soon as possible. That is all.*

That was all he said. You can imagine the various replies, but at least there was the excitement of some action nearby. Next day, the 9th, instead of two brews and a cookout, Pager and I stood alerts from 6 to 10 AM. Nothing happened. We stood alerts on the 10th and 11th and flew one CAP flight, but again the Iranians did nothing amiss. We finally got our precious beers and flight deck picnic on the 12th. The Navy provided a surprising variety of beers to choose from; I went with the Philippine beer, San Miguel.

The next day was special, too. We all knew the departure and return dates for our deployment, and we had plenty of time to count the days and figure the middle, so everyone knew the halfway point was October 13, 1987. Many of us marked off each day on a calendar, like jailbirds in a movie. The standard joke was that a Navy deployment was "like prison with paperwork."

The old salts would remind us that Navy deployments sometimes stretched to nine months during the Vietnam War. By the time I joined the fleet in 1981, the standard deployment was seven and a half months. That was better, but surveys of people leaving the Navy said family separation was their biggest complaint. I was impressed when top brass responded in the mid-1980s by cutting the standard deployment to six months. Believe me, six months is still a long time away from everything, but it's better than eight or nine.

Two months in the Indian Ocean had fine-tuned the pilots, RIOs, and sailors of VF-2 into a well-oiled machine, cranking out sorties in support of US national policy. For me it was an endless loop of events: Earnest Will, no-fly days, ready room movie points (fire hydrant!), AOMs, visits to workshops, coffee over auto-dog, paperwork. Repeat. Repeat.

Sounds routine, but this machine needs constant attention. One of the key people keeping a Navy squadron on track is the Schedules Officer. The Scheds O (say "skedzo") can be a pilot or RIO, but is always a mid-level lieutenant who has been around long enough to know how things work. VF-2's Scheds O for the 1987 deployment was Bing, a RIO perfect for the job. Bing was a few years older than the standard JO, owing to a two-year delay in starting flight training caused by a blown-out knee in a rugby game. While nursing his knee, he taught high school. Bing looked like a rugby player, and he liked the team spirit of a squadron. His callsign was a natural from his name, Bob Ingham.

Bing had smarts, good sense, and great attitude. Stir in his teaching experience, and the mix was a man who could handle a job that looked simple but wasn't. He had to juggle flights and alerts, keep tabs on "crew day" (the time a pilot or RIO can be scheduled), know which pilots were and weren't qualified for night landings, work within the bounds of sections and divisions, try to keep flight hours and traps equal for all, balance a dozen other inputs—and just when he had the next day's schedule figured out, an event like the Iranian helicopter skirmish or a pilot catching cold would force a rewrite. Bing handled it all and kept his humor. And if you ever got in a bar fight, you wanted Bing on your side.

We Bullets were not a happy-slappy troop of clones; we had our challenges, stresses, and disagreements. But there was an undercurrent of cohesion and camaraderie. One evening, after the squadron had been flying for thirty-six hours, there were ten people in the ready room for the movie—a big crowd during Earnest Will ops. At "The End" we adjourned to the wardroom for pizza. That's called midnight rations, but to us it was midrats. Navy men have a knack for giving good food a name that kills your appetite. (See "auto-dog.") We sat around telling flying stories and jokes I can't repeat here, until at 1 AM Jungle said, "The last event is about to recover. Let's go watch it in my stateroom."

Seven of us crowded in to watch on his 19-inch TV. Among the ship's few channels was the PLAT—Pilot Landing Aid, Television—which showed black-and-white footage of launches, landings, and deck movements. There was even a camera recessed in the flight deck that had crosshairs on the screen. Ready rooms monitored the PLAT to track squadron aircraft, and LSOs used it to debrief passes, but it also provided compelling entertainment to those of us not flying.

Jungle called the ready room. "Who's flying?" The duty officer told him, and he announced the pilots to the crowd, "Sax and Cowboy!"

We stared intently at the screen, and soon we could see the lights of an approaching aircraft. Tomcats always landed first back then, so it would be an F-14,

and it happened to be a VF-1 jet. The plane flew a smooth and steady approach, but the ship was rocking and so was the camera, so it looked as if the aircraft was bobbing up and down.

Once we realized it was a VF-1 jet, our criticism ratcheted way up and the commentary got vicious. That jet was followed by a second VF-1 jet, which got the same treatment. Then it was Sax's turn. Our brothers or not, Sax and Cowboy got no sympathy either. But in the past thirty-six hours we'd all starred on the PLAT, and soon enough we would be center stage again. As the A-6s and other air wing aircraft made their approaches, audience participation dwindled and we drifted off to staterooms and sleep.

We were facing a no-fly day, so everyone could sleep in. Except the crews that Bing had assigned to the alerts, and luckily that wasn't me!

The real-world backdrop to our Earnest Will missions remained tense. US Navy warships escorted tankers in dangerous waters, and Iran continued to menace. On October 16, Iran launched a Silkworm missile that slammed into the tanker *Sea Isle City*, wounding crew members—one a US citizen—and damaging the ship. In retaliation, the United States decided to destroy two former oil rigs in the Persian Gulf that Iran was using to support military actions.

The hit was set for October 19, when four US Navy destroyers would open fire. The platforms were more than 200 miles inside the Persian Gulf, which was no-man's land for aircraft carriers in those days. This put the action about 500 miles from the *Ranger*, which would be a stretch for such minor surgery, so our role was limited to an E-2 Hawkeye providing surveillance and a couple of F-14s in the Gulf of Oman.

Iran didn't react, leaving the destroyers free to shoot at the spindly platforms, with the *Ranger* aircraft as footnotes. It became apparent that ships' guns were not the ideal weapons for attacking targets that are mostly air, but eventually they made their point. I was curious about how such a minor military operation fit into the big picture, but it fit President Reagan's view of America's role in international affairs. It was yet another example of how events that seemed remote and political to most Americans could directly affect deployed military forces—in this case, us.

The ship had been scheduled to visit Mombasa, a seaport in Kenya, in late October. I'd visited Mombasa on my first deployment, but it was among the more unusual port calls for US Navy carriers. The enemy there was malaria, so we all started immunization two weeks before. The pills sickened some of us, but they'd rather barf than battle one of the world's worst killers. And all because of a mosquito.

It was all for naught. Things were heating up in the Gulf, so our port visit to Mombasa was first scheduled, then delayed, and finally canceled. We could stop taking the anti-malaria pills.

On October 22, VF-2 held "quarters" in the forecastle. The Navy pronounces it "foke-sul" and spells it fo'c'sle. Centuries ago, it was a fighting bastion at the bow of a sailing ship—a fore castle. In the *Ranger* it's a large room that the huge anchor chains pass through on the way from their enormous chain locker out the holes in the ship's bow. I'm avoiding nautical terminology here because … well, I don't know it, but those anchor chain links were massive. Carrier fo'c'sles were maintained in pristine condition, and squadrons used them for all-squadron formations (called quarters) for remarks by the CO, awards, and other all-squadron events. Ours started at 6:15 AM and finished around 7:00.

I was in my stateroom changing out of my uniform into a flight suit when there was a sudden announcement over the 1MC, with no preamble: "Helicopter in the water."

I'd never heard that one before. Seconds later someone in the passageway outside the room yelled, "Turn on the PLAT!" My roommate Seymour switched on our TV and we saw the view from the manned camera in the ship's island. Steaming next to us was a supply ship, and a CH-46 Sea Knight helicopter had settled on the water between the ships. Its rotors turned slower than normal, like a sick bird trying to fly. (Seymour's callsign came from his first initial and last name: C. Moore.)

The camera operator zoomed in on the action, and shouts of encouragement came out of every stateroom. "Come on! Fly!"

The Sea Knight's rotors turned half-heartedly for another minute or two. Then it rolled over. We could see commotion as the crew scrambled clear, and in another moment a second CH-46 swooped in to pluck them from the warm ocean—all in front of a PLAT-TV audience of hundreds, maybe thousands.

The CH-46 had been ferrying supplies from the supply ship to the *Ranger*, a routine operation known as VERTREP (vertical replenishment), when one of its two turboshaft engines died and it couldn't stay in the air. The crew of four all survived, but the helicopter sank. The incident was over.

★

Most carrier air wings back then consisted of two F-14 squadrons, one A-6 squadron, two A-7 squadrons, and one each of EA-6B, S-3, E-2, and SH-3, plus a few aircraft on detachment from other outfits. Air Wing 2 was unusual; instead of the two A-7 squadrons, we carried one Marine Corps A-6 squadron.

One sunny October afternoon, a Marine A-6 Intruder was on a routine flight as the *Ranger* carved a wake in the Arabian Sea. Suddenly it wasn't routine. Over the radio came something like this:

"We're having trouble with our engines. They may flame out. We're 30 miles south of the ship."

There was a pause. Then:

"Yup, lost them both; we're ejecting."

This wasn't the kind of radio comms we were taught in flight school, but it was effective. A chopper rose to the occasion and quickly fished the uninjured pilot and B/N out of the sea. Their accounts indicated a simple mechanical failure. As with the sinking Sea Knight, ops continued without a hiccup.

October 24 started early for Pager and me, and for more than thirty other pilots and NFOs. The battle group's primary mission at this time was to support Earnest Will, but there were lots of people out there who didn't like us, so we had to be ready to defend the carrier from whatever stunt they might pull. For "they," read "bombers of the Soviet Union." Unlikely? Sure, but you never knew.

The scenario had a name: the Outer Air Battle. A key aspect was to set up a defensive grid of Tomcats to spot enemy aircraft with our long-range radars. A blip on the screen would be like poking a hornets' nest. The fighter with the blip would streak toward the enemy with a finger on the trigger, while Tomcats behind him raced to bring their missiles into the fray.

To make it realistic, six or eight Tomcats had to be airborne for hours, because in reality we didn't expect to know when the bombers would arrive. The fighters would be supported by E-2 Hawkeyes, EA-6B Prowlers, and herds of A-6s and S-3s as tankers. It was complex, and it took a lot of airspace to do it realistically. The *Ranger* had steamed farther into the Indian Ocean, so we had the elbow room.

The briefing started at 5 AM. The intricate plan had been elegantly reduced to a repeating series of events on a few kneeboard cards. It also included spares—backup jets, in case one of the go birds went down— and that's where Pager and I were slotted. We had dragged ourselves into the briefing, collected our kneeboard cards, and paid semi-attention while visions of a delicious breakfast danced in our heads. We would man our jet, watch the scheduled Tomcats launch, shut down our jet, and enjoy breakfast and a nap.

We started our jet and sat there discussing whether to have pancakes or eggs, when we noticed a break in the flight deck routine. One of VF-2's go birds was down, unfit to fly. Suddenly a flight deck crew ran over to our jet and started waving urgent hand signals. We were going flying!

Okay, okay, which jet went down? 202? They were long-range CAP. Okay, I have that card.

In just a few minutes we went from max relax to launching off the cat into a beautiful tropical sky.

What's our heading? One-zero-zero. Okay, climbing to 26 K.

That was enough to get us started. As long-range CAP we were key players in an exercise that involved half the air wing while top brass watched it all. Distances were in hundreds of miles, so we had time to get our heads in the game and figure out the briefing cards and our role in the drama. Good thing, because the exercise was done in radio silence. We flew hundreds of miles away from the ship, orbited on our assigned station, left it on schedule to meet our tanker, topped off, and flew back to our station, all in an eerie silence.

I set up my radar and watched it with an eagle eye, because we'd been briefed that an "enemy" would be arriving to test our defenses. No one wanted to be the CAP that missed that target. So I stared at a blank scope for an eternity.

After a couple of hours, with no idea how long the flight would last, I'd had it with being strapped in. I ran my ejection seat to its lowest position, undid my lap belts, and squatted on the seat, frog-like. Man, it felt so good just to move! I kept my shoulder straps attached in case we had to eject during my brief relief. Safety first.

Pager was faced with mostly tedious flying, but at least the autopilot worked, so he had some help. And about every ninety minutes we visited a flying gas station and tanked up. That gets your full attention, day or night.

Hour after hour we flew. We chatted a little. Pager told me how he got into Naval Aviation: His dad had taken him to a Blue Angels air show when he was around 12 years old, and he wanted to be one of those guys. He went to the Naval Academy, then flight school, and did well enough to get Tomcats. We traded a few other stories, but mostly we flew in silence.

Whatever happened to breakfast? Well, we didn't get the feast we'd anticipated, but for some reason I had brought a decent supply of snacks in my helmet bag: two fruit rolls, two Kudos candy bars, two Twix, and two oranges. We shared them, and they got us through. Peeling those oranges after four hours of flying filled the cockpit with a fantastic fresh perfume.

A few hours later I did my frog imitation again, squatting on my seat. It was a relief to simply change my position.

Speaking of relief, eventually we had to answer the call of nature. Luckily we routinely carried piddle packs—a thick plastic bag that could be sealed. It contained a sponge before use, and after use contained a wet sponge. A low-tech solution to a basic need.

At last the exercise ended and we turned toward the ship. Two senior VF-2 pilots joined on our jet and let Pager lead the flight into the break, a measure of trust for a new pilot. He flew like a seasoned veteran.

Our flight time that day was 7.6 hours, which would stand as the longest flight of my career. (Other Tomcat crews have flown longer.) The only excitement was at the start and finish: the rush to launch and the cat shot, and when we led a small formation of squadron-mates above the ship at the end. In between we flew at a sedate 225 knots, five miles above the featureless ocean, hundreds of miles from land, with only some majestic clouds to keep us company. If doing that in an F-14 Tomcat fighter can be dull, it was. But we had to stay sharp and pay attention to the complex plan, the navigation, and the things our instruments were telling us. If it was dull, that meant we were doing it right. If

not, a lot of exciting things could happen—an aborted exercise, the dreaded "CAG…talk…you," and possibly the loss of an aircraft. It had happened before.

This time the exercise was a success. We proved that a large air defense grid could be set up and maintained for a long time. And late that afternoon, the formidable "enemy" finally showed up—a fat, friendly cargo plane loaded with mail and spare parts.

By early November, we could see light at the end of the deployment tunnel. VF-2 had stood at the leading edge of world events, and we could look back with satisfaction at having performed well.

Still, there's always time for a last-minute glitch or two. One afternoon, Jungle was actually cleared to fire on a low-altitude, high-speed target flying south into the Gulf of Oman from the Strait of Hormuz. It didn't make sense to him, so he didn't fire—at what turned out to be a French F-8 Crusader from the *Clemenceau*. Another night, it was Hooter who thought it didn't make sense, when he was cleared to fire on a "target" that looked to him like the lights of a large aircraft. He was right; it was a commercial airliner.

The *Ranger* departed the North Arabian Sea on November 11, completing an exciting and eventful phase of the deployment. It had been four months since we left San Diego—it seemed like longer—and it would take some time to get back there, but at least we were headed towards home.

CHAPTER 11

SUNSETS ON THE FANTAIL

When a carrier goes home and another takes its place, that's called a turnover. It's not just hello-goodbye; It's planned many months in advance and it plays out on a scale that's almost continental. Dozens of ships and thousands of people are involved. But sometimes things change, as we saw when our visit to Mombasa was scrubbed. So you're cautious about getting your hopes up.

And then the relieving carrier dots the horizon, and you know you're on your way home.

For us the handoff happened on November 11, 1987. The USS *Midway* (CV-41) steamed into the North Arabian Sea, and we steamed eastward, toward the USA. At day's end, the sun would set behind us, over the aft end of the ship called the fantail. "Sunset on the fantail" was a Pacific Fleet heartwarmer, for it meant going home.

Farewell, Gonzo Station! Now our focus shifted from Earnest Will and its potential contingency operations—that's called "combat"—to such thrills as writing end-of-deployment reports, planning for port calls on the way home, and getting everyone from here to there safely. As the details jelled, someone realized that we could actually arrive in San Diego before the New Year, which would make this a five- and-a-half-month deployment. Incredible!

Hold on. Until we tied up at the pier, we were still on deployment and still flying as part of America's global military presence. We had to compartmentalize our excitement about going home, so when we briefed and flew, when we stood alerts, when we all did our jobs, we could deal with the ever-present risks of Naval Aviation. I stood alerts almost every day, and flew three times during the eleven days it took to get to our first port visit at Pattaya, Thailand. I did a lot of compartmentalizing.

Eleven days? It doesn't look that far on a globe. But there were countries and islands and territorial waters to go around and thread through, and it all added up to more than 4,200 nautical miles. Do the math; it works out to an average speed of 16 knots, day and night. That's good, considering that we weren't alone. The carrier had to juggle the logistics of supporting an entire battle group, and also had to turn into the wind whenever we flew. My point: The Pacific and Indian oceans are vast.

I was the senior lieutenant in VF-2, and one of my collateral duties was Senior Watch Officer—oversight, scheduling SDOs, that sort of thing. With port visits coming up, I had to assign my junior officers to watches: this guy to shore patrol, that guy as boat officer, and so on. Over the course of three weeks, we would be in Thailand for five days, Hong Kong for four, and the Philippines for three, so some of us would be standing three watches. To share the burden, I did something I didn't have to do: I signed myself up for the 0200-0600 watch on a picket boat in Pattaya. I'd be in a small motorboat with a few sailors, patrolling the waters around the carrier.

Not many Americans have heard of Pattaya, and fewer have been there, but it's renowned throughout the Pacific Fleet as a scenic delight. I could see why as the *Ranger* anchored a mile offshore on the morning of November 22. It was my first look at this port-of-call, and what I saw was a modern city that lured tourists from Europe and Asia to its beautiful tropical beaches and myriad hotels, shops, restaurants, and clubs. And our battle group enjoyed them all!

In those days, before satellite phones and the Internet, this was my first chance in three months to actually talk with my wife, Laura. After dozens of delayed letters, it felt incredibly close to hear her voice real-time. The telephone seemed like the greatest invention in human history.

And then it was time to eat some non-ship food and down a beer or two. The VF-2 officers got together and booked a big hotel room as our on-shore headquarters. We called it an "admin," and we shared one in almost every port as a convenient place to meet, stash purchases, nap, and get away from the tropical humidity.

Five days off! Pure luxury after the months of work. And what better place to relax than exotic, friendly Pattaya? We spent money we'd saved, ate great food, enjoyed the clubs, and just got away from it all. Well, not all, but standing my boat officer watch wouldn't be enough to dampen my spirits.

Neither was my stint as beach guard officer. I'd given myself that job, too, so for six hours one evening I sat with four senior enlisted men in a room near the resort district to keep small problems from becoming bigger—shipmates who overindulged, sailors still in their teens and new to the world, guys who thought the snacks and booze in the mini-bar were free. We paid the bills, got their names, and collected later.

At midnight I caught a boat to the *Ranger,* and at 2 AM reported for my picket boat watch. A lieutenant from the EA-6B squadron showed up at the same time. "Someone made a mistake," I said. "I've got the watch." He did a crisp about-face and left, smiling.

I stepped carefully down the ladder and joined four sailors in the boat, an open twenty-six-footer with a binnacle amidships for the wheel, throttle, and a few gauges. These small boats did everything, even occasional man-overboard rescues. The diesel engine rumbled steadily as we prowled around the towering *Ranger.* How can this steel mountain float? I mused. But here it was, floating in the mirror-calm water as if in a surreal painting. We chatted about hometowns, girlfriends, and odd features on the ship's hull that we'd never noticed before. The four hours passed quickly. And, better believe, nobody messed with the ship that night!

I slept in the next day, went ashore for awhile, and was back in the rack by midnight. At 2 AM my phone jolted me awake. "Lieutenant Baranek"—Uh-oh, this can't be good—"we're supposed to have the picket boat officer at 2:00."

Smack on the forehead; in a flash I knew what had happened. The schedule said 0200 November 26, and that's when I stood my watch. But it meant the night that *began* on November 26, so 0200 was tonight, on the 27th. I will spare you my internal monologue as I threw on my khakis and raced to the boat platform to stand my watch. I'd been so proud of taking this one for the team, and now I was taking it twice. No wonder that guy was smiling the night before.

Hold on; it gets worse. Halfway around our first lap of the ship it started to rain. Perfect, I fumed. We finished the circuit and grabbed raincoats at the platform. And then the clouds tore open and there was hardly a difference between the air above and the bay below. I guess the fish thought so, too, because big ones were suddenly leaping out of the water, some even flopping into our boat. Last night seemed surreal, but this night really was.

Our patrol ended early as the ship prepared to raise anchor and get underway. Soon we were in the South China Sea, headed for Hong Kong.

Port calls, brews, beaches—yes, but also two flights and two alerts in the five days to Hong Kong. The deployment wasn't over. Again, compartmentalize the distractions and complete the mission safely. These flights were routine, even the CAP flight as we passed still-hostile Vietnam. But we needed them to keep that razor edge sharp. Our battle group could be recalled anytime.

Next stop: the bustling port of Hong Kong. We arrived at noon on December 2, steamed deftly through the crowd of ships, boats, and assorted watercraft, found our parking space, and dropped anchor. Thousands of shipmates made the hangar deck as crowded as the harbor, while a steady stream of shuttle boats slowly drained the flood of people eager to step ashore. I lucked onto an early boat for a port call even better than Pattaya: Laura was flying over to meet me! Wives and girlfriends loved to visit Hong Kong, with its vibrant culture and perfect mix of "exotic refinement." Oh, and excellent shopping.

Cell phones were rare in those days, so the ship and its squadrons served admirably as traffic cops, helping people aboard and ashore to find each other. I found Laura at the boat landing on Kowloon, and there was no daylight between us for half an hour. An imp between my ears kept whispering, *Get a room!* We did, and it was a great reunion.

New to Hong Kong, we wandered through Stanley Market and as many other tourist magnets as we could cram into a four-day shore leave. We even rode the subway for a few stops to have dinner at a "real" Chinese restaurant in the burbs. It was tough to kiss goodbye, but exciting to know that the deployment would end in three weeks.

Anchors aweigh! The run to the Philippines was déjà vu: sea duty as usual and liberty in port. Then the sun was setting in our wake again as we hightailed across the International Date Line. At this point in our journey, when we counted the days and hours, the Date Line cruelly caused us to add a day. No, it doesn't really extend the trip, it's just a calendar trick.

We bypassed Hawaii, and twenty-four days out of Hong Kong we were in San Diego in time for New Year's Eve.

Hold it; first there's the fly-off. Squadrons needed to return to their home stations in anticipation of life after the deployment.

For the final week at sea, nobody flew. That let the ship stay on course without having to turn into the wind, and it gave the maintenance people some breathing room to get as many aircraft as possible ready to launch for the fly-off.

Throughout the ship, there were meetings and more meetings as we ironed out wrinkles in the plan for the big leap from ship to shore. We all yearned to get home asap, with no aircraft left aboard to be ignominiously plucked off the deck by a dockside crane. But we wanted to do it safely. There had been tragic mishaps on flights like this, and no one wanted to be the next one.

At 6:30 AM on December 29, those chosen to fly the fly-off met for the last briefing of the deployment. We weren't scheduled the usual way. This time, pure seniority reared its head and I would fly with Hap.

Ship and squadron personnel were as excited as the chosen aircrews. They performed flawlessly one more time, moving some sixty aircraft around the deck like chessmen and launching them on a tight schedule—one squadron to one airfield, then the next to its airfield, and so on. That also made things easier for the air traffic controllers.

VF-2 launched all twelve of our F-14s, a tribute to the herculean effort by Maintenance. The ship was still several hundred miles off the coast, so we had plenty of time to rendezvous. We flew in loose formation most of the way, then tightened it up as we roared closer to Miramar. San Diego's ATCs were old hands at this; they knew how to handle a large formation barreling in from deployment.

Hit the Pause button. Now you're not in a Tomcat, you're in a crowd at Miramar, and you all know the Tomcats are coming; that's why you're a crowd. Any minute now, they'll darken the sky like a cloudbank. They're made partly of titanium, so you're about to gape in awe at what's called a "titanium overcast."

And here they come! Twenty-four howling jet engines deafen you as a dozen fighters darken the sky, each seeming to scream, "Baby, I'm home!" They make one pass over Miramar, then split up into the break. How many people ever get to see a sight like that?

And now back to real time, the men in those Tomcats, looking down into the crowd for a glimpse of a loved one in the sea of cheering faces? Hap was totally focused on flying a tight formation, but I was looking for Laura.

As we lowered the landing gear, the RIOs all reminded their pilots NOT to lower the tailhook as they'd been doing by habit for half a year. We landed on that 11,000-foot, rock-steady runway with no deck cables to yank us to a halt.

As we taxied clear, several junior officers from our host squadron were standing by the taxiway with a cooler and signs saying, "Welcome Home, Bullets!"

One of them signaled us to raise the canopy, and Hap was game, so I opened up. The "welcoming committee" raised a pole with a bag clamped on the end. Inside were two cold beers and two condoms. Welcome home, indeed!

Hap and I stowed the two smaller items and popped the two brews. It was the only time I ever drank in an F-14. The cockpit didn't have a lot of room, but the room service was terrific.

After we parked and climbed down from the jet, someone handed me a dozen roses to give to Laura. I found her in the jubilant crowd, and again there was no daylight between us. Scenes like this were playing out for the other squadrons at other bases, and next day the *Ranger* arrived for her share.

Our deployment was over. "Only" five and a half months. There *is* a Santa Claus. And his gift was a brand new year.

CHAPTER 12

HELLO, BLACKBIRD

An F-14 on a catapult can lurch from zero to 150 knots in two seconds. An F-14 squadron fresh from deployment is more like a two-trailer semi leaving a rest stop. The move from carrier to base slows things down a few days, of course, but so do the higher-ups in the chain of command. They intentionally slow things down for a month, with four-day work weeks and fewer flights to let us catch our breath.

That's how it was for VF-2 as 1988 began. I had only four flights in January—one of the lowest workloads of my career. But to keep it exciting I also had another "leadership encounter."

Remember those photo flights before we deployed? (They're in Chapter 3.) We had sent the photos to the Tailhook Association magazine, and they published a couple in the fall 1987 issue. The COMFIT Chief of Staff must've gotten to those pages in January. COMFIT was our name for the Commander, Fighter and Airborne Early Warning Wing, US Pacific Fleet. Led by an admiral, COMFIT managed the F-14 and E-2 squadrons on Miramar. Boil its name down to one impossible word, and you get COMFITAEWWINGPAC, which is why we said COMFIT.

One morning the SDO called me to the ready room. He told Hoser, me, and another pilot to get over to the Chief of Staff's office.

A former E-2 pilot, the Chief of Staff was a captain with a nice office and no apparent sense of humor. The three of us stood in front of his desk not knowing what to expect.

He asked if we took those photos.

"Yes."

He zeroed in on a photo of two Tomcats. Both had their landing gear lowered. Well, for one of them, make that "uppered." It was inverted, with its legs pointing up. And that was his point. He had consulted the F-14 flight manual, which said when landing gear are extended the plane is limited to between 2 g and 0 g. He pointed out that flying inverted was *minus* 1 g, so by definition we'd violated a NATOPS no-no.

I hope our mouths didn't actually hang open as we stood there in stunned silence. They sure were open when we all started talking. "Well sir, not really, we were in level flight so it was 1 g," or something like that.

He was probably right. But we had a saying around Miramar: "Arguing with a fighter pilot is like wrestling with a pig: you both get dirty and the pig loves it." That goes for RIOs, too. He had no desire to get dirty so he just yelled, "Get outta here!" We didn't argue with that.

We walked back to the squadron talking about how it was a cool photo but maybe not a good idea. There's a fine line.

On a clear day a few weeks later, Hoser and I launched for a PMCF. That's a post-maintenance check flight, and you do it to make sure a problem has been fixed. A PMCF was demanding because the flight had to verify that *all* the major systems were working, requiring pilots and RIOs with a certain level of experience, who were formally designated.

We took off and headed southwest, over the open Pacific. Everything worked well: fuel automatically transferred between tanks, cabin pressure stayed in the green, wings swept automatically. Then we did the special stuff: slowing to stall speed, dumping cabin pressure, shutting off the engines—one at a time, mind you!—to check the various systems affected by losing an engine. But what if the shutdown triggered a glitch in some other system, or maybe the engine itself wouldn't restart? That's why they chose experienced guys for PMCF.

This day, everything worked smoothly. We climbed to 34,000 feet for the prescribed high-speed dash to see that everything worked under the strain. Hoser jammed the throttles to full afterburner and we rocketed out over the Pacific.

"Want to see how fast we can go?" Hoser asked.

"Sure!"

We approached the speed of sound, Mach 1, known long ago as the sound barrier until Chuck Yeager broke it in 1947. Our powerful Tomcat broke it again and kept on going—Mach 1 … 1.2 … 1.4 … 1.5 … 1.6.

Oddly, up here at 34K there was little sense of speed. Just some wind noise from the canopy frame. It didn't matter; I was focused on monitoring the systems.

As the airspeed indicator rose, so did the TACAN that showed how far we were from Miramar: 80 nautical miles … 100 … 120. At Mach 1.5, we were clocking 15 miles per minute, an incredible mile every four seconds.

As those numbers went up, my fuel numbers went down: 9,000 pounds … 8,000 pounds … you get the idea. We were burning 1,000 pounds of fuel every minute, and of course I was keenly aware that we were heading *away* from our base.

I was crunching numbers in my head and finally said, "I think we need to head home." Hoser agreed.

We had hit Mach 1.74 at 34,000 feet. That's 1,230 miles per hour. It's also 1,080 knots, but that doesn't sound as impressive. How about 1,800 feet, or six football fields—*in one second?* Tomcats have flown faster, but it was a decent mark and remained the fastest I have ever flown.

There are faster machines. A few weeks later Hoser

and I met a couple of them. You'll recall how we stopped for fuel at Beale AFB and visited the SR-71 squadron. That's also in Chapter 3. They'd taken our names, and now they wanted us to represent the F-14 community at a conference. The SR-71 community wanted reps from the four types of US fighters—Navy F-14 and F/A-18, Air Force F-15 and F-16—to spend two days at Beale discussing "operational matters." They asked each rep to fly their aircraft in.

VF-2 gave it a thumbs-up. "You made the contact," Skipper Dodge said. "Take a jet and go."

On a mid-February afternoon, Hoser and I landed at Beale, a two-mile stripe of tarmac near the small town of Marysville, California (pop. 12,000). It was great to be back at the home of SR-71s and U-2s, and the Air Force made it even greater when they handed us the keys to a dark blue government sedan with zero restrictions. We changed out of our bags and headed for Chico, a not-so-small town of 40,000 some sixty miles north. It's a college town, so we had no trouble finding a bar. The place was oddly quiet; exams tomorrow? Just as well. We tossed back a couple and headed back to Beale.

The conference the next day was fascinating. We learned about the SR-71's missions, capabilities, op— Hold it. There's a grim little building on the base where Nazi POWs admired the view through iron bars in the 1940s. I don't want to be its next resident, so let's just say the SR-71 and U-2 crews were very professional, and they respected us fighter pukes and shared info that we needed.

The guys at Beale appreciated our coming to their conference, and they knew we were itching to see their aircraft. So finally we headed for the flightline and a waiting U-2 and SR-71, two jets that do their jobs at opposite ends of the airspeed indicator. Their only family resemblance was their black paint. The high-altitude jockeys gave us a walk-around of each aircraft, then we split up. I was courteous enough to look at the U-2 cockpit first. Yes, it could fly above 70,000 feet and stay there for twelve hours or more, but it just didn't push my buttons. After a cursory visit I slipped away to the sexy one.

Every reader knows what the SR-71 looks like. If not: It looks sleeker than most spaceships. It's big; 107 feet long. Stands high off the ground. Packs a pair of huge engines. Wraps itself in sensuous lines and curves. Looks speedy standing still. Give all that a dull black paint job, and it looks both elegant and sinister.

One glance tells you this racy bird can do some incredible things. 2,000 miles an hour? Mach 3? Better than that. 80,000 feet? That's 15 miles high. Right at home up there.

I climbed the boarding ladder eagerly. Before stepping into the cockpit, I paused to take in the undulating lines of this magnificent machine. I can see it even now.

Then I stepped down into the cockpit—and into the 1960s. The front and rear cockpits were complex but almost quaint, busy with old-school analog gauges and switches. No surprise; the Blackbird and its crews were working their wonders before the Tomcat was even imagined.

After we'd all tried on the Blackbird for size, we were chatting beside it, and I noticed one of the guest pilots kept glancing over my shoulder. Finally he asked, "Can we look at your jet?"

It was like Shakespeare asking to borrow your pen. "Of course!" I replied. Hoser and I led the group proudly to our Tomcat for a walk-around tour, with a sit-in at no extra charge. We all noticed that the large round TID in the F-14 rear cockpit looked a lot like the main display in the back seat of an SR-71.

Our Tomcat looked lonely on the flight line, so we asked the other fighter jocks where they parked. A bit sheepishly, they all said their squadrons didn't have the fuel money to fly to Beale, so they drove. How great it was to be in VF-2!

Hoser and I felt the need for another road trip, so we headed south to Sacramento. In the suburbs we spotted a restaurant and pulled in. The place was packed and a DJ was blasting music. We grabbed beers and settled in. A few minutes later the music stopped and the DJ blared, "We've got some real F-14 Tomcat fighter pilots here, and this one's for them!" He cranked up "Danger Zone," the *Top Gun* movie theme.

Hoser and I looked at each other with question marks popping from our heads. I had to find out what was going on, so I headed for the DJ. Shouting over the music and the crowd, I asked him who requested the song. He pointed to a booth where four young guys sat drinking beers.

I got Hoser and we squeezed amiably into the booth with them.

I asked, "Hey, are you guys the F-14 pilots?"

"Yeah, sure are!"

"What squadron are you with?"

A couple of them stammered out something like, "Oh, uh, we're not with squadrons, we just finished training." No pilot or RIO would say that.

It was a short interrogation. Our faces said we weren't buying it, and they could tell. They quickly fessed up: they were enlisted intelligence analysts attending school at nearby Mather Air Force Base and, well, they thought they would try the F-14 maneuver to "meet some chicks."

We wished them luck.

The second day started like the first. We talked about tactics—the F-14 maneuver was not one of them—but we'd already heard all the gee-whiz stuff. After an hour an SR-71 back-seater—an RSO, or Reconnaissance Systems Operator—quietly asked Hoser and me if we'd like to go watch flight ops. Guess what we said….

As we headed for the hangar, he told us they were launching two Blackbirds thirty minutes apart, a rare event. One crew was getting dressed, which involved more complex clothing than the simple Nomex bags we wore. These guys required layer upon layer to control their own temperature, and to protect them if they ejected at high altitude. We chatted with the pilot and RSO as they suited up with the help of two trained assistants. They seemed relaxed as we swapped flying stories. And these guys who worked in the stratosphere at Mach 3 couldn't get over the thought of night carrier landings!

We got another walk-around, and it was as fascinating as the first, with the Blackbird's amazing engineering and performance details to keep us wowing. Then we climbed in an Air Force station wagon with our escorting pilot and RSO. We would be the "mobile unit," eyes on the ground to spot problems and radio the info. As we drove slowly past the hangar, the SR-71's engines spooled up and it eased majestically out of its hangar, hung a left, and fell into trail well behind our humble wagon. I believe I've said before how cool that Blackbird looked, but I'll say it again. That long nose slowly easing out of a hangar was an awesome sight, as dramatic as any "reveal." Normal ops for those guys, but I'll bet they still thought it was cool every time.

We led the Blackbird to the hold short, the area where you hold short of the runway and do your final checks. I was cleared to take photos once we left the hangar area, so I popped in some earplugs and got out of the mobile to shoot a few.

Then the Blackbird took the runway to do what it did best. The takeoff roll started slowly, but once the pilot lit the burners the speed and sound increased, and soon the sleek machine was in its element—airborne. The pilot held it level at low altitude, building speed until the end of the runway. Then he stood the sleek black rocket on its tail, and we watched it shoot for the heavens. It looked like a visitor from the future even twenty-five years after its maiden flight. In a moment it was gone.

What a spectacle! The second SR-71 treated us to a replay half an hour later.

That was an impossible act to follow. Hoser and I didn't even think about going back to the conference. We thanked our hosts for their hospitality, got into our flight gear, and launched our own machine into its element. Beale Tower cleared us for an unrestricted climb, and I'll bet we looked good, too, as we yanked into a near vertical climb. In a moment we were gone.

CHAPTER 13

CHANGES ON THE GROUND AND IN THE AIR

Doc rolled our jet into a 90-degree bank and pulled for a hard left turn. "Mark," he said, "waypoint 3!"

I looked down at the highway rest stop directly below us. We were only 500 feet above the cars, trucks, and people, so I could see them clearly and there was no doubt they could see and hear us. How could they not? We were roaring over their heads, almost low enough to part their hair. Three hundred sixty knots is 600 feet per second, so it's not like we spent a lot of time there. I just noted the rest area and got back to the mission.

My mind was thinking, *Yee-ha!* But my mouth was professional, "Outbound course 087, altitude 900 MSL. Next waypoint is a road and railroad intersection coming up in two plus eighteen. Fuel is 1,200 pounds above ladder. We are four seconds ahead of plan; no correction necessary."

We roared east over the empty terrain of central California, searching for that intersection.

Welcome to the photo-reconnaissance mission. Here's the briefing. Satellites and aircraft like the SR-71 and U-2 provided strategic reconnaissance; that's the big picture. Carrier battle group commanders needed their own aircraft to support their own requirements. For decades, the Navy had relied on aircraft designed for that role, but they aged out. Now there was something new: a reconnaissance pod that could be carried by the F-14. Tuck a pod under the belly, and *voila*—it's a recon plane.

Known by the snappy acronym TARPS, for Tactical Air Reconnaissance Pod System, the pod was huge: seventeen feet long and weighing 1,800 pounds. Only

certain F-14s were wired to carry it, and only one of the two F-14 squadrons on each carrier had them. Like all TARPS squadrons, VF-2 was proud to be one of them.

Once I joined the squadron, I wanted to get TARPS qualified. So did Doc. Back to the RAG we went, sitting through classes for the fundamentals, then graduating to my favorite schoolroom: the back seat, for twelve flights like the one over the rest stop.

If we ever did this for real, it would be challenging. We would have to come back with clear, sharp photos of command centers, transportation hubs, factories, military bases, and other targets, and they would be well defended. The photo mission might be teamed with a strike at one of those targets or a shot at their defenses, so timing was critical. As a recon platform, the F-14 was an equalizer. Instead of the old setup with an unarmed fighter converted to recon, the F-14 with a pod still packed a weapons wallop of its own.

It was great to be paired with Doc, one of the sharp new guys I remembered from my RAG class. Doc brought the skill and enthusiasm you want in any fighter pilot. He took his flying seriously, and he enjoyed it immensely. This was 1988, but TARPS missions would pop up throughout the rest of my flying career.

While I was learning the TARPS mission, I was also picking up a new ground job. I'd always thought the best department to be in was Operations, because these officers managed the flying and dealt directly with missions, weapons, and training. Next-best would be Maintenance, part of the hard-working team that kept the squadron flying. Way down on my list was the

Administrative Department. They shuffled the paperwork. Businessmen would call Admin an "overhead function," but the overhead function I joined the Navy for was the flying.

Then job changes were announced. Take a wild guess. Right—I was the new Personnel Officer in the Admin Department.

Well, it wasn't all that bad. My boss, the Admin officer, was my former pilot, Hooter. We got along well, and we enjoyed working together on the ground as we had in the air.

I quickly discovered that Personnel had a lot of problems. It was run by an E-6, a First Class Petty Officer with three junior enlisted men supporting him. That should have been enough, but it wasn't; they were overwhelmed. Squadron instructions were being ignored. Programs had deteriorated to "good enough." There were glitches in award ceremonies and errors in sailors' service records.

One of my Personnelmen briefed me on my new job, and when we came to the performance evaluations that were essential to a sailor's advancement, he had one word for them: "pitiful." Worse, they were so late that there wasn't time to correct them. So supervisors throughout the squadron had been adding to the problems of the Personnel Office. And the buck now stopped with me.

COMFIT rated the VF-2 Personnel Department the worst of all ten F-14 squadrons at Miramar. Not "near the bottom" … the bottom. Our next formal inspection would be in November, so we had eight months to fix our shop.

I gritted my teeth and resolved to do my best, and soon realized that, hey, I'm enjoying this challenge. There was nowhere to go but up, right? As I got to know my Personnelmen, it was obvious that they appreciated a positive attitude and some attention.

I'd like to claim that I led our team to glory single-handed. But I gladly admit that the biggest boost was the arrival of a Chief Petty Officer. Chief Holland was

the quintessential pro. He trained the Personnelmen, boosted their confidence, held them accountable. He mentored the E-6 into an effective supervisor, and even taught me how to "read a service record" so I could spot errors. Once trained, I rolled up my sleeves and pitched in. Figuratively; we usually wore short sleeves at Miramar. But I really did read service records.

We faced a fat backlog of problems, but we were off to a good start. And, fortunately, I kept flying—four flights in January, ten in February, fourteen in March. In May I hit the jackpot with twenty. The post-cruise lull was over, and VF-2 was in full turnaround mode for the next deployment in February. The Navy kept its squadrons busy!

The first big event of the turnaround was an air-to-air gunnery detachment, a "gun det." We flew seven days a week, starting with a briefing at 6:50 AM. Miramar squadrons often deployed to El Centro for gun dets, but we flew this one from Miramar.

It went like this: Three Tomcats would peel off from a tight formation and shoot real 20mm bullets at a banner towed by another Tomcat. It was demanding, and for me there was an added wrinkle: These would be my first flights with a new pilot. Fresh from the RAG, Lumpy had been with VF-2 several months, flying with other RIOs. Now he was mine.

Each gun det flight began with a briefing. Our first one covered the basics, with special emphasis on keeping the other Tomcats in sight at all times. RIOs were coached on getting a radar lock on the banner so the gunsight could track it. Gunnery flights were more complex than normal training; we'd be shooting real bullets from our guns.

We fired up our engines and taxied to an arming area where Ordies armed the guns. We then taxied to the hold short to wait for the "tractor," the F-14 towing the banner. For many years, banners were towed by A-4s flown by other squadrons, but everyone liked the simplicity of towing our own banners. Soon the tractor was airborne, with a banner fluttering at the end of a

1,200-foot cable and one of the shooters flying escort. The banner was bright white with orange highlights, and with a Tomcat escorting it, nobody could fail to notice. Safety first.

Lumpy and I launched with the other shooter and crossed the coast in loose formation, looking down at thousands of sun worshippers dotting the beach on a beautiful day. This would be our last calm moment until we landed.

In our assigned area over the ocean, the tractor set up at a steady airspeed and altitude while the escort joined us on the "perch," nearby on the right and 2,500 feet higher. When everyone was set, the flight lead rolled in. In the second position, Lumpy and I watched until he was passing the banner. Then it was our turn.

Lumpy yanked our jet into a steep left turn toward the banner, then a quick roll to the right to point our nose toward it as we swooped in. He was good at this, deftly setting up a shot from less than a mile away. By then I had locked the short-range radar on the banner.

Lumpy was making split-second decisions and adjustments to put us in near-perfect firing position. He also knew *not* to shoot if the run wasn't near-perfect. Something didn't look right. Lumpy decided not to shoot.

We zoomed past the banner, quickly reversed, and climbed toward the perch as the third shooter made his approach. The three Tomcats rolled and pitched through the pattern like a team of acrobats, but instead of a tumble into a safety net, a mistake could result in a fireball.

On our next pass, the sight picture was right and Lumpy squeezed the trigger. Our Vulcan 20mm cannon fired with a loud *BRRRRP!* that vibrated the cockpit. With a firing rate of 100 bullets per second, it put a lot of lead in the air. To conserve ammo, the guns were set to fire a half-second burst with each trigger pull, which was still a lot of bullets.

At the end of the flight, the banner was dropped near a runway and we counted the hits. I know what you're thinking: Whose hits? Someone had long ago discovered that if you dipped a bullet's nose in paint, it would leave a telltale color smudge as it holed the banner. So the Ordies dipped them and each crew recorded their color. This made a gun det a lively competitive event, as well as good training.

Air-to-air gunnery was perfect to start the squadron training program. It took a lot of skill and teamwork, and it put a lot of stress on the squadron, a warm-up for more complex training to follow.

On the last flight of a gun det, each squadron was graded as part of the base-wide "High Noon" gunnery competition. With COMFIT as referee, the Ordies kept track of how many bullets were loaded, and how many (if any) were unloaded after the flight. The banner was examined and each pilot was scored on his percentage, how many hits for how many shots fired. Lumpy shot only when his sight picture was perfect. During our High Noon flight, he squeezed the trigger only twice out of about ten passes, but the result was an impressive 50 percent hits. Hey, he didn't make up the rules.

Lumpy's real name was Paul Akerlund. He was commissioned through Navy ROTC at the University of Washington. He decided he wanted to fly after talking to a college professor who had flown during World War II. He wasn't sure whether to go Air Force or Navy, but then he saw videos of Navy Phantoms on aircraft carriers, and that tipped the balance. Why the callsign Lumpy? If you drank three beers, closed one eye, and squinted at the Lumpy Rutherford character on TV's "Leave it to Beaver," you'd see Paul Akerlund.

Lumpy arrived at VF-2 with a Washington classmate, Brian Kocher, who was a RIO. Brian's callsign was Billy due to his youthful appearance—Billy the Kid. Billy's career arc would intersect with mine eight years later, when he would play an important role in an important part of my career.

Lumpy's 50 percent score wasn't a fluke. In a great example of how the entire squadron contributed, VF-2's Ordies and avionics technicians groomed the jets, taking them to the "gun butts," a long, low building, to test-fire the 20mm cannons, and boresighting the cannons to the HUD. This support, along with disciplined trigger fingers, helped the squadron to score 48 percent hits, almost unheard of. Our performance in High Noon looked good.

On the other side of the world, the flashpoint that was the Persian Gulf exploded once again, reinforcing the dangers inherent in Operation Earnest Will. Iranian forces had mined the shipping lanes, and on April 14, 1988, the frigate USS *Samuel B. Roberts* (FFG-58) struck one. Four days later US Navy ships destroyed a military facility on an oil platform, as our battle group had done in October. This time, however, Iranian aircraft, ships, and boats struck back at US forces with missiles and guns. Several Iranian vessels were destroyed, while the only American loss was a Marine Corps helicopter and crew lost in an accident.

The sudden flash of shooting hostilities reminded us to be ever combat-ready, especially on deployment. That one-sided outcome showed the value of this mindset.

Meanwhile, back in my world in Hangar 1 at Miramar, I was a RIO and Personnel Officer. If I wasn't flying I was checking on performance evaluations, tracking squadron manning with arcane reports, and updating squadron instructions. If I did fly, after debriefing I sat at my desk in my bag and checked personnel records, proofread award write-ups, pored over Navy instructions on the new weight standards, or slogged through some other task that helped the squadron run.

Flying and paperwork; if I had a coat-of-arms, it would show a paper airplane.

INTEL BRIEF: AIR-TO-AIR MISSILE COMPARISON – 1987

Aviation enthusiast or not, you may have trouble keeping track of the missiles we carried. They're in the Glossary, but this table adds detail. The F-14 wasn't cleared to carry the AIM-120A AMRAAM, introduced in 1991, but it's shown for comparison. Newer versions of the AIM-9 and AIM-120 are more capable…and more expensive.

	AIM-9M	AIM-7M	AIM-54C	AIM-120A – *for comparison*
Name	Sidewinder	Sparrow	Phoenix	AMRAAM**
Radio call	Fox 2	Fox 1	Fox 3	Fox 3
Guidance	Passive infrared homing	Semi-active radar homing	Semi-active and active radar homing	Inertial and active radar homing
Length	9.3 ft	12 ft	13 ft	12 ft
Body diameter	5 in	8 in	15 in	7 in
Weight	191 lbs	510 lbs	1,024 lbs	348 lbs
Speed	Mach 2.5+	Mach 3.5	Mach 5	Mach 4
Range	9.7 naut mi	38 naut mi	100+ naut mi	30-40 naut mi
Warhead	20.8 lbs	88 lbs	135 lbs	50 lbs
Unit cost	$94K	$221K	$1.4M	$247K
IOC* for this variant	1983	1982	1986	1991
IOC for earliest variant	1956	1954	1974	1991

* IOC: initial operational capability

**AMRAAM: Advanced Medium-Range Air-to-Air Missile

How much does a weapon system cost? There are many ways to determine that. This table uses cost data published in 1990 by Aviation Studies Atlantic in London. All other information in the table is from various websites, retrieved in January 2019 but accurate for these late-1980s versions.

How far will a missile fly? The definition of a missile's range can also be complex. As a pilot or RIO, you would want to know the distance from fighter to target at the moment you launch the missile. That's the launch range shown above. The target will usually be speeding toward you, so the missile won't actually fly that far to hit it. In one famous example, an F-14 fired an AIM-54 Phoenix at a target 126 miles away, and it was seventy miles away at impact. That was world-class range, especially for the 1970s.

As another example, think how far a missile would fly if it missed the target. For safety reasons we considered this maximum possible distance when planning missilexes.

We also kept in mind the "no-escape zone," the range at which we could launch a missile and it would hit the target no matter how the target maneuvered to dodge it. Those range numbers are classified. All I can say is, "shorter."

Each missile also has a minimum range. You don't want it to detonate the moment you launch it, so there is a safety delay before it arms. You also have to give it time to wake up, acquire the target, and fly itself to the kill with its own control surfaces.

The F-14 carried a versatile load of missiles, and like all American missiles, they were much improved by the hard lessons of Vietnam.

CHAPTER 14

THERE ARE TWO Fs IN FFARP

The gun det was a hard act to follow, but in a few weeks VF-2 followed it with FFARP.

Some people think of the Tomcat as an interceptor, but when the aircraft was designed the "fighter" role was equally important. As a fighter, it would fly missions such as sweeping the enemy out of the skies ahead of our bombers and escorting our bombers in hostile airspace.

That's why Tomcat pilots and RIOs went to Topgun, and why squadrons invested a lot of their training flights in dogfighting. To provide that same steep learning curve for an entire squadron, there was FFARP, the Fleet Fighter ACM Readiness Program. Forget the double F. Just say "farp."

FFARP was four weeks of ACM, run by VF-126, one of the adversary squadrons. Their pilots had completed a tour in F-14s or F-4s, and many had been through the Topgun class. The Navy's adversary squadrons worked with Topgun to give the pilots and RIOs an intense learning experience.

For VF-2, it was doubly intense. The year before we went through FFARP, adversary squadrons had received F-16N Fighting Falcons, adding some serious muscle to their fleet of A-4s and F-5s.

The program started with a couple of lectures, then jumped to flying. Right from my first 1v1, I could see that the F-16N was a tough opponent. I'd been sparring with A-4s and F-5s, where an F-14 could usually exploit an advantage—thrust-to-weight maybe, or sustained turn rate—to stay alive until we could get a good shot. The F-16N gave up nothing to an F-14, so in every 1v1 you were hoping for perfection by the Tomcat guys and a mistake—*any* mistake—by the adversary pilot. He rarely obliged.

Lumpy was a very good pilot. We flew one 1v1, then another, then two 2v2, all a mere warm-up for the challenging 2vUNK and 4vUNK flights that made up most of FFARP, where two or four Tomcats faced an unknown (UNK) number of bad guys.

There's a lot of shooting and killing coming up. Okay, the only thing that dies is blips on radar screens. The computer simulates what detonates.

These were Cold War days. The MiG-23 had been around awhile, but now the Soviets were flying the MiG-29 and the Su-27, so our training adversary planes had to fly like they did. The new Soviet fighters were nimble in a dogfight and could fire forward-quarter missile shots—from straight ahead to 45 degrees on either side. But in most FFARP flights we still could not use our AIM-54 Phoenix! Our forward-quarter tactics were evolving, but for now we would launch AIM-7 Sparrows and then maneuver to dodge enemy missiles similar to ours.

On Memorial Day evening, a holiday, the VF-2 ready room was jam-packed with thirty fighter pilots and RIOs, all talking at once and shooting our watches in classic fighter sign language. Out of the din a brilliant plan was hatched that, to this day, still surprises me. We cooked up a trick tactic to defeat the bandits' forward-quarter missiles. We knew that, when a missile was "launched" on the TACTS range, the computer would check where the radar was pointing and assign the missile to that target. We also knew that if there were two targets, it would select the closer one.

Our plan was to fly in a tight three-plane formation, with a "missile sponge" in front and the two shooters behind it. Once we heard the tone telling us the bandits launched a missile, our lead would turn around and vamoose, dragging with it a missile that would never catch up. After ninety minutes of arguing and high-fiving we left, excited about this brilliant tactic.

Most of VF-2's Tomcats wore the Navy's glossy light gray paint, which looked sharp in photos but stood out like beacons when you saw them in the sky. So a couple of lieutenants went to a teaching supplies store (yes, a store where schoolteachers buy supplies) and bought watercolor paints in three shades of gray. On a sunny Saturday morning ten of us met on the flight line, dipped rollers in trays of paint, and camouflaged our once-glossy jets.

Cool? That's an understatement. Our Tomcats were slick—no tanks or AIM-54 rails—and now they were wearing war paint. And we had a trick tactic up our sleeves. Bring it on, FFARP, we're *ready!*

At dawn Monday morning, Lumpy and I and our four co-conspirators met in VF-2's ready room and briefed for the first flight of FFARP's demanding second phase. The sweet smell of success kept us alert as we rehashed how "the tactic" would work. The missile sponge was noted as aircraft #1 on the TACTS Range. Those guys would fake out the missile and then fly home. The first crew that mattered was Lieutenant Commander Kevin Saxon (Sax) and Skipper Serhan (Rip), #2 on TACTS. Number 3 was Lumpy and yours truly. On the radio the controllers would use those numbers instead of trying to sort out callsigns.

We launched and flew east toward the range, checking out our radars—all good! Everything was running smoothly and we soon heard those magic words: "Fight's on."

Our controller called, "Bullets, single group estimated one-zero-five degrees, thirty-two miles."

Estimated? He knew exactly; our TACTS pods told him. He was sandbagging to make it realistic.

Number 1 replied, "Bullets, contact that call." We headed southeast at 23,000 feet, accelerating through 350 knots.

I was focused on my radar…starting to break out contacts…anticipating some kills before the merge…a great dogfight. The breakfast of champions! Then I looked outside, at our formation, and #1 was *right there*, just above us and offset. We were a tight wedge, perfect for our sneaky plan.

As we streaked toward the foe, we maneuvered to set up our missile shots. Just inside 20 miles we heard the telltale "boop." The bandits had launched a missile! Number 1 peeled off to lure it to nowhere, and left two Tomcats with a clear shot at the befuddled enemy! Rip took his radar lock, I took mine, and our pilots launched AIM-7s.

As the missile timers counted down, the controller calmly spoke.

"Three, you're dead."

Three? Wait—that's me!

You don't question the TACTS controller during a run, but in a flash I realized that our tactic had somehow flopped.

On the VF-2 squadron frequency I blurted, "Great f***ing tactic!" Yes, that was a violation of radio etiquette, but my disappointment was profound.

Like a good battle casualty, Lumpy followed protocol and peeled off, leaving Sax and Rip to face the bandits. They shot another missile and bugged out. It may have been the shortest run in FFARP history.

Once the knock-it-off was called, Sax radioed our controller in the TACTS trailer. "Pass to all aircrews, do NOT use the tactic. Use standard forward-quarter tactics."

We sent our erstwhile missile sponge home and set up for another run, a standard 2vUNK. That one went okay, but I fumed all the way back to Miramar to debrief. Other crews manned our jets, and when they finished they landed in El Centro where we would be based for the rest of the det. I jumped into my Corvette and drove over.

There was no serious discussion of our trick tactic. It was a flop because we obviously didn't have a good understanding of how TACTS assigned missiles to targets. Properly chastened, we resorted to the tactics taught at Topgun and the adversary squadrons, and the rest of the det went well.

So what about our other brainstorm; was our camouflage effective? The bandit pilots told us it was. A few gloss-gray F-14s didn't get the war paint makeover, and the bandits said it was much easier to spot them than the watercolor birds. We also flew several jets painted in the new Navy-standard low-visibility paint, and that was effective, too. You couldn't hide a 63-foot-long F-14, but you could make it harder to see.

A few days into the program we were assigned to a fighter sweep mission, with everyone flying above 25,000 feet. The bandits were simulating MiG-23 Floggers, known for their high speed, so they started at the eastern edge of the range and came in as fast as their F-5s would go. On this day, that was Mach 1.1, nearly 700 knots at their altitude. To get maximum range for our missiles we also ran fast, and our slick Tomcats exceeded 1.1, so the closing speed was 1,400 knots. Both Tomcats had good radars and we had good SA, so I felt comfortable despite the pedal-to-the-metal closure.

At 20 miles I switched the radar mode from track-while-scan/auto to manual (pulse search). Sounds technical, but it's just a click of a switch and it gave me an accurate picture of the formation.

Rip said over the radio, "Locking the front right guy." I quipped to Lumpy, over the ICS so nobody else would hear it, "No problem, I'll lock the front left." And I did. We were closing at one mile every two and a half seconds and I had to manually track the formation on radar. In my earlier days that would have severely strained my proficiency, but after 1,600 hours in the

Tomcat I even had enough brainpower left over to drop in that wisecrack.

Sax and Lumpy both launched missiles and we turned left to duck the bandits' missiles, carefully managing our heading to maintain radar illumination for our missiles. We scored two kills and survived, and I'll settle for that any day.

We all preferred the flights where we mixed it up at the merge, but when the scenario called for it we took a spoonful of Professionalism and followed the latest forward-quarter tactics. One day a senior officer was flying with the adversaries, expecting to mix it up with Tomcats like back in the day. He was a fighter pilot who had been around, and one of the perks he enjoyed was strapping on a jet now and then. He was itching for a scrap.

His itch didn't get scratched. It was one of those flights where we shot AIM-7s and turned away, and when our missile countdown timers showed zero, we bugged out.

In the debrief the senior snarled, "What the hell was that?"

Using the common term, our flight lead respectfully said, "We were flying counter-Flogger tactics, sir."

With a red face, the senior said, "Well I call them chicken-shit tactics!" No one said anything for a few heartbeats, and we gingerly finished the debrief.

The adversary lead, a skilled and respected lieutenant, said, "You guys did a good job." He said it after the senior left.

Not all flights were that cut-and-dried. One morning Sax and Rip led Lumpy and me on a 2vUNK that would test us all. We had good radars and I thought we had good SA as we faced a mix of F-16s and F-5s.

Our two Tomcats were hauling it at 500 knots and 22,000 feet, with more than a mile between us. An aggressive split. Rip and I worked the radars to paint the picture for our pilots and then launch AIM-7s. Out of the corner of my eye a blur caught my attention, just as Lumpy yanked us into a max-performance climbing left turn.

"Lumpy's engaged with an F-16," he calmly said over the radio. Lumpy sounded bored, like he was sitting in his grandmother's living room. But his flying was ferocious. In a clean Tomcat at that speed, he had a lot to work with, and he used it all.

I grabbed the ACM handle on top of the DDD and twisted to look up and left, and there was the F-16N in a climbing left turn. Dogfight! The F-16 pilot kept the fight tight so we couldn't get separation or any maneuvering advantage, while Lumpy did a fantastic job of keeping the pressure on him. I was impressed. In the blink of an eye, Lumpy had switched from a smooth intercept to a dust-up with an F-16.

Sax came up on the radio. "Visual, no tally." He could see us but not the smaller F-16.

Lumpy replied impatiently, "He's across the circle from us."

"I don't see no f***in' F-16!" Sax growled. Another violation of radio etiquette.

Lumpy kept the squeeze on the F-16 for a few more turns. Then Sax was back. "Belly Fox 2, F-16 engaged with the F-14."

"That's a kill, knock it off."

In the debrief, Rip and I learned that our radar had painted the trail bandits but missed the lead. Fortunately there were only three, and our shots killed the trailers. It wasn't the only ACM engagement I had during the det, but it was the most memorable.

El Centro got rather warm by noontime, so early flights were welcome. And for another reason, known as "lunch." We would change out of flight suits and drive to town, an easy five miles on an arrow-straight road. Once we invaded a small diner that served up a memorable burger: Monterey jack cheese and jalapeño peppers. The memory includes my Corvette with the top down and the late-morning sun streaming through the diner windows on five flyguys swapping lies about battling enemy aircraft over the Arizona desert. Hey, pass the mustard!

By now, you know we were challenged by FFARP—as it should be—and we took it seriously. But late in the program, like the rest of us, Lumpy was tired of the restraint required by the recommended tactics. So naturally he proposed another one!

On the final morning, four Tomcats launched under a gray overcast. We orbited as usual, while everyone checked in and our TACTS pods were okayed. This was one of the flights on which we simulated carrying Phoenix missiles.

Lumpy and I and one other Tomcat were the lead section. At "fight's on" we plunged into a steep spiral. But instead of a normal post-hole maneuver, both RIOs pulled the circuit breakers to disable our pods. Instantly we vanished from the TACTS control screens.

We continued the corkscrew until we were flying southeast along the western edge of the range. We had plummeted from 23,000 feet down to the deck—the real deck, the desert floor on the eastern side of the mountains. We were flying about 1,000 feet above the ground. I'd flown lower, but for what we had in mind, this worked. We had a lot of ground to cover.

I had eyeballed the airspace and estimated the intercept geometry, so when the INS showed we were near the US-Mexico border, I radioed, "Lumpy flight, left to 040." This heading would aim us toward the center of the TACTS range.

We were doing Mach 1.1—more than 800 mph at this low altitude. We were below the briefed hard-deck altitude, but a little thing like that wasn't going to stop us. I did not want to miss this intercept, so I had my AWG-9 radar in pulsed-doppler-search with the antenna looking 10 degrees up and scanning the full azimuth.

We had put our pods to sleep, so we had no info on where the bandits were. But I'd watched hundreds of intercepts unfold on the range, and I had guessed right. There they were, almost dead ahead at about 20 miles.

"Lumpy, ten right, twenty miles, ten degrees up." Our wingman rogered.

Now we had to get back on the system to make this count. On the VF-2 frequency I said, "Circuit breakers in." Both RIOs punched them in and the pods woke up. Our pilots started a climb to boresight the targets.

The TACTS system had us now. At 15 miles we each fired our imaginary Phoenix. Above us we could see the two F-16s silhouetted against the overcast. As we watched them, the controller radioed, "Five and six are dead." In our imaginations the silhouettes flared into fireballs.

The rest of that run was anticlimactic. The other two Tomcats engaged the remaining bandits and did well. The good guys won.

On the short return to El Centro I was thinking ahead. Would we get hammered in the debrief for not taking it seriously?

I needn't have worried. Someone said, "It looks like your pods dropped track for awhile, probably due to terrain or something."

We just said, "Yeah, look at that. Well, lucky for us they came back in time for the shots."

Lucky indeed. But the real reason we weren't questioned was that everyone was looking forward to debriefing the final run, where all aircraft simulated armament of guns only! I still remember the merge on that one. F-16 and A-4 silhouettes turning and burning and speckling the sky like bugs on a windshield in summer.

It was a great end to the det. And summer in San Diego was just getting started.

CHAPTER 15

SUMMERTIME AT MIRAMAR

Meanwhile, back on Planet Miramar, extracurricular activity was heating up. How come? Longer days, El Niño, some primeval force….

One primeval force was Commander Rip Serhan. We had known him for more than a year as the squadron's XO, and when Skipper Dodge moved on to bigger things, Rip "fleeted up" to CO, right in the middle of FFARP as we were about to move from Miramar to El Centro. We squeezed a ceremony and reception into half a day, and got back in step without missing a beat.

Our new XO was a pilot, Commander David Jackson, callsign Action. He'd flown F-8 Crusaders when he was a JO in the 1970s. Though he had converted to the Tomcat and served at the Operational Test and Evaluation squadron, he never lost the old-school fighter pilot spirit that goes with the F-8.

Things perked along for me as well—the FFARP flights, TARPS training, at-sea periods, air defense exercises, ACM, you name it and I was doing it and averaging three flights a week.

You name what a fighter jock might do off-duty, and I was probably doing that, too. Like the evening we set up a VF-2 night out at a San Diego Padres baseball game. There were always some Miramar people at Padres games, so tailgating at section F4 was like a night at the O-club. This time I counted thirty of us—officers, wives, and girlfriends. I was wifeless; Laura and I had house guests, so she stayed home and I'd be leaving early.

We were having a great time, enjoying the cool evening, the hot food, and the warm camaraderie. I quaffed

a couple of beers, and eased out of the stadium as the eighth inning started.

What's a yellow Corvette without the top down? And what's a fighter jock without a little showmanship? There was another VF-2 RIO on a motorcycle in my rear view mirror. I could not resist. It was burnout time. You know, not exorcising my demons, but *exercising* them!

SCREEEE! Uh-oh. On the slick asphalt my Corvette started to slide sideways. Quick, off the gas; steer into the slide. Man, that was close!

I drove sedately away from the scene of the crime, intent on just blending in with the traffic. Then a voice startled me. "Pull over!" it commanded. The voice belonged to a motorcycle cop right next to me, and there were two more riding my bumper. So much for getting away with it.

I pulled over. The cop checked my license and military ID, and told me to sit on the ground behind the car with my legs crossed. Flashback to SERE school.

One of the other policemen asked about my Corvette. I answered politely but was too nervous to chat. The lead guy came back and said a supervisor was coming for a field sobriety test.

I thought, *This could get serious.* I'd had just two beers in three hours, but maybe they'd charge me with something else. Driving while stupid?

By now the game was over. From the traffic stream, some VF-2 tailgaters spotted the yellow Corvette and pulled over to help. One of the cops walked over and suggested they leave before *they* got in trouble. They took the hint.

The supervisor arrived and barked orders at me like a drill sergeant. "Stick your arms out to the sides, tilt your head back, stand on one leg, and then bring the index finger of your left hand to the tip of your nose. Okay, go ahead and…"

Squeal of tires. Flash of headlights. *CRUNCH!* A rubbernecker slammed his car into the patrol car.

We both jumped out of the way. He jammed my IDs into my hand and growled, "Lieutenant, I think you can make it home."

And I did.

Many squadrons had events like that, for themselves, but there were also higher-profile events around Miramar. One squadron organized a road rally, another sponsored Wednesday night happy hours at the O-club. Nice try, guys, but VF-2 organized a bash at the O-club known as the Bullet Blowout. It had been a few years since the last one, so the two-time Bullets like Jungle and Brutus suggested it was time for the next. We all agreed.

We picked a Friday and chose sports as a theme. VF-2 officers paid for food and kegs of beer. For our guest DJ, I invited Cookie "Chainsaw" Randolph, a well-liked voice on San Diego's KGB-FM. The Bullet Blowout was going to be *big!*

Laura decided tennis would be our sport. I don't play tennis, but we dressed in tennis-suitable outfits anyway and headed to the club to help set up. The weather was perfect and the large patio was filling up with happy Fightertown people. It was VF-2's party, and we had a big flag with the squadron logo on it— every squadron had one—so we hung our "drinking flag" on the fence.

Half an hour into the party, our flag suddenly whooshed over the fence, like a tablecloth snatched away by the world's quickest magician. A dozen Bullets saw it and dashed through the club to the parking lot, where a few young guys were jumping into a black SUV.

As it roared away, one of us grabbed the car's side mirror and broke it off, two more threw beer bottles, and I jumped into my Corvette for a 1v1 through the maze of streets toward the main gate.

You've seen those action movies where the frantic pace suddenly jolts to slow motion so you can savor all the details. That was us, a pulse-pounding chase scene in real slow motion at 11 miles an hour. That's not a typo. The speed limit there was 11mph, and we both knew Miramar police were aggressive. Neither driver wanted to get nailed on base.

The SUV eased through the gate into the rush-hour traffic. Then he gunned it. I was a block behind, still on base, so the range to the target increased rapidly. An eternity later, I eased through the gate and floored it to redline in first and redline again in second. Well into third, I glanced at the needle. It was passing the 100 mark. That got my attention so I knocked off the chase and returned to base flagless, at legal speed.

Bad enough to suffer the indignity of having our flag stolen; worse to learn next day that the culprits were a bunch of RAG students. The ransom was to buy the beer at happy hour, which we paid. You've got to have your drinking flag, even if the flagnappers are doing the drinking.

That kind of action went with the territory and the Bullet Blowout was once again a huge success. Now back to business: the Fighter Derby.

It was another base-wide competition, like the High Noon gunnery event, but Fighter Derby was a 2vUNK scenario: intercept to engagement, one run on the TACTS Range. COMFIT did a good job of giving all squadrons an equal challenge.

It had been two months since FFARP, but we were ready, and once again we camouflaged our jets in watercolors. Lumpy and I flew as wingman for Sax and Rip, and we had a good run. No trick tactics, just solid 2vUNK and good execution. Based on informal debriefs it sounded like VF-2's runs were good, but it would be a few weeks before the official results came out.

Then came the highlight social event of the year: the Tomcat Ball. Lead-in events and athletic meets set the stage for the main event, a formal dinner for officers and their dates, with more than five hundred people attending. It was a huge, raucous party, culminating in the awarding of the Mutha Trophy to "the most outstanding and spirited fighter squadron." The award was given not for performance in competitions, but for fighter spirit, and we all wanted to win it.

Squadrons performed all kinds of stunts to get attention in the lead-up to the ball. The 900-foot-long gun butts bore a red, white, and blue WELCOME TO FIGHTERTOWN U.S.A. greeting—until the year VF-114 repainted it in their colors of orange and black for the Mutha competition. Another year, a squadron painted their name on top of their hangar…and another squadron modified it. Let your imagination play with that one.

The Bullet Blowout was a lot of fun, but it was important to stage it before the Tomcat Ball so we could get some unofficial "Mutha points." Losing and ransoming our drinking flag—well, we lost Mutha points on that.

At one of the gates to Miramar, an E-2 Hawkeye posed proudly on a pedestal, a tribute the Pacific Fleet E-2 squadrons that also called Miramar home. Over its head loomed a massive disc with radar inside, and on its tail stood four little rudders. The distinctive Hawkeye was a stirring sight.

Well, it was until a week before the Tomcat Ball. Someone painted it in VF-2's distinctive colors: a red, white, and blue fuselage stripe, and blue rudders with white stars. Those markings dated to the early days of the squadron, when our forebears were flying biplanes from the first US aircraft carrier, USS *Langley* (CV-1). The fuselage stripe was known as a *Langley* stripe.

Once again the COMFIT Chief of Staff called the squadron and told us to get over there to discuss this transgression. As the senior lieutenant in the squadron, I talked to a few other guys and quickly determined it wasn't one of us. With halos over our heads, two other lieutenants and I marched over to COMFIT to face the Chief of Staff.

He was mad as a hornet in a hailstorm. "I know you fighter guys like to have a good time," he thundered, "and I put up with your pranks. But when you damage property that's not yours, that's crossing the line! *Why did you paint the E-2 in your squadron colors?!*"

No wonder he was mad. Call it righteous indignation; he was a former E-2 pilot! This would not be easy.

"Sir," I ventured, "we didn't do it. We wouldn't paint an E-2 in *our* colors."

Oops. Shouldn't have said it that way.

For two long seconds, the fuse burned. Then the detonation. "Get outta here!!"

It was probably good for everyone that VF-2 was scheduled for a det to Fallon, Nevada.

CHAPTER 16

TAKING THE GLOVES OFF

"Los Angeles Center, Navy november echo two-zero-one, three F-14s, level two-three-zero."

"Two-zero-one, roger two-three-zero. Understand you're en route Navy Fallon."

"Two-zero-one, that's affirmative. We're going for two weeks of great flying."

"Sounds like fun. Good luck to you guys."

"Thanks, Center."

Three VF-2 Tomcats cruised above the jagged Sierra Nevada mountains on the California-Nevada border. We rarely bantered with controllers, but traffic was light on this Sunday afternoon, so he mentioned Fallon and got a snappy reply.

On his radar, a Tomcat was a nondescript symbol that could have been an airliner or a Piper Cub. But if you could see us with the naked eye, well, we hoped you couldn't. We'd spent a lot of time painting our Tomcats in flat blue and gray camouflage.

I was flying with Coney in the number three position of this loose formation, excited about the upcoming flying.

Unlike LA Center that day, controllers around Fallon had their hands full. Air Wing Two squadrons were gathering for two weeks of challenging training before deployment. The deployment was still five months away, but that time would pass quickly. Each squadron brought maybe three-fourths of its aircraft, so as we taxied in after landing, the flight line was like a crowded carrier deck. VF-1 and VF-2 each brought eight jets.

Fallon was evolving. A Navy air strike in Lebanon in December 1983 did not go well, so the Navy ramped up its air wing training, and the remote base at Fallon, Nevada, was a perfect home for it. Reno was 70 miles away, so Fallon had wide-open airspace, ideal for large training events. The base had been upgraded to world class, and we were ready for some world class aviating.

I'd been here before. In 1981 we got good training at Fallon flying large coordinated strikes. But the threats we faced and the tactics we flew harked back to the skies of Vietnam a decade before. Blue was friend and red was foe, and debriefings weren't a whole lot more than swapping our impressions of what we did.

Not so in 1988. Fallon was like FFARP on steroids. The surface-to-air threat had matured, and so had our tactics to defeat it. Staying alive was more complicated now.

The Navy learned a lot from that Lebanon lesson. It launched the Navy Strike Warfare Center, which was a lot like Topgun. Don't bother with the abbreviation for this one; we all called it "Strike U." Debriefings also got a makeover, thanks to an instrumented TACTS range at Fallon.

The FFARP experience helped us meet the Fallon challenge. We put more time into planning the missions and honed our skills in flying them, and we learned more in debriefs, due to the TACTS range and the quality of Strike U instructors.

One of the changes that I most appreciated this time was that we would be allowed to use AIM-54 Phoenix missiles in the scenarios. The F-14 was a big airplane. It had to be, to carry the Phoenix missile and the AWG-9 radar that went with it. But so far the missiles had been "reserved" for defending the carrier. Meanwhile, threat aircraft and missiles had evolved such that the Phoenix was required for superiority. And in combat you don't want a fair fight, you want superiority. So we would simulate carrying the much-improved new AIM-54C. Not the Tomcat's maximum load of six Phoenix, but a more realistic one or two. That was enough.

The town of Fallon was just a few miles from the base, so that evening some of us checked out the bars and casinos. Not Rip; he and some others hit the ground running. They had a mission to plan, so they worked at Strike U most of the night to get it right.

Bad weather grounded us on Monday. Tuesday was a go, so at 5 PM Lumpy and I briefed for a fighter sweep. We would roar into enemy airspace ahead of the strike group and kill or scatter the enemy fighters. We were the wingman in a section—that's two planes—and both Tomcats simulated carrying Phoenix.

The mission commander ran an impressive briefing. He was an A-6 bombardier/navigator, and he'd be responsible for the event from brief to launch to touchdown to debrief. I was a second-tour lieutenant and might soon be leading an air wing strike myself, so I watched him carefully. Would I be able to do that?

I walked out of the brief with four kneeboard cards full of information—timelines, callsigns, radio freqs, navigation, aerial refueling, and more—common for a coordinated strike. Lumpy and I preflighted in twilight, and soon the Fallon flight line came alive with the shriek of dozens of jet engines spooling up. It got quieter with the canopy closed, but then the radios crackled with people checking in and making a few final adjustments. No banter, just business.

An afterburner at night is a brilliant blowtorch. Imagine one after another of them shooting into a darkening sky on long cones of flame as the Tomcats launched!

Lumpy and I topped off at the tanker, then began the strike in inky blackness. We were sweepers, so all we had to worry about was our own formation instead of a sky full of bombers and escorts. But there were bandits ahead of us, so we made sure we stayed in our altitude block and hoped they stayed in theirs.

"Fight's on."

We pushed north on our assigned route. Both sweeping Tomcats had good radars, so it was a matter of working with the AWG-9 to make the magic happen.

The radar controller in the E-2 called, "Contacts orbiting Bullseye three-two-zero at fifteen, second group Bullseye zero-one-zero at thirty." Bullseye control let everyone gain SA, as long as they knew where the bullseye point was, and where they were in relation to it.

We had good SA, so our lead RIO responded with our plan. "Sweep committing Bullseye three-two-zero at fifteen." We turned left to control the intercept.

I could see them on my scope. Symbols 40 miles from us. They turned south: Enemy fighters defending their homeland.

E-2 controller: "Bullseye three-zero-zero at ten is hostile. Second group Bullseye three-three-zero at twenty-five, heading south."

Sweep lead: "Sweep 1 breaking out lead-trail. Targeting the lead."

Me: "Sweep 2 has the trailers."

In seconds we were in range and both sweep RIOs announced, "Fox 3." I hit the red LAUNCH button. Roaring away on a blazing cone of flame went—nothing. All we got was the *boop* tone from the TACTS range.

Now and then the TACTS range would score a shot as a miss to simulate a variety of real-world glitches, and we experienced that. After the simulated missiles' time of flight, they pronounced only one bandit dead. We took follow-up AIM-7 shots, then left the area according to plan—a very smooth run. Just another late night at the office.

Our sweeping Tomcats were only a small part of the strike. Jammers, escorts, bombers, tankers, and more did the heavy lifting. There was only one run, but the flight lasted 1.7 hours. There's nothing simple about launching and recovering an armada of warplanes at night. The debrief started at 10 PM, and if anyone was tired they didn't show it.

We didn't launch any real missiles, but on the simulating screens at the debriefing, our avatars did. There they go, a pair of mighty Phoenix missiles streaking away from our Tomcats. With the bandits more than 20 miles away, the missiles climbed immediately after launch as we watched the action on the TACTS display. The missiles looked like space rockets as they climbed to their programmed altitude before turning downrange.

For me, that was the best part of the debrief. It would be unprofessional to complain, but at midnight we were still going strong.

FFARP had been busy, but Fallon was busier. It was also much further from San Diego, so I was glad I didn't drive my Corvette. To get around I either caught a ride in one of the few rental cars, or rode the base shuttle bus.

One day I had an afternoon flight, then an early brief the next morning, then took a break in the ready room—and then lightning struck. The radio barked that a VF-2 jet had crashed.

I cannot overstate the impact of those words on an aviation squadron. One of our jets, with our friends flying it, had crashed. We controlled our emotions and immediately put into effect the Aircraft Mishap Plan, a detailed list of procedures kept in a binder at the SDO desk of every squadron.

People dropped what they were doing and looked for a way to help. The SDO was in charge, until the Operations Officer, XO, and CO hustled into the ready room. Info trickled in: aircraft 201, flown by Jungle, had crashed during a 2v2 ACM engagement. His RIO was Zip, a nugget who'd been in VF-2 less than a year.

Beneath our grim efficiency, every one of us was a maelstrom of emotions. What to do? Did they make it? Wife and kids? Finally the word came that two good parachutes had been spotted. The relief was profound.

Instead of mayhem, everything was well-timed teamwork. The Plan told us what to do and when. Phone whatever we knew to higher-ups within five minutes. Send official messages to Naval Aviation activities asap, and update frequently. Squadrons actually practiced using the Mishap Plan for just such occasions. It sure helped.

The Tomcat had slammed onto empty Government land. Other aviators saw Jungle and Zip on the ground and walking around. Good news! But still we scurried about, nailing down details, freezing the aircraft logbooks, and juggling endless details needed for the inevitable investigation.

On our recent deployment, a day's flying was cancelled after one fatal mishap. That was a good decision. This time, with pilot and RIO okay, events continued without missing a beat. Even in VF-2.

I hustled to my next briefing and walked in late. No one discussed the mishap; we had a mission to brief and fly. Lumpy and I were on Hap and Slush's wing, flying escort.

Our part of the flight didn't go so well. Maybe I was distracted. Maybe we all were. We debriefed without excuses and chalked it up to experience.

Later a group of us gathered at the O-club, where two new rocket riders, fresh from medical checks and phone calls to their wives, were telling their story. Jungle and Zip were clearly happy to be alive. Soon eight Bullets peeled off and headed into Fallon for a quieter dinner and thorough debrief.

Surrounded by relieved squadronmates, fortified by beer and pizza, Jungle and Zip told their story. The audience was riveted.

Two F-16s kill one F-16 during an intercept, and Jungle and Zip go after the other one. It's a dogfight. Soon the F-16 uses its incredible thrust and goes vertical and Jungle follows. The midday sun was overhead, but now, nose up, it hits him straight in the eyes and blinds him. He loses sight of his prey, and dodges to avoid a collision. Still nose up, the Tomcat's airspeed bleeds off. Suddenly it, as we say, "departs controlled flight." That's what airplanes do when they get too slow.

Like every aircraft, the F-14 has some bad habits. One of them is the way it behaves when departing controlled flight. It gets violent. So now Jungle is fighting for control as the Tomcat tumbles out of the sky. Zip is on the ball and totally aware of what's happening, and backs up his pilot with the boldface procedures.

They started at an altitude that was legal for dogfighting. That's what soft decks and hard decks are all about. Then they climbed. But after the departure the Tomcat is plummeting. The turbulent air isn't sucking smoothly into the engines and one of them quits almost immediately, making the departure even more violent. Those engines were the Tomcat's Achilles' heel.

Zip doesn't want to screw this up, so he waits a prudent moment, then jettisons the canopy and yanks the ejection handle. Blowing the canopy off is part of the procedure for ejecting from a spin, but sometimes a RIO forgets it in the excitement of the moment.

Zip doesn't forget. His seat fires first, then Jungle 0.4 seconds later. Two chutes pop open. The Tomcat explodes in a fireball on the sand, and Zip has to yank desperately on his parachute lines to steer himself away from the bonfire. Jungle said the sight of the explosion "was amazing."

We later estimated that Zip and Jungle ejected about 3,000 feet above the ground—literally the last few seconds for a survivable ejection in this situation.

We listened in silent amazement as the pair recounted detail after detail, spicing the saga with humor appropriate for their survival with hardly a scratch. Zip said he had difficulty walking after he landed. He looked down, expecting to see his leg horribly mangled. Instead he saw that his kneeboard had slid down around his boot.

A gray pickup soon approached, which Jungle thought was a quick response from the rescue crew at Fallon. It turned out to be a local rancher who saw the fireball and the parachutes, and drove over with his wife. He looked at Jungle and drawled, "Boy, you got a stick in yo' head." Jungle reached up and felt a twig jabbed into the skin of his forehead. He and Zip decided it was in too deep and left it for Medical to remove.

These lighter moments brought guffaws around the table. It was an enjoyable dinner, and a hell of a lot better than what could have been. After all, we could replace an airplane, but we couldn't replace our friends.

Earlier that afternoon, shortly after the crash, I had called back to the small cadre of VF-2 people who stayed at Miramar. I related the bare bones of the incident to Hooter, and he said the scuttlebutt around Miramar was that Jungle was pulling the jet out of its departure when his nugget RIO punched them out too soon. I knew Jungle would set the record straight when he got back to Miramar.

One evening some Bullets were contributing to a small Fallon casino. Bored (read: losing), a dozen of us crossed the street to watch the new Bruce Willis movie, "Die Hard." We behaved ourselves, but a few points were called. "Fire hydrant!" A fireball in the desert, an inside joke at the movies—the good folks of Fallon took it all in stride.

I had seven tactical flights during the two-week det, which made it good training. Sometime after Fallon, we learned that all Miramar Tomcat squadrons had completed the competitive exercises, and we looked forward to the results.

There were four tactical competitions each year at Miramar, and for 1988 the results were looking good:

- Fighter Derby (2vUNK intercept to ACM): VF-2 won
- High Noon (air-to-air gunnery, shooting the banner): VF-2 won
- TARPS Derby (reconnaissance): VF-2 won
- ECCM Competition (in the simulator against bombers and jammers): VF-2 second place

Our air wing commander summoned VF-2 and VF-1 to the O-club to announce which fighter squadron he would nominate for the Admiral Joseph Clifton Award, which recognized the Navy's top fighter squadron. We hustled over with high anticipation to accept the honor we just *knew* must be ours.

It wasn't. "I've selected VF-1 as my nominee for the Clifton!" he announced.

I hope our faces didn't show what we were thinking. Actually I hope they did. Soon enough our T-shirts sure did. We had some made up and wore them proudly. They listed our first-place wins. Fighter Derby … High Noon … TARPS Derby … CHAMPS!

Well, can't win 'em all.

CHAPTER 17

CHALLENGES AND CHANGES

"Los Angeles Center, Navy november echo three-zero two, flight of six, level two-seven-zero."

"Three-zero-two, roger two-seven-zero."

That's all. No banter, no snappy replies like two months before, when we left for Fallon. Now Hap and I were escorting four A-6 Intruders on a long-range strike at 3 AM, and this time we had our game faces on. If you could see us, you'd better be a skilled pilot, because it was pitch dark and the weather was ugly.

A lot had happened since Fallon. First there was Topgun FAST—Fleet Air Superiority Training, a program that I ran when I was a Topgun instructor (described in *Topgun Days*).

Lectures for the F-14 and E-2 squadrons, and simulators for some of the F-14 aircrews, all packed into one week. There had been some changes, and it was great to see my project continuing to thrive.

Meanwhile, my Personnel Officer duties were a growing concern as the formal inspection approached. Annual evaluations of the twenty-eight first class petty officers would shape their careers, so they had to be correct and on time. The new XO and I were working together to change squadron policies and programs. Like the metaphor of building an airplane while it is flying, we were fixing problems while bucking a headwind of routine tasks. And I was still averaging three flights a week.

Then in mid-October it was Tailhook time. Most of the Bullet aircrews and thousands of other carrier aviators past and present invaded Las Vegas for the annual Tailhook Association convention. It was a long weekend of fun and camaraderie, not yet marred by the headlines of later years. Many of us took our wives along. Laura and I toured the squadron hospitality suites and enjoyed losing a little in the casinos. Well, I lost. She won.

Shortly after Tailhook, VF-2 and Air Wing 2 boarded the *Ranger* again for a month of advanced training. At sea I was promoted to lieutenant commander. One evening at quarters in the fo'c'sle, fellow RIO Czech and I were called out of ranks and Rip announced our promotions. I'd been a lieutenant for more than six years, so I was ready for the change—and for the half-stripe between the two stripes I'd worn on my sleeve for so long.

Lieutenant Commander David Baranek. Sounds respectable, doesn't it? How about "hinge," does *that* sound respectable? Ask a lieutenant, and he or she will tell you: Open the top of a lieutenant's skull, remove the brain, and close it up with a hinge for further removals, and you have a lieutenant commander. Czech and I had become "hinges." I'd known many a hinge, and I vowed not to become one.

So there we were, Hap and his hinge—I mean, RIO—on that long-range Intruder escort to a strike in filthy mid-November weather at 3 AM. The briefing had started at 10 PM, with Hap and me assigned as a spare. I was tempted to give it my full inattention, but there was always a slim chance we might launch.

At 2 AM—you knew this was coming—we launched.

The *Ranger* was off the coast of Baja California when the cats started hurling us off her deck. The quarter moon had set before midnight, so we launched into blackness. Nights weren't always pitch black, but those flights are the ones you remember. Hap and I rendezvoused overhead with the strikers and a KA-6 tanker. The group pushed northeast and everyone took on a few thousand pounds of fuel.

Why refuel when we just took off? For one thing, we had burned some 2,000 pounds of fuel just getting a thirty-three-ton Tomcat five miles up. On a car trip there's always a gas station nearby, but in the sky there are only the tankers. The plan for this strike called for everyone to top off at the start, and that tanker immediately returned to the carrier. Another waited in the darkness ahead.

After tanking we climbed higher for the long flight. The A-6s were assigned a target in Utah's Wendover Bombing Range, a trip of 600 nautical miles each way. For the Intruders it would be good training for deployment. No bandits were lurking behind every cloud, so for the Tomcats it was a dry run.

Los Angeles is nothing less than spectacular when you see it from the sky at night. We had to take in the view through breaks in the clouds, and they soon obscured the ground completely. As the weather worsened, the flight spread out, first into two-plane sections, then loners, then at different altitudes to avoid collisions. Good radio contact seemed to be the only thing holding us together in the severe weather.

Then things got complicated. It was time to refuel from an Air Force KC-10.

Hap didn't say much, but I'm sure he felt some of the trepidation I did. In the North Arabian Sea we would spot the tanker's lights from 50 miles and join in a controlled formation, but now our air traffic controller had us hold while the strike leader discussed Plan B with the tanker crew.

On ICS Hap asked me about our radar. "You said the scope is good. Can you see the A-6s and bad cells of weather?"

"Yup, I'm staying in search and watching everything in front of us. I can see the tanker sometimes." That made us both feel better.

I hadn't flown much with Hap, but I was comfortable with him in this mess. True, he hadn't logged much time in Tomcats, but he'd learned a lot about them as an adversary in the Philippines. He was an Air Force kid, and after college he wanted to fly. The Air Force recruiters seemed to be dragging their feet, so he joined the Navy. Both services were steering him toward training as a back-seater, even though he had 20/15 vision. He finally won Navy pilot training and excelled.

As the KC-10 crew searched for a clear area, our strike plan was falling behind schedule. Several aircraft were in heavier clouds and felt their safety was compromised, so they diverted to NAS Lemoore. The *Ranger* had made sure it would be open for just such a situation, but refueling was delayed due to storms, so they landed and waited.

Hap asked if I thought we too should divert for safety. I said I was comfortable but would keep it in mind. It was good to get that option on the table.

The KC-10 finally found a big gap in the clouds, and we all gathered for a fill-up. When it was our turn, Hap eased up to the basket. Something in my peripheral vision got my attention. The KC-10 was flying along the side wall of a well-defined cloud. To help us get oriented, they had turned on the spotlight that illuminates the tail, a holdover from the aircraft's origin as an airliner. It projected a circle of light on the clouds with a silhouette of the tail fin.

This was our "Bat signal" for aerial refueling.

With all tanks full, the remaining aircraft continued the mission. The A-6s dropped their bombs while we circled nearby. Then we all went home and hit the *Ranger*'s deck in the morning sun. Despite the dropouts, the air wing could chalk up a 600-mile strike. Hap and I logged 5.1 hours.

Four weeks at sea, thirteen flights, home in time for Thanksgiving. Life was good.

The next big event had been eight months in the making: the formal inspection of the Personnel Department by COMFIT. The inspection team was led by a senior chief petty officer who knew Navy personnel procedures inside and out. I'd met with him before, and was still getting used to his strong Cajun accent. He had no grudge against VF-2; we just had to get our act together.

Our own team lead, Chief Holland, was calm and confident. He had made sure the VF-2 Personnel shop was ready for the trial.

The inspection took a day and a half, and the difference since the last one was night and day. No major faults and only a few minors. The senior chief debriefed us, and he chose his words carefully. "The VF-2 Personnel office was the worst on base, without a doubt. After this inspection, you are … in the top three and headed straight to the top."

You could have heard our *Whew!* a mile away.

It was a nice parting gift for me. A few days later I became the Assistant Operations Officer. I'd be working on the squadron's flying mission and aircrew training. My boss, the Ops O, was Sax. I knew him from my first F-14 tour, and we made a good team.

By year's end I was ready for a break, and got it in December: two flights, two weeks of leave.

With a deployment approaching, the pace of flying picked up: twenty-three flights in January, fifteen in February, all more or less routine training missions. Except one.

In January 1989, off the California coast, one of our jets had a minor landing gear problem after the cat shot. They followed procedures, left the gear down, tried some troubleshooting, and radioed the Skipper and others to talk it over. Safety procedures prevented their return to the ship. It would've been smart to go to Miramar for mechanics and tools that weren't on the ship. Instead they landed at North Island, ten miles from Miramar. The aircrew hopped on a late-night helicopter bringing parts out to the *Ranger*. They were back onboard in time for midrats. Maybe they thought they were being cautious, but the decision didn't make sense because our jet was stuck at North Island.

The next morning Rip asked Lumpy and me if we felt comfortable flying the jet to Miramar. We said, "Sure!" We grabbed our flight gear and jumped on a helicopter, and soon we were preflighting the Tomcat at North Island.

Because of a simple broken wire, we couldn't taxi by steering the nosewheel. So Lumpy steered the jet with his feet. Tap the left brake, she turns left. The aircraft had not been refueled and had 3,600 pounds in its tanks—a fraction of our normal fuel load of 20,000 pounds. On a quiet Sunday morning, with Miramar just a short hop away, we figured no problem.

Lumpy tap-danced us onto the runway centerline. Once airborne, we left the landing gear down and contacted San Diego air traffic control, expecting a nearly direct flight of about ten minutes.

It didn't happen. "November echo two-zero-five," said the controller, "I'd like to confirm you are a single F-14 direct Navy Miramar." Did he think something unusual was going on?

"San Diego, two-zero-five, that's affirmative."

"Two-zero-five, I'm going to route you to the east to clear some approaching traffic for Lindbergh." That's San Diego's commercial airport. "Steady up zero-eight-zero, climb and maintain five thousand."

I rogered his instructions and checked fuel with Lumpy. "Do we really have 2,900 pounds?"

"Yup."

Our landing gear added a lot of drag, but NATOPS said to leave it down. Standard procedure for daytime at Miramar would be to land with 2,000 pounds of fuel, and we would have cut it close if all went smoothly. But all did not.

After what seemed like forever, the controller cleared us to turn north. This was progress, though we were now a long way from Miramar.

I asked the controller if we could proceed direct.

"Negative, two-zero-five, I've got a couple more coming in. Continue north."

Great!

A few minutes later, with our fuel below 2,000 pounds, I again requested direct.

"Two-zero-five, are you requesting special handling?"

I was stuck. If I requested special handling or declared an emergency, COMFIT and who knows who else would've been notified. We would've been chewed out for taking off with so little fuel. On the other hand, if something didn't change we would run out of gas.

"Negative," I replied.

Lumpy and I were keeping a close eye on the distance to Miramar and calculating flight time and fuel flow. We finally heard the magic words: "Two-zero-five proceed direct Miramar. Cleared to switch Miramar Tower."

Another mile-away *Whew!* Thank you, thank you, thank you. That's what I felt. But what I said was, "Roger, switching."

We landed with less than 1,000 pounds of fuel. Hey, we could have buzzed around up there for another six to ten minutes!

The next day Rip told me he regretted asking us to make the flight but I just said, "Well, the jet's here now." I didn't tell him how much I'd sweated the fuel!

Next stop: Hawaii.

CHAPTER 18

ONCE MORE ACROSS THE PACIFIC

Leaving for deployment doesn't get easier with practice.

My fourth was beginning, and it was as wrenching as the first three. I left behind my wife, car, house, dog, and so much more that I loved and enjoyed. Along with some 5,000 shipmates I loaded my stuff, said my good-byes, and got underway.

Ahead lay six months of mission-focused flying with little distraction from the rest of the world. Wide-open airspace…foreign ports…boisterous ready-room movie crowds…auto-dog and midrats…2 AM cat shots…hostile shores to patrol…blasts in Zone 5 just because we could.

One month of all that would've been enough. Okay, two. But the Navy said six, so off I went.

On Friday, February 24, 1989, the *Ranger* left San Diego in the morning and squadrons started flying out to her in the afternoon. Next day, Lumpy and I flew two traps for daytime qualification—day qual—and landed back at Miramar. We'd already said our farewells, so we hung out on base. And we didn't have cars. We weren't going to leave them at the squadron for six months.

That evening, some of us were going to get our night quals and stay aboard for good. Lumpy and I launched at 10:30. Things didn't run smoothly. At midnight we were back at Miramar.

"Hi, Laura! Guess where I am. Can you come pick me up?" She had mixed feelings, happy to have me home for another night (well, who wouldn't be?) but not looking forward to another farewell. It never got easier for our wives, either.

Sunday we flew aboard for keeps and the *Ranger* steamed west for Hawaii.

Nine days en route. Seven flights. Four alerts, one at midnight, another at 4 AM. It was only fair for the Operations Officer to share the pain. And the Ops O was, suddenly, me.

Sax had a family emergency and stayed behind. That kicked me upstairs to Acting Ops O of VF-2. I'd been the assistant for more than a month, so the job seemed like a natural, and the Ops Department had a good team.

It was traditional for the Ops O to lay down some ground rules at the start, so I was on the agenda for an AOM the day after we left. I'd seen Gatsby and Streak do it in VF-24, and now it was my turn. I was the youngest and most junior lieutenant commander in the squadron, but most of my audience were junior officers who had never been on a deployment.

Listen up, guys. Ready room etiquette. Flight scheduling. Strike planning teams. I covered the "house rules," then threw in a few things that had stayed with me from Topgun. Don't blab about our squadron's problems; what happens in VF-2 stays in VF-2, got it?

Nothing profound, but it did help implant the deployment mindset. It was a good warm-up act for the XO and Skipper. When they were done, we were all in the right frame of mind.

Our first stop was Pearl Harbor, and most squadrons arranged admins. VF-2 booked a suite on the top floor of a hotel on Waikiki Beach, a great place to meet up, leave packages after shopping, and crash at the end of the day—for some; when all beds and couches were full, the floor became an option.

We invited the CAG, his staff, and other senior officers to a sunset party on the hotel's rooftop deck. It was a great evening with a good crowd. After awhile the party moved to our suite. Before long, hotel security told us we were too loud. We calmed down a bit. A little later, they told us we were still too loud. The crowd was thinning anyway, so things settled down for the night.

Around 6 AM, Security made its move. Four burly guys and a manager told us to leave for violating the policy against a party in the room. Strange timing; we'd be checking out that day anyway. However, hint taken. We left.

Rip suggested we tell other squadrons to avoid that hotel. I said we should recommend it. Throw us out? Let's see how you like our friends!

I've shared what it's like on a carrier flight deck: the uncanny quiet when I walked to my jet and could talk to my pilot in a normal tone of voice before the shriek of engines began, the bottomless enthusiasm of my plane captain greeting me and working the preflight, the smell of the catapult steam, and so many other sensory inputs. They still made an impact, even with 450 carrier landings and 1,700 hours of flight time in my logbook.

Back in those days, the carrier USS *Midway* was one of the oldest active carriers, but her fighter squadrons were right up to date, with brand-new F/A-18 Hornets. The *Midway* and its air wing were homeported in Japan and happened to be sailing in the western Pacific the same time we were, so a carrier-vs-carrier exercise was arranged. The *Ranger* played the good guys, so VF-2 flew our Tomcats like Tomcats. The *Midway* played the enemy, so her very capable Hornet strike fighters were reduced to pretending they were a much tamer threat—the Yak-38 Forger.

Action, VF-2's new XO, planned the air defense part. The main component would be four VF-2 Tomcats lurking 150 miles from the *Ranger*, each with four Phoenix to blast the attackers. Their CAP station would be based on the *Midway*'s expected position, acutely aware of the air traffic control routes and boundaries of the Philippines, Taiwan, and Hong Kong. Scoring the kills would be Action and his RIO, Billy, along with three other crews in his division.

Action assigned a division of VF-1 jets to another station next to his, just to keep it fair. Lumpy and I were in Sax and the Skipper's division, so we were assigned as a deck launched interceptor (DLI). Basically table scraps, the way things looked.

On a Friday afternoon, eight Tomcats roared off the *Ranger*'s deck, licking their chops for some easy kills. Then aircraft were moved around the flight deck, and Lumpy and I manned the DLI slot with little enthusiasm. What could possibly get through that screen of eight Tomcats bristling with Phoenix? We'd sat through the briefing; now we would sit in a jet for two hours.

At least we played the game. Our Tomcat was lined up on the catapult, ready for launch on short notice. We started the jet, checked all systems, then shut it down and opened the canopy. Engine starter, electrical power, and ground crew were all there. The jet was now set, "cocked" like a pistol. How long do we have to sit up here?

Ten minutes after we shut down, the Air Boss yelled over the 5MC, "Launch the DLI! Launch the DLI!"

No time for a "What the hell?!" Something must've gone wrong. Lumpy signaled the plane captain to start the engine while I shouted, "Canopy's coming!"

I was head-down, prepping for immediate launch, when Lumpy on ICS said, "There's a guy on the right holding a sign." A sailor held up a vector board with the latest info: an 8 in a circle for the radio frequency, and the vector 020°/80. How could the targets be only 80 miles away?

Four frenzied minutes after the Boss sounded the alarm, we were ready to launch. All eyes were on the pilot, so when Lumpy gave a thumbs up, everybody sprang into action. Remove the tie-down chains. Check the weapons. Check everything. Zone 5. Lumpy salutes. We brace. And the cat kicks the Tomcat off the ship!

I set my radar to a narrow scan and dialed up button 8. "Two-zero-six airborne, state tiger," which meant our state, our condition, was full fuel and full weapons. Full, indeed: two Phoenix, two Sparrows, two Sidewinders, and bullets. They were all simulated, of course, but still I loved saying, "state tiger."

"Two-zero-six, bandit zero-two-zero, 65 miles."

My radar had just painted the contact, so I said, "Judy." That code word tells the controller I'll take it from here.

"Lumpy, I've got a single on the nose at 60 miles, 25,000 feet. Let's start a climb. Wait, there's another one about 5 miles behind him."

Lumpy said, "Phoenix selected," and climbed into a sky full of clouds.

We had a few miles to catch our breath. Lumpy said, "I wonder what happened with Action and the CAP."

A few miles don't last long in a rocketing Tomcat. Soon we were close enough to launch on the first target, with another one in trail. I said to Lumpy, "I'll call the launch at 30 miles," then over the radio, "Two-zero-six, Fox 3, zero-two-five at 28, descending." One Phoenix was on the way. A few seconds later, "Two-zero-six, Fox 3, zero-two-zero at 31." Two Phoenix en route. I didn't know if anyone was plotting our shots, but I wanted the *Ranger* to know the DLI was getting the job done.

Lumpy switched to Sparrows. More contacts dotted my radar. The incoming jets acted like a dedicated enemy, boring into the target despite the missiles coming their way, and it was simple to keep track of them on the radar. Even the two we targeted kept coming at us like ghost Yak-38s.

I told Lumpy, "The first guy is ten right at 5 miles, should come down the right side. I'm taking a lock on the third guy so we can shoot a Sparrow."

Over the radio I said, "Two-zero-six, Fox 1, zero-one-five at fifteen."

Lumpy spotted one of them. "Tally, F-18, right one o'clock." Can't fool Lumpy; he knew it wasn't a Yak-38.

A few minutes more of this, and we'd shot our second Sparrow and both Sidewinders, and then called a gun kill or two. That was enough. No dogfight, but I'll bet they were tempted. I know we were.

"Two-zero-six, Winchester, state twelve point eight," I radioed. Translation: "We're out of weapons, and we have 12,800 pounds of fuel left." We'd been airborne twenty minutes and scored seven or eight kills.

In an airplane, you can't just pull over and park. To wait for something, you hold by flying in circles. While we orbited, I dialed up the *Midway* on our TACAN—and was surprised to see she was 100 miles away, much closer than we'd been told in the briefing. No wonder we launched the DLI!

I would not have wanted to be the person who told Action where the *Midway* should be, which was so far off that it screwed up the whole plan. On the other hand, that's why we train. Better now than when it counts.

Our flight was a short 1.5 hours. There was little to learn from it, so the debrief was brief.

The *Ranger* stopped in the Philippines, then headed into the South China Sea for a port call in Singapore. In three days we were passing the closest we would get to Vietnam, 200 miles to our west. We knew the Soviet Union had stationed MiG-23 Floggers at Cam Ranh Bay. Those were capable aircraft that could threaten ours, so we launched Tomcats to establish a barrier CAP to the west.

The E-2 Hawkeye got into the act, and reported multiple contacts airborne from Cam Ranh airfield. The Tomcats turned that way and got radar contact, then turned back to keep out of Vietnam airspace. The E-2 kept its hawk eye peeled, and did a great job of keeping the Tomcats out of trouble.

It was cat and mouse as the two flights sparred and feinted, each on its side of the airspace fence. When the Tomcats got close, the bogeys turned away. Finally the other guys crossed the line into international airspace, where the Tomcats closed in on them and confirmed they were MiG-23 Floggers. In 1989 this was big news.

It was starting to look like an ACM training event, and Tomcats from VF-1 and VF-2 were in it. The Floggers maneuvered aggressively; it seemed like they were training to prevent smooth formation join-ups. But if they were trying to gain offensive position on the Tomcats, they failed. We had intercepted Floggers here on the 1987 deployment, and those had also maneuvered aggressively, but this time things were getting hotter.

And busier. Both VF-1 and VF-2 squadrons launched more fighters, and soon some tankers joined the mix.

Lumpy and I briefed and launched, excited about joining the action, but it was not to be. What a lousy time for a rare IFF breakdown! The IFF is a transmitter that identifies you as a friendly, and the sky was abuzz with blips from both sides, so without it we could not enter the arena. We held overhead of the *Ranger*, fuming, while I tried everything to fix it. No go. By the time we hit the deck, the aerial swordfights were ending. And we missed it all.

Those who didn't miss it came back with some good photos and a lot of observations. CAG tapped several former Topgun instructors to work up a full report. I was one of them, and a newcomer was another.

Loner had joined VF-2 in the month before deployment. His callsign was accurate; he didn't show the sanctioned adolescence that many junior aircrews did. He took his work very seriously. We'd been Topgun instructors together, and now were together again in VF-2.

Put VF-1 and VF-2 together, and you'd have a bunch of strong aviators, some of them legendary in the Tomcat community. Together they had dominated the Floggers—no surprise, given the effort Grumman put into making the Tomcat as agile as possible. So, no surprise that our classified report took on a sporting tone.

Two weeks later the 4-star admiral in charge of US forces in the Pacific wrote a sharp message to all forces under his command. Citing our report and a report from a Navy ship that had encountered a Soviet Navy ship, he called the tone "inappropriate" and reminded us that the Soviet Union was the ideological enemy of the United States and a military threat.

Oops.

INTEL BRIEF: FLIGHT DECK CYCLE AND THE FUEL LADDER

"Bingo."

When you heard that, it meant "go home." Someone's fuel had burned down to a predetermined low, and the flight was over. No anxiety; we planned our bingo levels with plenty of fuel to return to base and then some.

Fuel planning is essential for any kind of aviation, as important as knowing how to operate stick and throttles. Over the years I enjoyed many F-14 flights where fuel planning was simple. We'd be in a familiar area with our choice of airfields to divert to if necessary, so we could fly missions that lasted as long as our fuel.

It wasn't like that when flying from a carrier in the middle of the ocean. "Blue water ops" gave you no divert options, of course, but did give you something else unique to carrier flying: the "deck cycle." Think of a carrier as a very busy airport. You take off by being thrown into the air like a kid's paper airplane, and you land by slamming down and being jerked to an eye-popping stop by hooking a cable. Meanwhile, aircraft are being moved about the deck, maintenance is being done, ordnance is carted around, and it's all got to be coordinated like clockwork. So the length of almost all flights has to be based on the deck cycle, the time between the start of one series of takeoffs and the start of the next. Airborne aircraft landed after the next cycle launched.

This often made fuel conservation a priority. Aerial refueling helped, but it wasn't always available. Some missions lasted longer than one cycle and were known as double-cycle or even triple-cycle. You couldn't fly them without refueling.

For me, the deck cycle was usually 1 hour, 45 minutes. We called this a "1-plus-45 cycle." But since you landed after the launch, actual flight time was more like 2.1 or 2.2 hours. Yes, we measured the cycle at 1 hour and 45 *minutes*, but we recorded flight time in hours and *tenths*; just one of those things.

Sometimes the deck cycle was only 1+30, and sometimes we had flex deck ops, which meant the flight deck would recover aircraft as soon as possible after they returned. That was usually associated with fun flying.

To deal with the typical cycle, every aviator that I knew set up a fuel ladder. I started mine by listing my expected recovery time, usually fifteen minutes after the start of the following launch. Then I figured my "max trap" fuel, the amount of fuel that would put us at the maximum acceptable weight for an arrested landing. In the F-14A, the max trap weight for many years was 51,800 pounds, later raised to 54,000 pounds. Squadrons sometimes made a rule that we could burn down to a certain fuel level, say 4,000 pounds, but in most cases I recall the rule was "max trap on the ball."

To figure max trap, I started with the weight of the specific aircraft I was flying, because each jet was different by hundreds of pounds. Next I added missile rails and missiles or bombs. For example, with Tomcat number 162600:

162600 base weight:	43,180 lbs
Rails for missiles / fuel tanks:	1,580 lbs
Missiles and bullets:	1,940 lbs
Total weight:	46,700 lbs

That total aircraft weight would be 5,100 pounds less than the max trap of 51,800, so our max trap fuel was 5,100 pounds. The F-14A normally burned JP-5 fuel, which weighed 6.8 pounds per gallon, so that max trap fuel was 750 gallons.

One more piece of information was that at "max conserve," the throttle setting to remain airborne the longest, the F-14A would burn roughly 1,100 pounds of fuel every fifteen minutes, which works out to approximately 650 gallons per hour if you're interested.

So if the next launch was 5 PM (1700), my expected recovery time was 5:15 (1715). Figuring back from that, I'd have the fuel amount that I should see each 15 minutes, and I would draw a fuel ladder on my kneeboard card that looked like this:

1600	10.6
1615	9.5
1630	8.4
1645	7.3
1700	6.2
1715	5.1

I usually calculated my ladder for the final hour or so, not the entire flight. During the flight, we would monitor fuel and if it reached an amount shown, we were "on our ladder" and limited to max conserve on the throttles, which meant flying around at 225 knots.

We sometimes saved fuel for dogfighting at the end of the flight. For example, if we had 10.4 at 1630, then we had 2,000 pounds to play with—a nice package. After all, we were flying fighters.

CHAPTER 19

CRYSTAL BLUE CONES OF FLAME, FIFTY FEET LONG

Lumpy and I didn't get to see the Floggers that day. But the day wasn't over.

With the *Ranger* cruising along at 20 knots, we were soon out of range of Cam Ranh Bay and its Floggers. Still, there was a chance that other aircraft could approach, so that evening I was scheduled for a Barrier CAP mission.

I'd always been fascinated by afterburner photos and had learned a few lessons about how to get a good one. Burner plumes show up well at night, but you need enough light to see the plane and maybe identify the squadron; otherwise it's a blowtorch in a blackout. We were scheduled for a launch around sunset that should provide the perfect opportunity.

I'd shot a lot of photos in my career, and back in those ancient times they were on something called film. You could push the button and then wind it to the next frame, or you could buy an autowinder and just push the button. I liked the latter.

As you would expect, the F-14 accelerates quickly in full Zone 5. That would make it difficult to take a smooth photo, so I planned to pull the nose up in a climb to keep speed under control.

I was flying with Lumpy, and we were the wingman. But I was the senior guy in the flight, so that made me the mission commander. The lead was Pager, my pilot from the 1987 deployment, and his RIO was Jumby. On missions like this we usually had a little extra fuel, so after the mission brief I described the photo op and asked if they were game. They were.

My Tomcat launched first. We joined up at 10,000 feet, Pager took the lead, and we headed toward our station. Our friends had sparred with Floggers just a few hours before, but it was nightfall now and we expected no action. My brain kicked into multitask mode, and half of it zeroed in on the photo op.

A few miles from the ship, we shifted to hand signals and our second radio to run the shoot as I had briefed it. By now, ten minutes after sunset, it was dark enough for the burner plumes to look fantastic but light enough to get the Tomcat into the scene. Pager swept his wings to 50 degrees as planned, while Lumpy kept our wings in auto so we would have a maneuvering advantage. As we cruised at 300 knots, Pager selected full Zone 5 and pulled his nose up 30 degrees.

In a split second Pager's afterburners flickered to life and spurted long cones of blue flame. I started shooting and directing Lumpy. "Move up…good…forward…little down…good."

I was clicking away with my autowinder, but the spectacle was so riveting that I kept pulling the camera down to just let the photons flood into my memory. The burner plumes didn't look like fire as we are used to seeing it. They were bright blue cones that appeared to be made of crystal, extending fifty feet behind the Tomcat.

I could clearly see the shockwave discs in the burner plumes, slowly moving forward and back as our speed and altitude changed. There was a complex pattern inside those twin cones, yet they looked delicate. They weren't; the exhaust temperature was nearly 2,000°F and it blasted out of the nozzles at more than 1,200 mph. Delicate? They were fire-and-brimstone icons of raw, powerful thrust.

I'd asked Pager to pull the nose up for two reasons: it would control airspeed for smoother flying, and it would look incredibly cool. I was right on both counts. In maybe a minute I'd shot all twenty-four frames on one roll of film. I radioed that I was done. I should have hollered, "Cut!"

We were near our planned CAP altitude of 25,000 feet, so both pilots came out of burner and went back to normal operation.

Soon we stabilized and checked fuel. Uh-oh. We'd burned all our mission fuel and actually cut into our fuel ladder. Pager and Jumby too. This was one part of the photo op that I had not planned carefully—how long to stay in burner. We asked the ship—casually—about aerial refueling but none was available. It was a common request, so it didn't raise any alarms.

The night became velvet black as we headed to our station at a very conservative speed. Lumpy and I tried to think of a story about what happened to our fuel, but couldn't come up with anything that made sense. Ordinarily I would have relished the excitement of an intercept, but not tonight, thanks. The anxious stress of tracking our fuel state was enough.

By this time you've noticed a common theme: the preciousness of jet fuel in a fighter. And you've probably guessed why. Fuel is heavy stuff, so the less you carry, the better you fight. And it's especially precious in a Navy fighter. Out here on the open sea, if you're running out of gas, there's only one place to land.

We orbited silently, waiting for visitors that never came. When the ship asked our fuel state, I padded it. Those guys kept track of aircraft all day; they knew what we should have, so that's what I told them. About an hour later we headed gingerly back to the ship. All went smoothly and we never needed a cover story. Only the refuelers knew.

A few days later we pulled into Singapore and I dropped the film at a one-hour photo shop. I was elated to see the results! You will be, too; the best one is in the photo section. Of all the photos in a long flying career, those were some of my best.

After three days in Singapore the battle group continued west, into the Indian Ocean and North Arabian Sea. We were back at Gonzo Station, but some things had changed in the seventeen months since we left. Operation Earnest Will ended in September 1988, so there wouldn't be nonstop flight ops for forty-eight or seventy-two hours. Around the same time, Iran and Iraq signed a cease-fire that ended their eight-year war, but that had little effect on us. One ugly fact persisted: Iran was a sworn enemy of the United States and a vocal threat to regional stability.

As the tip of the spear for American policy, all elements of the *Ranger* Battle Group had to be razor-sharp and ready for whatever might happen. Iran's military muscle still demanded respect. VF-2 flew its fighter missions, and also kept its reconnaissance eyes peeled to update info on Iran's weaponry and defenses.

A week after arrival, VF-2 flew a TARPS mission through the Strait of Hormuz, still a potential flashpoint. Sea and air traffic was within range of nearly every weapon in Iran's arsenal. The waterway was both a practical chokepoint—the world's most important oil chokepoint—and a hugely symbolic waterway for Iran. Our TARPS mission had to be well-prepared, with a VF-1 Tomcat escort, a bomb-laden A-6 for instant response if needed, and an EA-6B for electronic warfare, all supported by E-2 radar and S-3 tankers.

I didn't fly this mission. My squadronmates did. I helped to plan and brief the mission, but was scheduled as a spare. And this time the spare didn't launch.

I flew about every other day—intercept training (dull compared to everything else), ACM, escorts for simulated strikes, and such. No 0200 launches to CAP stations. Some night events, though, to keep the edge sharp.

I enjoyed flying with Lumpy, a very good pilot with an entertaining sense of humor. On boring flights we would swap jokes and rehash Saturday Night Live skits. It helped ease the tension of sitting on a time bomb.

A few weeks later I did fly into the Strait of Hormuz as the TARPS jet for an intel update. Sax had returned from emergency leave, so I'd be flying with him.

Our route had to conform with international rules for flying the strait. I plotted the left and right limits on a chart and picked waypoints within the corridor. Intel told me the targets for the TARPS cameras. Complex performance charts became my friends as I calculated aircraft weight, drag index, altitude, air temp, and more. I prepared kneeboard cards with navigation points and timing, radio frequencies, airspeed, fuel flow—you get the idea. A lawyer from the admiral's staff even got into the mix, to okay the chart and check me out on the rules for transiting the strait.

I briefed the aircrews on all that and more. Then we all grabbed lunch and got into our gear. This time, my "gear" included something unusual: an old, snub-nosed .38 pistol. I'm not Rambo, and our mission definitely was not combat, but it seemed prudent in case things went terribly wrong. I'd gone through pistol qualification at Miramar, and at SERE school they taught us when to use it. It was a weapon of last resort, they said. Okay, but this was the Strait of Hormuz.

Sax and I launched at 12:15 PM into a sunny sky. Heading 305°, we climbed to 20,000 feet and joined on two S-3 Viking tankers. The rest of the package arrived and we all refueled en route to Waypoint Alpha. We climbed to mission altitude at 28,000 feet.

The E-2 Hawkeye stayed behind, keeping its radar eyes on the entire area and relaying info to the ship. Now and then we'd hear a question or comment from higher headquarters, and I was told later that the flight was monitored in the Pentagon. Talk about your 10,000-mile screwdriver!

"Hey Bio," said Sax as we approached the strait. "I saw you checked out one of the squadron pistols. Are you carrying anything else?"

"No, just what the SDO gave me. Are you?"

"Look at this."

I looked up and saw Sax brandishing a long-barreled .44 revolver and a 9mm automatic. He said he had plenty of ammunition, too. If we found ourselves on the ground in hostile territory, I'd be sticking close to Rambo—I mean, Sax.

It was a hazy day, and our route kept us well off the Iranian coast. I couldn't see anything of interest, but I hoped the big TARPS cameras could.

With the multiple waypoints, I was busy navigating. Most legs were longer than three minutes, but a few were less than two. Was I nervous? Better believe it. This was a high-profile mission loaded with details and parameters and international implications, and top brass was looking over our shoulders. Oh, and there was also Iran.

The four-hour mission went smoothly; all the pieces fit. The TARPS long-range cameras peered through the haze and got us the updates we needed.

Good mission. After debriefing I had another flight that evening, an air defense exercise with Lumpy that put another 2.4 hours in our logbooks. Near midnight we grabbed some pizza at midrats. It was great to be 30 years old and busy. I could eat whatever I wanted and not gain a pound!

There were always other Bullets at midrats, so there was plenty of good conversation. Skipper Serhan showed up that night and we chatted about the TARPS mission. Soon our table talk evolved—or maybe degenerated—into a joke-a-thon. It was great to see Lumpy and the Skipper, two very different personalities, trading jokes and stories. Call it bonding. A squadron needs that.

"Did you hear the one about the two construction workers on a noisy job site, so they had to communicate using sign language?"

Want to join in? Google "eye left tit in the box." Thirty years later that joke still makes me smile.

CHAPTER 20

LEAVING SO SOON?

What do you do on a no-fly day? Department head meeting.

First item of business a day after my TARPS flight through the strait: start thinking about the post-cruise report, a summary of lessons from the deployment. We had one more month on Gonzo Station, and sometimes it seemed like we just got here. There would be two more TARPS missions into the strait, some exercises, and almost daily flight ops, but we could see the light at the end of the tunnel. The 1989 deployment seemed smoother than 1987, but six months was still a long deployment.

With Earnest Will off the schedule, we found other ways to keep busy. We spent a week training near Diego Garcia, an island in the Indian Ocean, where we could drop bombs and launch missiles over open sea. We sharpened our air-to-air gunnery skills on banners towed behind our Tomcats. We flew four days against a friendly air force near Gonzo Station, sneaking in fast and low to mix it up with our wily adversaries—great training and a lot of fun. In July we flew dogfights against the Royal Thai Air Force as we passed through their area.

Whatever the mission, the danger of carrier ops was always there. Pager could vouch for that; one night he and Rico had to take the barricade—in the dark! The barricade is a nylon web twenty feet high, stretched across the flight deck like a giant tennis net. It's the last resort.

It's not there all the time. In a normal carrier landing, the pilot shoves the throttle to max as the wheels hit the deck, so he'll have full power to get back in the air if something goes wrong. So the deck has to be clear. But if things have gone wrong, if the tailhook and deck cables can't do it, the barricade has to be rigged. And quickly.

During a routine flight, Pager and Rico boltered on their first pass. That means they didn't catch a wire. No real reason. The ship then experienced shifting winds and had them hold overhead. Soon they were low on fuel, so Pager plugged a tanker but it couldn't transfer fuel. When the tanker retracted its hose and extended it again, the hose fell off. It would have been comical if they weren't low on fuel at night in bad weather in the middle of the ocean. Yeah, otherwise the hose falling off would be humorous.

The powers that be did not want to take chances and decided he'd have to hit the barricade. And with the barricade he couldn't take off and try again.

In the ready room, we heard what was happening. All eyes locked onto the PLAT TV. Lightning flashes outlined the heavy clouds in the area. Word spread quickly and more people came in as the airborne drama unfolded. Though he was near the ship, we couldn't see Pager's plane but we could hear their radio voices. He and Rico sounded cool under pressure as options diminished along with their fuel. A barricade landing would do little or no damage to an aircraft, but the crew had only one chance to get it right.

The *Ranger*'s flight deck crew swarmed onto the deck and rigged the barricade in a few well-rehearsed minutes. Pager and Rico got radar vectors for the approach. Now we could see their lights on the PLAT, a few miles behind the ship and coming in smoothly. The flight deck was still crowded with people checking the giant net, so the controller told Pager to circle for a short delay and asked their fuel state.

This time Rico's voice had an edge to it. "Nine hundred pounds." In Ready 2, we all yelped, knowing that was only a few minutes' fuel.

Storms were churning up unpredictable winds. The ship turned this way and that, hunting for a steady wind. The controllers gave the Tomcat more vectors. Time ticked away. And finally ran out. Both Pager and Rico said, "You've gotta take me now."

The LSO took over. "Paddles contact," he said; he could see the Tomcat. The net rose. With a steady and reassuring voice, the LSO talked Pager down. "You're working just a little low there…. Hawk that line-up and get it on centerline. … Call the ball."

Seconds later the Tomcat hit the deck and careened into the barricade. At 150 mph it wasn't like tumbling into a featherbed, but thanks to the net's design and the skill of everyone involved, they were safely aboard and the jet had hardly a scratch. That's why we train.

A lightning bolt punctuated the PLAT screen as the audience broke into cheers. A few minutes later, Pager and Rico were greeted at midrats by an enthusiastic crowd. They had the best story that day.

Want to watch it happen? Go to YouTube and search "blue water ops barricade." It's fuzzy because it's 1989 night-vision, but it's the actual video.

By early June, Lumpy and I had been flying together for more than a year. We were comfortable, but it wasn't going to last. Skipper Serhan announced an almost complete shuffle of pilot/RIO and lead/wingman assignments. Food moved into Lumpy's back seat and they would fly wingman for the XO and Zip.

My new pilot was Lieutenant Bill "Chevy" Shivell, making his first deployment. Chevy and I would be the wingman for Munch, a lieutenant commander, and his junior RIO, Bagman. Chevy had one of the best landing

grades in the air wing, and I soon found him to be a capable pilot, eager to learn more about the Tomcat.

And then, on June 8, I became the Operations Officer.

Ops O and Maintenance Officer were a squadron's two "major department heads." In an aviator's career, this was an essential step toward command of a squadron. I felt very fortunate, because I was the most junior lieutenant commander in the squadron. Skipper Serhan and I got along well and he had confidence in my abilities, and the decision was his.

It wasn't a complete surprise. Assistant Ops usually fleets-up to Ops O. I'd also been the acting Ops O several times when Sax was away, so I felt prepared for the real thing. Still, it was like the first time you drive a car by yourself, after weeks with an instructor. Maybe a little trepidation, but more a sense of freedom. Responsibility. Adventure. Satisfaction. And more. Not much trepidation.

Not many movies, either. Every evening the next day's air plan would be published and we'd write our flight schedule during the movie. It was a sacrifice I happily made.

In June the *Ranger* left Gonzo Station in its foaming wake and transited to a happier place. Perth, in Western Australia, lay more than 4,000 nautical miles southeast. On the way I made another memorable flight, and it wasn't in an F-14.

Slush was a high-profile junior officer in VF-2, a tall, lean RIO who was also loud and made no apologies for it. Most guys in a fighter squadron have opinions about everything, but Slush made sure everyone knew his, and loved to argue with anyone who would engage. I'm not insulting him; this was simply his "brand." He was in VF-2 when I got there, and was actually a good RIO, so he fit in perfectly. His callsign was a mash-up of the words "slut" and "lush," and he wore it with pride.

In mid-June Slush asked me if I wanted to fly in the C-2 cargo plane for a photo-ex with a VF-2 Tomcat. He had been talking to the C-2 crews about it. I jumped at the opportunity and soon it all came together. I had to admit, Slush made things happen.

I showed up at the C-2 detachment's ready room in bag and flight jacket, carrying my helmet. Jockey, a VF-2 JO, was there with a video camera, as well as photographers from the E-2 squadron and the *Ranger*. We briefed the event, climbed aboard the C-2, and catapulted into the midday sky.

Two oddities about the C-2 Greyhound. A conventional tail on a plane that big wouldn't fit into a carrier hangar deck, so the C-2 has four small rudders, but only three of them move. And C-2 passengers don't sit facing forward; they face aft for safety. Sitting backwards for a cat shot felt strange after my hundreds of "normal" cats. In a Tomcat you get squashed into your seat. In a Greyhound you feel like the airplane is leaving without you.

Soon we were flying at 5,000 feet and 150 knots. The photographers from the E-2 squadron and the *Ranger* put on gunner's belts—thick braided restraints—and clicked themselves to safety lines with large hooks on the back. The rest of us stayed strapped in our seats, and when everyone was ready the rear cargo ramp was lowered. The ramp measures about ten feet wide by eight feet high, but when your brain knows that you are flying in an airplane it looks like the portal to another dimension.

In a few minutes an E-2 Hawkeye eased into the portal. It's similar to the Greyhound, but with its huge radar disc it looks like a C-2 under an umbrella. With its complex shape and slender fuselage, the E-2 looked cool gliding behind us. The COD crewman let the rest of us stand up, but we had to stay well back from the open ramp. He didn't have to tell me twice, and I could see just fine from the safe zone.

The E-2 posed for us for maybe five minutes, then left the stage for its primary mission. The ramp stayed open and everyone moved back to the safe zone. Jockey and I put on the gunner's belts and clicked onto the safety line. I gave the whole setup a good pull and

figured it had worked this long, so I would probably be okay. We plugged our helmets into comm cords, although we could only listen, not talk. I stepped to the edge of the ramp and sat down.

First impression: It wasn't very windy, but I was glad I had my jacket. I resisted the temptation to hang my feet over the edge; it wasn't the time or place to be funny.

Slush and I had set things up with VF-2 Maintenance. They would prep our two most colorful Tomcats and load them with two Phoenix, two Sparrows, and two Sidewinders. I settled into my lofty perch and didn't mind waiting for my subjects, a pair of shiny Bullet Tomcats bristling with weapons.

The best laid plans of mice and me: In my helmet I heard that both of the colorful jets had maintenance problems, so they launched the spare. It turned out to be one of the dull-gray "tactical paint scheme" jets, with Hap as the pilot and Darth as his RIO.

They climbed above the solid cloud deck, located the E-2, and flew by underneath us. Hap had his head in the game, and swept his wings so it looked like he was going 600 knots, when he was really doing about 250. I started hitting the shutter button.

They had just taken off and needed to save some fuel for the rest of the flight. Darth radioed that they would make a few more passes and burn down (meaning "reduce their weight") so they could fly at 150 knots. With an unobstructed view from the open ramp, these fly-bys also yielded some decent photos, but I saved most of my film for the main event.

After burning down, they approached at a slower speed, head-on to the C-2's yawning back door. Hap skillfully eased into position, and in seconds he was stabilized about 40 feet behind us. With the jet so close, I could see that it was dirty and had no external weapons, but it's what showed up, so I started shooting.

Like the Zone 5 photos off Vietnam, several times I lowered my camera and just looked. For years I had seen them in close formation, but had never seen a

Tomcat like this without the Plexiglas canopy wall between me and the jet. Few people had. It was an attention-getter: a crystal-clear view of this sleek fighter just a few feet behind us. It seemed like I could reach out and touch it. I thought about this thirty-three-ton metal machine held aloft by its wings, but got back to the task before going existential.

I gave Hap hand signals to move a little up, a little to one side, and I could see him nod his head.

I spent fifteen minutes sitting on the cargo ramp and shot all four of my rolls of film. As you can imagine, I was very careful changing rolls of film on an open ramp a mile above the ocean. I'm pleased to report that there were no "oops" moments. The *Ranger*'s photo lab developed the film as soon as we landed, and the mission was a success.

Once we left Gonzo Station, we were no longer the primary carrier. We dropped to a lower priority for spare parts and fuel, so the air wing flew less. During the first half of deployment I flew about once every other day, forty-seven flights in ninety days. During the second half, I flew only twenty-seven flights. Less flying left more time to work on that post-cruise report. But the sunsets were on the fantail and Perth was on the nose.

We were still on deployment and had to stay ready for anything. Some of the flights were still pretty cool. One morning we launched a large, long-range simulated strike. Both A-6 squadrons launched four jets, VF-2 launched five, and so did VF-1. The strike package flew to various waypoints above the featureless Indian Ocean on a gorgeous day. During the low-stress transits, I captured a few photos and some video of the other four Bounty Hunter Tomcats.

As the ship approached Australia, I was scheduled for a TARPS mission to Mount Augustus, a prominent peak 200 miles inland. I was flying with Donnie "Big Time" Cochran, a former Blue Angel who was VF-2's Maintenance Officer. When we approached Augustus we dropped to the lowest altitude allowed and took a good look at it. Then we turned around and headed back to the *Ranger*, hundreds of miles away.

As we crossed the coast we noticed what looked like a big bite out of the coastline below. Big Time asked, "Do you know what that is, Bio?"

I checked my chart and replied, "Looks like it's called Shark Bay."

There was a pause and he said, "Shark Bay? Let's get out of here!"

On June 29 the carrier anchored off the port city of Fremantle, and shuttle boats carried excited sailors ashore. Fremantle and Perth welcomed us like long-lost friends. VF-2 set up an admin in one of Perth's great downtown hotels.

The second day ashore, Goober and I were evaluating Australian brews in the admin, and decided we needed to see more of the city than the local grog shop. Goober was Tony Moore, and like Slush he'd been in VF-2 almost a year when I arrived. He had a good sense of humor but was serious about his RIO position and wanted to do well. His father had been an Army officer, but one day Goober saw a Navy poster that showed F-14s on a carrier flight deck. That started him down the path that led to the Navy, to VF-2, and to the admin in Perth.

Gotta be honest. Goober and I decided that we needed to make it *appear* that we were seeing more of the city than the local beer store. So we jumped in a taxi and went to the Perth zoo. There we raced from place to place and shot a roll of film. Satisfied that we'd documented this excursion, we got back in the cab and returned to the admin and our beers. We were at the zoo about twenty minutes.

On my second deployment, with VF-24 in 1983, we spent one four-month stretch at sea. For me, the 1989 deployment was payback. See if you agree:

Pearl Harbor: March 8-10
Philippines: March 26-31

Singapore: April 7-10
Diego Garcia: May 11-16
Perth: June 29-July 6
Pattaya Beach: July 15-19
Hong Kong: July 24-28
Philippines: July 30-August 1
Pearl Harbor: August 14-17

As a bonus, Laura flew to Thailand to join me in Pattaya Beach, and then to Hong Kong. She traveled with Goober's wife, Lucy, and other wives from the ship and air wing, fearlessly negotiating airports and transportation modes that most Americans had never heard of. We had a great time exploring these exotic ports together.

The deployment ended with a fly-off August 23, and the *Ranger* arrived at her berth the next day.

When I was new to VF-2, I would watch Skipper Dodge run the squadron, and I would wonder how one person could manage it all and still fly. After a few months as Ops O, I no longer wondered. I started to think, *I could run a squadron!* A new dream began to coalesce, one that I had not dreamed before: command of a fighter squadron.

CHAPTER 21

FAREWELL TO FIGHTERTOWN

Here I am in September 1989, nine years to the month after my first Tomcat flight in the RAG. I've done four deployments, logged more than 1,900 hours in the F-14, and I'm the Ops O of the best Tomcat squadron at Miramar. Yeah, that's what I said.

The latest deployment was a fading memory. And I was ready to make some new ones. The Tomcat Ball was coming up in September, and a week later, the Tailhook Convention.

After the deployment, VF-2 enjoyed a long weekend off, then a light schedule for two weeks. Then the bell rang and recess was over; back to work to start training for the next deployment. That's what Navy squadrons do. What the Ops Department does is plan it all—turn-around training, aircrew turnover, aircraft turnover, building-block training missions, fuel allotment, and a whole lot more.

It wasn't all Bio. Czech was Assistant Ops. He did the planning for detachments, such as the week-long det to Holloman Air Force Base, New Mexico, where VF-2 would be adversaries for Air Force squadrons. Pager's job was Pilot Training and Food's was RIO Training, and both did their jobs so well that I actually enjoyed writing their fitness reports.

But the buck stopped with me. We had a $3 million fuel budget, and we wanted to burn it within $100. So on the last flying day of the fiscal year, I got an update on where we stood and went to the radio in Maintenance Control to advise planes as they taxied in. "202, go to the fuel pits and top off. 205, come straight to the line." We hit the $3 million mark by a lunch-money margin.

I took my job seriously, sweated details, raised my voice when I had to. But this was what an Ops O did, and if you did it right, it was comfortable, like a weight vest that fits well.

Being gone for much of the year, we crammed the usual competitions into year's end. On November 8 a handful of pilots and RIOs reported to the simulator building for the ECCM Competition. They would defend a carrier from a large force of enemy bombers armed with cruise missiles and screened by jammers. That would be too much to stage for real, so the Navy put a lot of effort into making simulations realistic for both pilots and RIOs. And the scorekeepers could replay the action, like the zebras in a football game. The real good guys and the fake bad guys would slug it out in the same domed simulator that Topgun used for FAST training.

Fight's on. No, wait—the SDO rushes in to tell me one of the RIOs can't make it and there's no stand-in. Well, yes there is, and it's me.

The briefing beamed me down to the Indian Ocean, on the verge of a major attack on my carrier. It took only a moment to get into the mindset as the screens came alive. I recalled the FAST lessons I'd taught eighteen months before, and got to work. When the results came out, my pilot and I were the second-highest crew in VF-2, and the VF-2 team came in second among Miramar squadrons. Second? Maybe I should have taken that AIM-7 shot I passed up.

On November 21 we flew the High Noon gunnery competition, shooting at a banner. I flew with "Stretch"

Armstrong, a pilot who was new to the squadron. Thanks to the all-hands effort and sharp shooting by our pilots, VF-2 won the High Noon competition… again.

The evening before Thanksgiving, Skipper Serhan and his lovely wife, Laurie, hosted a dinner for lieutenant commanders and wives. As we were mingling before dinner, the Skipper was talking to Loner and me, pilot and RIO, both former Topgun instructors but with very different personalities—as the Skipper was about to find out.

"Do you guys have any plans for tomorrow?" he asked.

I said in my best eternal-JO voice, "I'm going to watch the *Twilight Zone* marathon on TV!"

Loner paused, and in a deep voice said, "I'm going to be serving food at a homeless shelter downtown."

Um, did I hear someone say dinner is served?

One December weekend we painted our jets in watercolor camouflage. It was Fighter Derby time on the Yuma TACTS Range. Loner was my section lead, with Herman as his RIO, and I would be flying with Stretch. This put a former Topgun instructor in each jet.

It was warm and sunny when we manned up, and once again I got a buzz strapping into a camouflaged Tomcat. On the flight over, our jets checked out perfectly. We entered the northwest corner of the range and immediately heard, "Fight's on."

Loner was a cool, disciplined expert and kept it fast as we tore through the sky at the start of our intercept. Stretch was a capable wingman, and Herman and I did our parts. Both Tomcats took missile shots, maneuvered, and took follow-up shots. Soon we exited the range, RTB Miramar. My total flight time was 0.9 hours! VF-2 didn't win Fighter Derby, but my two-plane section scored the most points of any section that year, and in the shortest time.

Last but not least for the year was the TARPS Derby. Simulating operational urgency, on short notice a pilot and RIO would be given a route and target to photograph and a time on target. Photos had to be taken along the route and all would be graded, including the time-stamp on each image. Like a road rally for jets.

On a December afternoon, Loner and I were told to be in the ready room at 7:00 the next morning for the TARPS Derby. No details, just be there.

We arrived early and at 7:00 a COMFIT rep handed us a simple piece of paper bearing something like this:

Route: VR-1262, points C-G
Altitude: 500' AGL
Airspeed: 480 KIAS
Target: road-railroad intersection at 35° 08' 55" N, 119° 13' 50" W
TOT: 0855

That fast? That low? That soon? It seemed almost impossible, but we knew it wasn't. Figuring backwards, we found we had less than thirty minutes to plan, so we grabbed some charts and started measuring and calculating. Maintenance had been alerted, so a TARPS jet was ready and waiting. With little time to double-check or study the route, we wrapped it up, jumped into our flight gear, and hurried to the jet.

The air was cool as we roared into the clear morning sky. The pressure of the mission was in the cockpit with us. No "mental free time" for chatting or sightseeing, but our experience was up to the challenge. I threaded us through the rush-hour air traffic gauntlet in Southern California, and soon we descended to start the route.

We had an INS, but we couldn't rely on it for this mission. When it worked perfectly, INS was like the GPS so familiar today, but on TARPS missions our primary navigation was visual. We used the charts we'd prepared and the visual navigation techniques we'd learned early in our training: look ahead between 10 o'clock and 2 o'clock and pick out landmarks, then come inside and find them on the chart. Repeat, and

BOTH S-3's FLEW 3.0 TO 3.3 HOURS

GAVE 6.5 EACH — 961 TOT. NM

TARPS F-14: POD, RAILS, ECA, 2/2/0/F AMMO 30 MAY 89

12:14, 20K, .64 IMN, 30 NM, 16.9K

BRG/RNG off 78	PT	LAT/LONG (28K 30K)	INBND HDG	DIST	m:s LEG TIME	m:s TIME FR.'A'	h:m ELPSD TIME	LEG FUEL	EFR	AFR / notes
[MV= 1°E]	PIM			-	-	-	0:00	-	18.5	18.0 †1204
	TANK	305/100		-	4.2K 70S		TOP OFF	20.0		12:30 19.8, 37:19.0
161/109	A	2530/5700	240 ~~300~~		45:00	0:00	0:45	1.0	19.0	16.7 13:02 5.8K PPH
151/51	B	2628/5649	349°	58	8:50	8:50	0:54			1311 15.8 360, 20 PRIOR KGS
144/40	C	2642/5648	352°	14	2:48	11:38	0:57			300, B-C KGS
167/36	E	2638/5630	245°	23	4:18	15:56	1:01			} 320 UNTIL PAST F
188/41	F	2633/5615	248°	14	2:38	18:34	1:04	FIRST HALF		1320 15.1
210/86	G	2600/5533	228°	50	7:10	25:44	1:10			1327 14.5 5800 PPH 420 KGS
213/116	H	2539/5509	225°	30	4:18	30:02	1:15	↓		14.0 1332 28K
227/148	I	2541/5415	271°	49	7:00	37:02	1:22	3.8	15.2	
"	TURN	-	90/270°	-	5:00	42:02	1:27			12.9 1344
213/116	J	2539/5509	091°	49	7:00	49:02	1:34			12.3 1351
211/83	K	2603/5533	042°	32	4:41	53:43	1:39			11.7 1356
209/57	M	2624/5551	036°	26	3:43	57:26	1:42			11.3 1358
202/52	N	2626/5600	075°	8	1:08	58:34	1:44			11.1 1400
195/41	O	2634/5610	047°	12	1:43	1:00:17	1:45	SECOND HALF		11.0 1402 360 O-S
167/36	P	2638/5630	076°	18	3:00	1:03:17	1:48			10.8 1404
144/40	S	2642/5648	065°	23	3:50	1:07:07	1:52			10.7 1407 320 S-U
151/51	T	2628/5649	172°	14	2:38	1:09:45	1:55			10.5 1410
156/80	U	2600/5658	165°	29	5:26	1:15:11	2:00	↓		9.9 1414
156/102	V	2540/5707	157°	22	3:08	1:18:19	2:03	4.2	11.0	9.6 1417
	PIM		RTB: 240 NM, MAX CONSERVE				OVHD		6.8	1500

BANDAR ABBASS INT'L 2713N/5622E, TACAN 78

HUMMER CAP - 2520N/5700E
exposure every 6 sec.
Q7 = FOSTER

A-6 TOOK 2.5 GAS

EA-6: 2.0?

@ ↓
RSP A-6 — 10.0
EA-6 — 9.1
iO3 — 10.5

ON TRAP, 15
TARPS - 3.2
A-6 - 5.0
EA-6 - 3.8

The back of the kneeboard card for a TARPS mission through the Strait of Hormuz in 1989, loaded with navigation, timing, and fuel information. Success depended on meticulous planning with this kind of detail.

After forty-five days at sea, everyone on the ship was allowed two beers. You could get yours behind that makeshift barrier, which explains why it's so crowded back there. The rest of the deck was a "steel beach," with barbecue, snacks, and everything except the sand.

These guys know how to party. From the left: Rico, Sax, Food, and Gus enjoy the pool they brought aboard in anticipation of a day on steel beach.

While waiting to land, we radioed an E-2 Hawkeye from VAW-116 and joined on him for a photo. The aptly-named Hawkeyes did a great job of controlling and coordinating virtually every flight.

Looking through the open rear cargo ramp of a C-2 as an E-2 Hawkeye approaches for a photo-ex. We were flying at an altitude of 5,000 feet and speed of 150 knots.

Another shot from the C-2: a VF-2 jet making a pass before burning some fuel to be light enough to stabilize behind the C-2.

With Darth in the back seat, Hap deftly eases the Tomcat's nose close to my perch on the C-2's open ramp. Did you notice the heart where the two exhaust trails meet? I didn't until I saw the photos later.

Hoping for a little squadron publicity, I shot this selfie for the Tailhook Association's magazine. That's what I'm reading in the back seat five miles above the ocean. The shot has had a life of its own in humorous incarnations ever since. *Credit: U.S. Navy photo by LCDR David Baranek*

Laura and me in Hong Kong in 1995, during a formal reception aboard the US 7th Fleet flagship, USS *Blue Ridge*.

November 1996: This Tomcat is hauling live 1,000-pound bombs low and fast during a det to El Centro for air-to-ground training. In a moment it'll pop-up above those hills and bomb the desert beyond—and then my jet will follow. By the way, that's the aircraft shadow at lower-left.

A red and white flash interrupts the ceremony as Skipper Oliver delivers his remarks during the change of command. Captain Checkmate strikes again!
Credit: U.S. Navy photo

Commander David Baranek, US Navy. This was my official portrait as commanding officer of VF-211, starting in August 1997. *Credit: U.S. Navy photo*

VF-211 Tomcat taxis to the catapult aboard the USS *Nimitz*. Steam from the cat bathes the taxi director as a squadron troubleshooter approaches the fighter. Flight deck personnel had to work effectively and safely in a hazardous environment.

Nickel 110 banks overhead as the USS *Nimitz* carves an arc in the Persian Gulf, turning into the wind to launch aircraft. Once the launch is complete, the recovery begins.

Fighting Checkmates F-14 goes to zone 5 (full afterburner) on the cat seconds before launching for an Operation Southern Watch (OSW) mission over Iraq during the 1997–98 deployment.

A few heartbeats after a cat shot, this was the view over my shoulder.

We started most OSW missions by tanking—usually from a USAF KC-10.

My primary pilot, "Twist" Oliver and me with a missile under my arm on the deck of the *Nimitz* before an OSW sortie. The big missile is an AIM-54, the small one above Twist is an AIM-9.

Aboard the *Nimitz*, a TV news crew from Norfolk, Virginia films interviews in the VF-211 ready room. The guy in the green jersey is Rob Engel, the civilian technician who kept our LANTIRN pods working so well. We called him Laser-boy due to the laser illuminator in the pods.

Aircrews debrief their LANTIRN video after an OSW mission. Left to right: pilot, RIO, and Laser-boy (our LANTIRN technician).

I'm enjoying a beer-and-burger break with Lobes on *Nimitz'* beer day. Behind us are Master Chief Reilly in the green shirt and Senior Chief Argiro in brown, two senior Maintenance Department stalwarts.

A Tomcat and several Hornets tank from a USAF KC-10 for a training exercise during the deployment.

This shows a typical loadout for our OSW missions: left wing—AIM-54C and AIM-9M (not visible); belly—AIM-7M and two cluster bombs; right wing—LANTIRN pod.

Nickel 100 approaches the *Nimitz* at low altitude and high speed. It can't land that way. First it peels off in a carrier break, enters the landing pattern, extends the wings, slows down, and *then* lands.

NG101 wears the "Santa Brutus" tail designed by Mach to commemorate being deployed during the Christmas holidays.

Six VF-211 Tomcats—including the jet I was in—on an all-Tomcat OSW mission. This was a much-appreciated tribute to the hard work of Checkmate Maintenance, for making more Tomcats flyable during the deployment.

Two Checkmate Tomcats in low holding over the *Nimitz* after an OSW mission. They look dirty, don't they? Our deck crews wiped down the jets, but the low-viz paint seemed to trap the grease and dirt that was all over the carrier flight deck. Okay by me; I liked the "working machine" look.

Each squadron was allowed one "colorful" aircraft. Based on the quality of the Santa Brutus design, I had Petty Officer Kreisher paint the Brutus character from VF-211's logo on the tail of NG-101. This photo also gives a sense of the F-14's size.

Last flight! In August 1998 I took my final flight as a Tomcat RIO and received a traditional "wet welcome" upon landing. Inflating my survival vest added to the festivities. *Credit: Alfredo Maglione*

This photo incriminates the perpetrators of the last flight wetting-down. They thoughtfully called Laura so she could enjoy the spectacle. What a memorable finish to a memorable flying career! *Credit: Alfredo Maglione*

quickly; we'd be covering eight hundred feet of terrain every second.

Our route west and south of Bakersfield, California, may look remote on a road map, but it's great for low-level visual navigation, loaded with useful features such as refineries, storage tanks, and a few distinctive roads—at least it was in 1989.

Settled into the mission, I assumed my responsibilities for navigation. "Our next waypoint is power lines crossing a road, coming up in twenty seconds. We continue heading zero-eight-nine. The next turn point will be at time 5 plus 32: six storage tanks. We are two seconds ahead of time. Fuel is above plan." I turned the TARPS cameras on at each waypoint. Totally focused on the mission, Loner and I were working well together.

Then, in full compliance with Murphy's Law, something bad happened: ground fog.

In an instant we were flying in whiteout. I could barely see the ground directly below me, and ahead was marshmallow. Forget the eyeballing. We had planned carefully, so we knew we weren't going to hit anything, but we couldn't be certain we were on the route and on time.

"Where are we, Bio?" Loner asked with an edge to his voice.

You haven't been lost until you've been lost at 800 feet per second.

If it had been anything but the TARPS Derby, I might have made a smart-ass remark. But I said, "We're on the route, on time. Continue heading one-zero-six."

At least our INS was still good. Moments later, still in the fog, I checked my clock. We were over the target—or should be, anyway. I turned on the cameras, but I couldn't visually confirm whether we were over the road-railroad intersection or downtown Bakersfield.

"Mark!" I told Loner. "We just flew over the target. Continue this heading for forty-five seconds to reach the exit point."

I radioed for clearance back to Miramar. As soon as we climbed above five hundred feet, we could see the thin layer of fog covering the area—just where we didn't need it.

Flying home, I had enough mental bandwidth left to reflect on the mission. We used all of the tools and skills available and did the best we could, but I figured that we'd blown it due to the fog on the final segment. I kept this to myself.

The film was developed and analyzed that day. At least we wouldn't have to wait very long for the verdict.

Surprise! Loner and I got a perfect score. Bigger picture: VF-2 won the TARPS Derby in 1989.

The timing of these competitions was almost theatrical, since my tour at VF-2 was nearly over. I had turned over the Ops O job to Loner on December 1.

Where to next? I'd been working with my detailer on my next set of orders. As a lieutenant commander with a good record I had a lot of options, but they were all staff jobs, not flying. My detailer asked if I'd be interested in the Joint Staff. That, he explained, was the official name of the staff that supports the Joint Chiefs of Staff in the Pentagon.

"Oh, JCS, I've heard of them," I said. "Keep talking."

He did. It was a "career enhancing" assignment, he said, and was competitive, with at least three people nominated for the job. I told him I was interested. A few days later he called to say I was in. Laura and I traveled to the Washington, DC, area for a weekend in mid-December and bought a house in the Virginia suburbs.

I was assigned to VF-2 until February 1990, but had only three more flights after the TARPS Derby mission. I didn't know the third flight would be my last with VF-2, but suddenly, there were my orders. I missed the champagne celebration.

I would soon begin my time as a staff officer. At times over the next few years it seemed like my flying might be over, but stay tuned—it wasn't.

CHAPTER 22

BECOMING A POWERPOINT RANGER

Read any good books lately on military staff officers?

There's a reason why you haven't. It may not be as exciting as flying, but it's a whole different world. Welcome to the Pentagon!

The transition from Fightertown to the Puzzle Palace was not easy, but getting there was great. I enjoyed driving across the country in my Corvette. Laura stayed in San Diego to wrap up some deals—she was a real estate agent—and when she came over we had fun discovering the historic sites and the modern delights of Washington, DC. I was excited about working in the Pentagon, and I had cheerfully accepted the job. I was assigned to the Counternarcotics Operations Division of the Joint Staff Operations Directorate—J-3 in military-speak.

When the job began I quickly realized that I had underestimated the culture shock of going from Navy fighters to the Washington Beltway.

The Pentagon was a bustle of uniforms—all of the US military services and even some foreign forces. Yet one of my first impressions was how similar we were, regardless of uniform. An Army special operations officer, a Coast Guard officer who had commanded a cutter, an Air Force B-52 navigator, a Marine Corps infantry officer, a Navy P-3 pilot and NFO—I worked with all these and more. Almost without exception, they had the same pride in their Service and enthusiasm for their experience that I had. Now we were action officers—AOs.

Our bosses were from all the services, too: captains in the sea services and colonels in the other branches. Their bosses were admirals and generals, with one to four stars on their uniforms. Every day I saw more stars than I had seen in my entire career.

No one was shooting at us, and after work we went home to our families and comfortable homes, but every staff officer faced challenges every day. If you dealt with operations, you faced tight schedules with resources that didn't meet demands. In counternarcotics we supported the War on Drugs announced by President Bush in 1989. But we wrestled the beast with one arm tied behind our backs by the prohibition against getting involved in law enforcement. So for us it wasn't a "war." One of our generals soon made that clear: Don't say "war on drugs," say "counternarcotics operations." Same job, different catchphrase.

My job turned out to be an interesting gig. My right-hand man was DM2 Hill, a Navy draftsman who had taught himself the ins and outs of PowerPoint and was now teaching me.

Being a new guy, I was put to work on two projects that were on the to-do list but had not launched. One was a weekly written summary of counternarcotics activities and policy issues. With my limited knowledge, I got busy gathering inputs from those who had been in the office awhile, and assembled my first summary. It was forwarded through the chain, and got kicked back with a variety of comments: say this, don't say that, and so on.

I tried a second time. Kicked back again. A third. Kicked back. Finally, one morning, an Army 3-star strode into the office. I recognized him as my boss's boss's boss's boss.

His gravelly voice matched his weathered appearance. "You the guy putting together the weekly summary?"

"Yes, sir."

He sat down in the chair next to mine and began. "Well, here's what I want…."

In less than five minutes I had the picture. Our weekly summary was off and running. There's a lesson here: Five minutes with a 3-star is worth weeks with colonels.

My other project was a daily briefing on counternarcotics activities. Barred from enforcement, the US military did what was called detection and monitoring, and there were dramatic chase scenes every day or two that added spice to my briefing. If we had no ops to report, we fleshed out the briefing with updates on counterdrug patrols by Navy ships, Air Force AWACS, and such.

Every day I spent hours on the phone talking to command centers close to the action, gathering details and explanations. Then at 5:00 I faced an audience of about twenty and told them what was going on. My Topgun instructor experience came in handy, giving me some resilience for speaking in front of a group. But my toolkit lacked an essential tool: knowing more than your audience. Every person in the room had been doing this longer than I had. The most dangerous phrase in my briefing was, "Any questions?"

The senior officer in the briefings was the same flinty 3-star who told me what he wanted in the weekly summary. He would ask occasional questions, but every now and then he would throw me an embarrassing comment. I would grit my teeth and continue without missing a beat. People came up to me afterwards and said, "Don't let him get to you, Dave. He does that to everyone." I would walk out of the Pentagon that evening, thankful that I had not lost my cool.

And then one day something changed. I felt like I was accepted. The 3-star started calling me "Goose." Someone must have told him about my F-14 background or that I was at Topgun when the movie was shot. Whatever, I was glad I survived my trial period. Lesson learned: Even a general can appreciate a good Navy flick.

Some trials I brought on myself. This one, for example. Some comedian once said that being a nice person is forgettable, but if you want to be remembered, be an asshole. One boring afternoon I spouted that gem to a fellow AO, and as I got to the "if," an Army lieutenant colonel walked by. He was only one rank above me, but he was a team leader, so he was higher on the org chart.

Next day I needed input for the weekly summary from this same lieutenant colonel. He'd been putting out fires all day and didn't yet have his input for me. That ticked me off; my summary would be delayed. But I tried to sound flip. "That's fine, sir. It's not for me anyway, so I don't care." He grimaced.

Next afternoon our office had a meeting in a crisis briefing room, with two levels of projection screens and multiple control consoles, the kind of place that would monitor World War 3. My own crisis was imminent. The lieutenant colonel was there, and as we shook hands he pulled me close and growled, "I don't like your f***ing philosophy."

Hmm…he's trying to tell me something.

I thought about it overnight and realized I'd acted like a beer-guzzling lieutenant at Miramar. But I had to work with this guy every day, so I'd better deal with him head-on. The next morning I knocked on his door, asked if he had a moment, and said I appreciated him calling me on my behavior. That's right—I appreciated his candor. He turned out to be a nice guy and great officer, as well as a fellow Corvette driver. The rest of my tour I counted him as a friend.

Another lesson driven home: Deal with personal conflicts head-on. My own actions had created the problem, so what did I have to lose?

Those first few months were like learning to fly missions in a new breed of airplane. You read the manual and listen to the experienced guys, but then you strap in and take off and the real learning begins. Keep flying and learning, and soon you feel comfortable in it. So after a few turbulent months in the Pentagon, things got better for me.

Briefings for the most senior officers were in "the Tank," a nickname from a briefing room of the 1950s. Counternarcotics was high visibility, and so was my audience: Secretary of Defense Dick Cheney, Chairman of the Joint Chiefs of Staff General Colin Powell, and other names in the headlines. I need not mention that I put a great deal of effort into those briefings. When I'd done five of them, my coworkers solemnly awarded me a certificate proclaiming that I was now a "Tank Ace." It was a very nice certificate, I still don't know if it was a joke.

Some days were merely busy. Others rose to stressful. My workday was ten hours long, but we rarely worked late or on weekends, so we had it better than some. AOs on some staffs worked seven days a week and fourteen hours a day—or more.

And then, one hot August day in 1990, Iraq invaded Kuwait. In a matter of hours, counternarcotics faded to a distant second on everyone's agenda. The activity level in the Joint Staff during Desert Shield was amazing, surpassed only by Desert Storm. Kick an anthill sometime, and you'll see what I mean.

We who were not fighting the real war followed the action. There was my old squadron, VF-2, deploying for combat aboard USS *Ranger*. I thought about the FNG lieutenants I'd known who were now flying in combat, and I silently wished them well. I thought about my timing, too. Half a year sooner I'd have been there with them.

Things went very well for US forces. Soon the war ended half a world away, and inside the Pentagon the war on—I mean, counternarcotics operations—regained much of its audience.

There were Tomcat guys in other Joint Staff offices, and some I'd known before at Pensacola, Miramar, or Topgun. One day in 1992 there was a buzz of excite-ment. The results of the annual Aviation Command Screen Board were due, and we would learn who would take command of a squadron. Your eligibility depended on when you were commissioned, and 1992 was the first year I was eligible. Let's see—good JO tour in VF-24, Topgun instructor, good department head tour in VF-2—I figured I had a good chance.

The results got to me in early afternoon. I mean *really* got to me. I recognized several names on the list… these guys would be Tomcat squadron skippers…and BARANEK was not on the list.

For years I had not thought much about being a squadron commander. Then it became a goal. Now it became a bitter disappointment, maybe the worst I'd ever felt. I told my boss I needed to take the afternoon off. I didn't tell him why.

I went home, told Laura about the list, and went upstairs to take a nap.

I woke up an hour later a new person. I realized that I'd enjoyed an incredible ten years of flying at Miramar, and flying had been my goal from the start. Commanding a squadron was a new goal, and if I missed the target this time, well, how many guys get chosen in their first shot at the list? Not many. So this was not going to taint my Navy experience. This was my first year. There would be a second.

It took an hour of dozing to arrive at this insight. It took a few weeks to hammer it home. I ran into another Tomcat guy in the Pentagon, a community leader I hadn't seen in years. We swapped pleasantries, and then he mentioned that he had also been disappointed. But this was his last chance; he would not be considered again. His vivid bitterness was souring what had surely been years of great flying and squadron experience.

Maybe he just needed a nap.

After two years I was nearing burnout on the Joint Staff. I sat down with my detailer, now across the street instead of across the country. He was the person who doled out officer assignments. He had nothing promising for—wait, there's an empty seat at the Marine Corps

Command and Staff College in Quantico, only twenty-five miles south of my house. Did I want it? I took it.

The Marine Corps school took 192 officers through a ten-month program on combat operations and defense strategy. Three out of four were Marine officers, and the rest came from other US services and twenty-four allied nations. The Marines treated us very well and it was a great set of orders.

As the end of the course approached, I told Laura I needed to think about my next job. Without hesitation, she said, "I think we should go to Japan." It took me one second to agree.

My second Aviation Command Screen Board came up, and again I was not selected to command a squadron. This time I didn't even need a nap.

By then I had a new detailer, a pilot I'd known at Miramar. He was ready for my visit. "I don't have any flying jobs for you, Bio, but I've got several good staff jobs back in San Diego." No flying jobs? No surprise. I'd done my turn at department head as VF-2 Ops O, so the only options for flying would be as a squadron XO/CO, and the Board hadn't picked me for that.

So I looked him in the eye and heard myself saying, "I want to go to Japan."

He did the best double-take I've ever seen. "Are you sure?" he stammered. "Once I start this process, you won't be able to change your mind."

I was sure. In moments he found me a good billet: Aviation Operations Officer on the US Seventh Fleet staff, based aboard the Fleet Commander's flagship, stationed in Yokosuka, Japan. Sold!

Moving to Japan was a great adventure. We lived out of suitcases for two months, drove on the "wrong" side of the road, and spoke no Japanese. You can handle all that and more if you keep a positive attitude.

We had not gone to Japan to live on a US base. With some effort we found a gorgeous house two blocks from the ocean, in a Japanese neighborhood seven miles from the base. We met our neighbors, and friendships sprouted that remain today.

Like the Joint Staff, 7th Fleet staff was a great experience in meeting people from different service communities who were as capable and proud as any in the Tomcat community. My job looked like it was going to be in the "reasonable" category, and I started making plans with my cubicle neighbor to take our wives to lunch often.

That didn't happen.

For one thing, my boss was Captain Craig Honour, a former F-14 pilot and squadron commander. I'd seen him in the club at Miramar. He had flown more than two hundred combat missions in F-4s in Vietnam, done some interesting test and evaluation flying after that, and commanded VF-51 at Miramar. As 7th Fleet Operations Officer, he oversaw a score of other officers, including several who had commanded ships, submarines, and squadrons.

Captain Honour was dissatisfied with his Assistant Operations Officer, and faster than you can say *ohayo gozaimasu* I was the new Assistant Ops. The job kept me busy at my desk seven days a week, twelve hours on weekdays and half days Saturday and Sunday. And informally, I ranked myself only the fifth-hardest-working person in Ops, but Captain Honour out-worked me, and out-striped me as well.

If that didn't kill the lunch-with-the-wives plan, this did. A new 7th Fleet Commander arrived shortly after me, and he decided his flagship should be away from home port 50 percent of the year. When we were underway, I spent seventeen hours a day at my desk. And still, I was not the hardest worker on the staff.

It was good to be part of a hard-working team and to be a solid contributor. But I have to admit that sometimes I'd be home and my alarm buzzer would growl at me at 4:30 AM, and I'd sit up in bed and growl back: "F**k."

When time allowed, we found that living in Japan was nothing less than fascinating. That's a different book.

Traveling through Asia on the admiral's flagship

was great, too. Laura was now living in the same hemisphere, so she often flew to meet me: Hong Kong twice a year, Bali, Sydney, Cebu, and more. That's a different book, too.

The new 7th Fleet Commander was a former submariner, Vice Admiral Archie Clemins. His vision was to update the staff with everything from new computers to new strategies for fighting a war. I was skeptical at first, but he was soon getting results I'd thought impossible.

Shortly after Admiral Clemins arrived, he planned a two-week trip to visit some of our country's allies, and he wanted to take two staff officers with him. Captain Honour nominated me for what turned out to be a memorable experience. Imagine yourself in a plush British helicopter with an admiral, cruising over the spectacular city of Hong Kong. Or sampling lobster and champagne on a Royal Australian Navy yacht in Sydney harbor. Or dining with ambassadors. For two weeks, my alarm would growl and I'd sit up and sigh, "Ahhh…."

Once Admiral Clemins had hit his main targets, he focused on his own people. What did it mean to us to be assigned to 7th Fleet staff? He sensed that it was a less-attractive option, when what he needed was the best available talent. To get top people he'd have to make it a springboard to greater things. So he put in endorsements for staff officers he thought would make good unit commanders. It wouldn't guarantee selection, but it sure would help. As a result, two former ship skippers were selected to command ship squadrons, two former aircraft squadron commanders were selected to command air wings, and one staff officer was selected to command an F-14 squadron. That was me!

In the late summer of 1995 I was sitting at my small desk in 7th Fleet staff spaces when my phone rang. It was Jake. He and I had met in Pensacola and gone through Topgun class together.

"Bio, this is Jake. Have you seen the command screen list yet?" He was stateside; the list wouldn't reach Japan for several hours.

Then the bombshell. "You're on it—congratulations!"

"What? Really??? Wow!" Jake had a sharp sense of humor, but I could tell this wasn't a joke. I'd been selected to command a Tomcat squadron!

Jake apologized for breaking the news before I'd seen the list, but I told him there was no bad way to learn you're going to command an F-14 squadron. He landed a cool job, too: command of the Strike Weapons and Tactics School.

As soon as we hung up I called Laura at our home in Japan, told my boss, and took a moment to think. Leaving 7th Fleet was months away, but planning started now. My new command would be VF-211, the Fighting Checkmates, based at Oceana. Laura left Japan in January 1996, went to Virginia Beach, and bought a house. I flew home from Darwin, Australia in February, went to Jacksonville, Florida to see family (Laura was there, too), and bought my second Corvette.

You're thinking now what I was thinking then: Let's get back into the cockpit!

CHAPTER 23

THE FIGHTING CHECKMATES

In the Navy, you can hold the rank of commander without actually commanding anything.

That was me. Commander Baranek had been wearing the silver oak leaves, and the three broad stripes on cuff and shoulder, since November 1994. Now it was March 1996, and I was a "dinosaur," chosen by the command screen on my final chance, as opposed to those selected early or on time. But I didn't yet command anything.

And I wouldn't for at least another year. First I'd need refresher training at the RAG and more than a year as a squadron XO. One step at a time.

I'd started my Tomcat experience at Miramar in San Diego, but in 1996 my old familiar Naval Air Station was morphing into a Marine Corps Air Station under BRAC, the Base Realignment and Closure downsizing. So the F-14 RAG was now VF-101 at NAS Oceana, in Virginia Beach, Virginia.

It's hard to describe the excitement I felt when I drove up to the F-14 RAG in Oceana for the first time. I was a PXO, a prospective executive officer. PXOs would check in and out of VF-101 at any time of year, so you never knew who would be there. This time there were four others, including some familiar faces—and a fellow dinosaur. Some PXOs were selected early and were still lieutenant commanders. They needn't worry; they'd be promoted before joining their squadrons.

I walked out to a hangar crowded with Tomcats, and so many sensations immediately flooded back. The RAG trained for all three F-14 variants—you'll sort out A, B, and D in the glossary—but VF-211 flew the

A model, the original Tomcat of the 1970s. They're the ones that got most of my attention.

PXOs had a full slate of ancillary training to check off. There was a leadership course, legal school, aviation safety school, and a lot more. Important for squadron leaders, but I'd gotten a little rusty in the six years since my last F-14 flight, so I needed the classes on systems and tactics. Turned out that I remembered the Tomcat as if I'd owned one. I knew its complex fuel system, its redundant hydraulic systems, and other features that the first-timers would have to master. So, like my previous RAG refresher, this one gave me some leeway about attending classes.

My first flight for this go-round was scheduled in May. I was as excited as Ensign Baranek reporting for his first flight at Pensacola in 1979. But wait—would I get airsick now, as that green ensign did then? And if so, would I get over it soon enough, as he did? And if not, would I get a new callsign? Barf instead of Bio?

Didn't happen, I'm pleased to report. After a few flights, I was at least regaining my air sense.

But it wasn't a perfect fit. There had been many changes in the F-14 and its mission since 1990. The air-to-air threat had become much smarter and tougher, so complex new tactics had to be mastered. The US Navy retired its A-6 Intruder bombers in the early 1990s, and the Tomcat was flexing its latent air-to-ground talent to help fill the role. I would be returning to the fleet in an air wing that boasted fifty strike fighters: three F/A-18 Hornet squadrons and one F-14 Tomcat squadron.

I got all the training I could get in the time available:

twenty-one flights in both air-to-air and air-to-ground. The guys in the current crop of RAG instructor pilots were professional and enthusiastic, as I knew they would be. They gave me a great refresher on the F-14 and a much-needed update on its new missions, plus a glimpse of the modern Tomcat aviator. You'll meet him later.

On July 5, 1996, Laura and I flew to San Diego. The first week was a whirlwind of renewing old friendships, getting to know new squadronmates, and prepping for the change of command.

The ceremony was on July 11, the date I became the XO of VF-211. The new Skipper was J.D. Oliver, a pilot who was in VF-211 as a JO. I knew him back then, during my junior officer tour in VF-24. Knowing each other made us both feel comfortable in our new jobs. There were others I'd known before, too—Mach, Chevy, Billy, Gunner Sharpe, and several maintenance guys.

My first flight with VF-211 finally came on July 15, a simple air intercept with Chris Ferguson, callsign "Fergy." If you follow the US space program, you know Fergy went on to fly three Shuttle missions.

A few days later I logged a milestone: 2,000 hours aloft in an F-14. No brass band, no ceremony; we were too busy for that. I didn't even know it until sometime later.

Routine training flights served as good refreshers, but looming over everything was the cross-country move to Oceana set for the hot and humid month of August. If you've ever moved all your stuff to a new home, you should try moving a whole squadron across a continent. It took a herculean feat of planning, timing, coordinating, sorting, packing, sweating, and cussing to move more than three hundred people and all of our tools, machinery, furniture, papers, airplanes, and you-name-its 2,500 miles from sea to shining sea and then put it all back together again and hit the ground running and the runway flying.

Navy squadrons are good at that, though. Every deployment on and off a carrier is like a rehearsal for it. Every training detachment is a preview. And every XO

is the assistant director. I was lucky; the director was a meticulous planner: Skipper Oliver had done most of the hard work before I arrived, when he was XO.

VF-211's Tomcats left Miramar the morning of August 6. Eleven Tomcats roared away, refueled from Air Force tankers over Oklahoma, and landed at Oceana 5.5 hours later. What a sight that must have been for people along our route! It sure was for us in the flyover.

On flights like this we used our official callsign, November Golf, and the side number of the airplane we were flying. Around our home field we used our radio callsign, Nickel. But whether November Golf or Nickel on the radio, you could just look at our Tomcats and you'd know who we were. See that checkerboard on our tails? We were the end of the game for the enemy. We were the Checkmates!

We landed to a warm welcome by the mayor of Virginia Beach and other dignitaries and Navy officers. They all expressed their delight that Oceana was the new home for all the Tomcat squadrons.

For me, landing at Oceana meant the end of temporary locations and turbulence that had begun when I left Darwin in February. My squadron was settling into its new home base. An advance team had been working for weeks getting our hangar spaces ready. Our digs were like what we'd left behind at Miramar: adequate, with minimal creature comforts. We'd had briefings on the local scene, and would soon know our way around the operating areas.

Five weeks later the Checkmates flew 800 miles south for a det at NAS Key West, one of the most valuable training areas on the East Coast. It was a bit longer stretch than from Miramar to El Centro, but the payoff was the same: getting away from the administrative distractions to focus on training.

Oh, perhaps I should mention that the weather in Key West was a little better than Oceana, too. Almost forgot that. But I can't forget the axiom I learned while walking the flight line in full flight gear: You can beat the heat in Key West but you can't beat the humidity.

The focus of the det was air-to-air training in support of our Strike Fighter Weapons and Tactics aircrew qualifications. (Hang in there; SFWT becomes clear in the next Intel Brief.) In the second week I had an early morning briefing for a 4vUNK, an SFWT check ride for Lieutenant Daryl "Salty" Martis, a former A-6 BN who became a RIO to help jump-start the Tomcat community with the strike mission. Salty briefed and led the event. I was flying as Dash 3 and my pilot was Lieutenant Dwight "Tricky" Dick, who had been in VF-211 for two years.

No one was happy about briefing at 7 AM, but we were trying to beat the midday steam bath. Salty was the personification of adrenaline in the flight briefing, and even though he was rather new to air-to-air, the briefing was a one-hour course on fighter weapons and tactics.

On the walk to our plane, Tricky and I talked about the det and the squadron, and he came across as very enthusiastic and polite—an interesting combination in a fighter pilot.

The four Tomcats launched and joined up, heading south over the Straits of Florida. The bandits took off after us so we wouldn't know how many there were.

Heavy clouds screened the morning sun but didn't mess up our training area. Our jets were in good shape, all systems working, as we checked in with our controller. If Salty was nervous, he hid it well. Same with Tricky, a lieutenant with his XO in the back seat. I was still coming to grips with the age difference between me and almost everyone else in the squadron except the Skipper.

Soon the bandits checked in, and Salty called "Fight's on." A moment later, "Salty flight, reference three-zero-zero."

Our controller radioed the bare-bones info, "Bandits three-two-zero, 43, tracking southeast." The first number was always compass bearing, second was range in nautical miles, and if altitude was provided it came third. Bearing, range, altitude—BRA. It kept you abreast of things.

Our wingman was a mile from Tricky and me. We were Dash 3, so Tricky kept our section a little farther from the lead section. You'd see us not as four planes but as two and two. Turning two pairs of fighters can result in a mess of airplanes if you don't do it right. Navy pilots do it right, and in moments four AWG-9 radars were pointed toward the threat, two searching high and two searching low.

"Salty single group, three-two-zero, 39, heavy." I was showing the same contacts—had the same picture.

The next call was covered in detail in the brief and was executed precisely. And it showed me how much things had changed.

"Salty, action."

Instantly Salty and his wingman yanked into a hard right turn, and Tricky led our wingman in a hard left. We all started the stopwatch function on our cockpit clocks, as the turn swept the enemy blips off my radar screen, which could not look beyond 60 degrees off the nose. The adversaries would see the dramatic split and would have to react to it.

In 20 seconds the four Tomcats turned back in. I aimed my radar again, and there were the bandits.

"Salty, new picture, two groups, near group BRA three-one-zero, 32, 26 thousand, far group BRA three-zero-five, 37, 20 thousand."

Again Salty's call showed me how much had changed. The simple words "new picture" keyed everyone that there was a significant change in the threat.

I worked my radar, silently impressed at Salty's ability. Each of our four Tomcats turned loose a simulated Phoenix, several bandits were kill-removed, and we engaged the survivors. Our second intercept was like an instant replay. We scrutinized it all on TACTS back at NAS Key West.

Salty was a good RIO, as were most RIOs in VF-211, due to good RAG training, but also a result of more structured training in the squadron. The SFWT program worked.

During the Key West det I flew nine air-to-air

training flights in ten days, so it was worth going on the road. There's a lot of seawater to fly over down there. But to practice bombing, you need a lot of dry land with nobody living on it. There isn't much of that in the populated East. So in November we *really* went on the road, all the way back to El Centro, California.

This was an air-to-ground training det. I was still new to this mission and each flight increased my knowledge base. Here's a memorable one.

On a warm afternoon, eight Checkmates are sitting in a no-frills briefing room in El Centro. Our mission is a division low-level that takes us to the Chocolate Mountain Gunnery Range, where we'll drop live 1,000-pound bombs—a great way to spend an afternoon!

The flight lead is Lieutenant Chris "Meat" Gordon, one of the more senior JOs. He enjoys being a fighter pilot, but I'd say he's on the serious end of the personality spectrum. Maybe more mature than the average lieutenant.

Meat has filled the entire whiteboard with info about the flight, starting with callsigns and frequencies on the left, piling up specifics of the low-altitude route in the middle, and finishing with a mountain of details about the pop-up and bombs-away at the end. We will enter the bombing range at low altitude and then pop up to sight the target and set up for safe delivery.

Meat's briefing board is crowded with details: to start the pop, light the afterburner, pull the nose up 45 degrees, turn to a heading of 120, and climb to 12,000 feet. He then describes a theme-park ride. The pilot rolls inverted and pulls the nose down into a 45-degree dive, then rolls upright and looks for the target while hurtling toward the ground at 500 knots. We rolled inverted at the top not because it was fun, but because the pilot pulling on the stick was the fastest way to go from a climb to a dive. But it was also fun.

For RIOs, Meat briefed the settings for a half-dozen switches in the rear cockpit. All of them had better be correct before the dive, because RIOs will be busy monitoring airspeed, altitude, and dive angle to help get the job done: bombs on target, on time.

We don't have to write it all down. Meat gave us the essentials on printed kneeboard cards at the start of the brief. Now he walks us through it all with the smooth confidence of a trained professional. And we listen carefully. Pieces of the exploding bombs will fly almost 3,000 feet back into the air, and no one wants to get fragged.

There are a few questions, and then we file out and suit up.

Today I'm flying with Lieutenant Kevin "Bugs" Aanestad, a first-tour JO who joined VF-211 when I did. He's my regular pilot for work-ups. Bugs treats me with a little deference, but as pilot and RIO we quickly become a well-coordinated crew. Despite his limited experience, Bugs is a skilled pilot and he loves flying Tomcats.

Thirty minutes later, it's easy to understand why. We're blasting along a low-level route, 500 feet above the desert at 480 knots. A half-mile to our left is another Tomcat, and a mile ahead of us are Meat and his wingman. This offset box is a good formation for sneaking in low and hot.

We're on route VR-296, northbound near the California-Arizona border. Ahead I see the dual ribbons of Interstate 10, and as we approach a turnpoint Meat's RIO says, "Meat flight, tac left, reference two-eight-seven."

The jets in front roll into their turns, and seconds later so do we. Each jet weighs more than 60,000 pounds, but they are very responsive at this speed and altitude. Snap-roll left, 5 g pull for a few seconds, roll out on the new heading. Multiply your weight by five, and that's how much you weighed for those few seconds.

The taxpayers down there on I-10 are getting a free air show. They're wondering how four Tomcats in a box formation can hang a left at breakneck speed and come out of it still in a box. It looks complex, but it's routine for the professional. Routine, but still cool.

The ride is rough in the hot air. Our jets are at MIL power with our wings swept back, so we are making a lot of noise and looking good. That's an air show winner. I doubt that our audience notices the bombs, even though each is almost ten feet long.

We parallel the highway for one minute, then turn for the final leg. At the designated point, Meat's RIO transmits, "Meat, action." He lights the afterburners and yanks the stick to start his pop. Seconds later his wingman does the same, followed by Dash three and finally Bugs and me.

Starting at high speed and adding Zone 5, we blast upward in an impressive display of power. At the apex of our climb Bugs rolls inverted. We're upside down only an instant—look up to see the ground. Bugs pulls us down toward the target and rolls us right side up. My altimeter starts to unwind like a runaway elevator pointer. I re-check my switches and soon begin my cadence on ICS: "Track." "Stand by." "Mark."

Bugs pushes the bomb pickle button on his stick. We feel a firm *Thump!* on our feet. That's the small explosive charges that shove a 1,000-pound bomb off its rack.

Bugs immediately does a hard pull-up, and rolls left wing down so we can see the target. We are rewarded with the orange flash of the bomb's fireball, visible even in the bright desert sun.

Meat checks everyone in and we set up to drop our second bombs. Then we return to El Centro for the debrief.

I logged eight flights at El Centro, but the biggest impact hit me on the flight line one crisp morning. Brief, man-up, and start went smoothly, so Bugs and I had a few calm moments in the jet before taxiing. Out of the blue, Bugs said on the ICS, "You really like flying, don't you, XO?"

It was a rhetorical question. He knew I did. But it stopped me in my tracks, like a frolicking pup at the end of its tether. Was that the image I was projecting? Carefree enthusiasm? A kid on a joyride?

I don't recall answering his question. I hope I did. But I owed Bugs more than an answer. His remark was a turning point for me. It drove home the fact that I was now the "adult leadership" of a fighter squadron. Sure, enjoy every minute of it, but don't let the fun overshadow the responsibility. I owe you one, Bugs, for helping me strike a balance.

There were plenty of new responsibilities as XO, and I took them very seriously. But you know by now, as Bugs did then, that I also enjoyed being in the air again. I had seen the dark side—my staff jobs—and it was great to once again strap on an F-14, hang out in a ready room, look up to see the ground, and just be part of a Tomcat squadron.

INTEL BRIEF: FACTS AND OPINIONS ON THE NEW SQUADRON ENVIRONMENT

A great deal changed from the time I left VF-2 until I returned to VF-211. I've already mentioned how the evolving air-to-air threat led to new tactics and how the Tomcat picked up an air-to-ground role upon retirement of the Intruder.

Another seismic shift saw the number of F-14 squadrons cut in half, while the number of aircraft per squadron increased. At one point the Navy had twenty-four deployable Tomcat squadrons equipped with twelve aircraft each, but by the mid-1990s more than half of these squadrons were decommissioned and the remaining squadrons were assigned fourteen Tomcats.

To handle the increased number of aircraft, each Tomcat squadron was increased in size about fifteen percent. Comparing two squadrons in my experience looked like this:

	VF-2, 1988	VF-211, 1997
Aircraft	12 F-14A	14 F-14A
Total personnel	272	321
Enlisted*	220	258
Chief petty officers (includes senior chiefs and master chiefs)	15	18
Officers	37 (15 pilot/RIO crews plus ground officers)	45 (17 pilot/RIO crews plus ground officers)

* The number of enlisted personnel shows those technically assigned to the squadron. Several dozen of them worked temporarily at jobs around the base or on the carrier, so didn't directly contribute to keeping our jets flying.

Something else that changed and wasn't a factor—really—is that we had females at all levels of VF-211, from junior enlisted to officer, as a result of policy changes in 1993 and 1994. For the record, we had one female pilot during my tour in VF-211; she performed well and blended into the ready room milieu.

The "typical junior officer" seemed to be different than when I was a first-tour lieutenant, but much of that was probably related to my age (separated from them by about fifteen years) and changes in American society. Our JOs ranged from polite and respectful to sharply cynical, but I had to admit that I probably operated everywhere along that scale as a JO. As far as flying, they were skillful and enthusiastic, a great combination.

Checkmate lieutenant commanders were a very strong group. Pilots and RIOs alike had a good deal of tactical ability and leadership skills, and displayed an impressive loyalty and commitment that really helped when I dealt with turbulence early in the deployment.

As XO, I was responsible for administrative aspects of the squadron; the common phrase was "heads and beds." (Head is the Navy term for bathroom, and I don't want to explain why the Navy calls a bathroom a head in a book about F-14s.) I formally inspected all squadron spaces at least once a week, reviewed correspondence and squadron directives, and dealt with administrative matters for enlisted and officers. The CO owned the squadron and was responsible for it, and as XO I was his deputy. When I became CO I was responsible for the squadron.

Of course I continued to fly, and averaged fourteen flights per month.

I'll write about our enlisted sailors in upcoming chapters.

The Strike Fighter Weapons and Tactics program brought a profound change to the F-14 community—in the ready room and in the air. In the wake of Desert Storm the Navy realized that the average fleet aviator needed improved training for both air-to-air and air-to-ground missions. Starting in 1995, F-14 aircrews were required to qualify at advancing levels through written tests and flights supervised by a Strike Fighter Tactics Instructor (SFTI), usually a former Topgun instructor. Every flight was important to an aviator's progress and was conducted according to a tightly controlled plan to use all available time (and fuel) for training. To clear these hurdles junior officers spent time in the ready room studying, which was quite a change from what I'd seen in the old days. But this system was all they knew, so it was a case of, "How high do you want me to jump?" The mid-grade officers, who had started in the old days, fully embraced the new way. As a squadron leader, I was grandfathered in at the highest level and enthusiastically supported the program because the result was a much more mission-effective aviator.

While SFWT may seem like a burden compared to the squadron environment of the 1980s, it did not reduce the passion of junior officers for flying and fighting the Tomcat. It provided a structure for their progress and ambition, which only fueled their enthusiasm.

Finally, the F-14As that we flew were little changed from the prototype that flew in 1970. We still used the AWG-9 radar and TF30 engines. Incredibly, over the years the engines were *reduced* in thrust to 17,000 pounds each, while the aircraft got heavier. The AWG-9 had benefited from marginal improvements.

Despite the age of our fighters, squadron personnel at all levels were proud to be in the Tomcat community and confident we would succeed in combat. That is not a boastful generalization, it's an informed opinion based on many candid conversations.

INTEL BRIEF: THE 569 BULKHEAD AFFAIR AND LANTIRN

In early 1997, Navy engineers performing routine inspections found alarming cracks on a bulkhead deep in the fuselage of an F-14. Some cracks are normal, but these were larger than expected, indicating a potentially serious structural fatigue issue, possibly a result of the additional stress of flying at low altitude and high speed while carrying bombs. If uncorrected these cracks could lead to structural failure.

This discovery led to inspections of more F-14s, which verified it was not an isolated issue, so Navy authorities notified squadrons that they would have to inspect their aircraft to determine the extent of the cracks. As a safety measure, affected aircraft were restricted to mild maneuvering until they were inspected and either cleared or repaired. Dozens of Tomcats were immediately grounded and headed for disposal.

The affected structural piece was the bulkhead at fuselage station 569, so the issue was referred to as the 569 bulkhead inspection or the fatigue life expectancy (FLE) inspection. Squadron maintenance personnel had to partially disassemble the aircraft to perform the inspection, which meant a major effort and required a lot of follow-up to ensure the aircraft was fully functional after it was reassembled.

The situation developed while VF-211 was in the final stages of workups, and the Navy announced the maneuvering limitations while we were on the *Nimitz* at the end of workups. We completed the det and flew home without issue, but dramatically altered our plans for the thirty-day period before deployment.

One ripple effect was to reduce the number of aircraft in each F-14 squadron from fourteen to ten, implemented over time. Although VF-211 deployed in 1997 with fourteen Tomcats, this decision affected us during the deployment.

Let's now switch to a very positive development, the integration of the LANTIRN precision targeting system into the F-14. LANTIRN is certainly in the running for most contrived acronyms, as it stands for Low Altitude Navigation and Targeting Infrared for Night, but I can overlook that, given its effectiveness as a weapon system. Developed in the 1980s for US Air Force F-16s and F-15Es, the system was adapted for the F-14 in the 1990s. It was a model of rapid development and low cost, and greatly increased the value of the Tomcat as a strike fighter.

As used on the F-14, LANTIRN was a pod mounted on a weapons station on the right wing pylon. The RIO interfaced with the system through a dedicated hand controller mounted on his left side instrument panel, and both the pilot and RIO could see the infrared display.

A few weeks before the 1997 deployment started, I spent twenty minutes using a tabletop trainer to learn how to use the hand controller. I then had one training flight at the start of deployment and I was LANTIRN-qualified.

LANTIRN was one of the main contributors to the Tomcat's effectiveness during its last ten years of service.

CHAPTER 24

CHECKMATE ONE

Key West and El Centro for workups ... three dets aboard USS *Nimitz* (CVN-68) out of San Diego ... that challenging air wing det to Fallon—VF-211 checked all of the blocks. Now it's the summer of 1997. I'd been XO for a year, and we were set to deploy in September.

For each of those training events we'd picked up the whole squadron and moved it, like a travelling circus. We'd flown our jets hard and pushed ourselves even harder. And then we'd returned to Oceana to train some more. Now it was time to "get well" during the thirty undemanding days before the deployment. That's how it was in the Tomcat community.

Except that, this time, that's how it wasn't. The Tomcat community had recently learned of cracks in the F-14's 569 bulkhead. The details are in the Intel Brief. During our final pre-cruise training event, a month-long det aboard the *Nimitz*, we learned how it would affect our squadron: We would have to take apart a dozen of our Tomcats before we could deploy.

At the end of the det we launched from the *Nimitz* flight deck off San Diego for the flight to Oceana, refueling over Oklahoma. As we cruised over the United States, it sank in that instead of spending thirty days fine-tuning our jets, the Fighting Checkmate Maintenance Department would be working round the clock on complex and demanding rebuilds.

As I learned early in my career, Naval aviators don't just aviate. When we're on the ground, we run the squadron. That's called "collateral duties." So here we were, prepping for the deployment, but also inspecting bulkheads and overseeing maintenance and shuffling

papers—and, oh yes, flying. I was up to my eyeballs in it.

Then things went to the next level. On August 29, 1997, Skipper Oliver would hand me the reins. I would take command of VF-211!

The weeks before this lifetime landmark were an incredible whirlwind of activity. I was lucky; Mach, our Admin officer, was very capable and headed a strong department. They handled the official arrangements for the change of command while I juggled a thousand other details.

Important details. High on the list was the invitations to the change-of-command ceremony. It was like graduating from high school, except that I wasn't looking for a gift, but saying thank you to people who had played a part in getting me here. I invited all of my previous squadron COs, Captain Honour, Admiral Clemins, and many more. If they could attend, great; if not, at least they'd know about it.

A few months before the ceremony, I was sitting in my office at Oceana when a yeoman knocked on my door. "XO, a woman is here to see you. Do you have a moment?"

I looked out and saw a nicely dressed woman with her son, one of our junior sailors who had recently stood before me at a disciplinary hearing. Not a major case—he was a sharp young man who just made a mistake. I braced myself for whatever his mother might say.

In walked this small but steady lady with her son right behind her. I stood to greet them and invited them to sit down.

"I live in North Carolina," she began, "an hour drive from here. My son told me about his little problem in the squadron. I just wanted to come meet the man who is in charge of my son's Navy unit."

The Skipper wasn't there, so I was in charge. "Your son is an important member of the squadron," I told her. "I know him and he's a good performer. He just made a small mistake and things have been going well since then." It was all true.

We chatted a bit more, and then she looked at her son. "This man is trying to help you," she told him. "I want you to listen to him."

I invited her to the change of command. She came, and I discreetly waved to her from the stage.

My family, some relatives, friends, and former neighbors all planned to attend. Our big house became HQ for the visitors. A few days before the ceremony, I disappeared, poured myself a glass of bourbon, and collected my thoughts to write a speech.

And suddenly it was Friday afternoon. Squadron members in dress uniform stood in precise ranks, while a crowd of about three hundred people gathered in Oceana's ceremonial hangar. Mach tuned up his most serious voice to announce the ceremony. It was the standard Navy squadron change of command: arrival of honored guests, parade the colors, National Anthem, invocation, and so on.

But wait—this was a *fighter* squadron, and the Fighting Checkmates at that. Halfway through Skipper Oliver's farewell speech a figure in red tights swooped from the side of the stage, flapping a red-and-white checkerboard cape and hiding his secret identity in a VF-211 flight helmet with the visor down. It was—gasp!—Captain Checkmate! Our unofficial mascot dashed dramatically past the stage as the audience cracked up.

The intrepid Captain Checkmate hadn't saved the world since an event at an Air Force base in North Carolina, where a Russian Su-27 was on display. He postured in front of the Flanker while a video camera recorded the encounter. That time, the bad guys won: A colonel with no sense of humor growled, "Get that guy out of here before I have him arrested."

He got a warmer welcome at our ceremony, and the outgoing CO was back on target in moments. Soon CAG had us both at attention at center stage, and command of the Checkmates was officially passed to me.

I took the podium, faced my squadron and the audience, and launched into my speech. I was comfortable in front of these people. Sure, I had been thinking about such a moment for two years, ever since Jake called me in Japan. But the gravity of it hadn't sunk in. Until now.

My speech ran almost seven minutes. Two minutes too long, maybe, but I didn't want to lose this chance to say what I said in closing:

> I am counting on your dedication. Supervisors, I need you to continue leading, teaching, and setting the example. Junior sailors and junior officers, I'm counting on you to do your job correctly all the time and to grow professionally and personally.
>
> As commanding officer I will give you all I've got. I am unspeakably proud to be the new commanding officer of Fighter Squadron 211. I know by our past performance that we can do great things. Ahead we have adventures, challenges, and successes.

Mach concluded the ceremony. There was a reception at the enlisted club, and I dropped in to share a drink and chat with some of the hardworking personnel who had brought us this far. There was another reception at the officers club, and I spent some time there visiting with out-of-town guests and the many Oceana aviators who joined us.

The whole squadron attended the ceremony, but only half attended the festivities afterward. The others were night-check maintenance personnel; they changed out of their dress uniforms and went back to work. A mention of it during the ceremony ensured that everyone knew. In about one hundred hours we would start flying fourteen Tomcats to San Diego, and there was a heck of a lot of work to be done. The ceremony was on a Friday afternoon and Monday was Labor Day, but the Checkmates were working 12-on /12-off, every day.

Fast-forward through that one hundred hours. I had a quiet celebration with family and friends at home Friday evening. Saturday was a workday, and I spent most of it at the hangar. This will sound trivial, but it wasn't: I had to get new pens. In squadrons, the XO wrote notes in green ink, so everyone knew they came from him. COs used red ink. So I had to trade in all my green pens for red.

The big party was Saturday evening. Laura was outstanding as planner and hostess for a huge bash at our house. The guest list included all VF-211 officers, the CO and XO of all Oceana F-14 squadrons, and folks from out of town. I also invited my neighbors, so we didn't have any noise complaints. The weather was perfect and it was a great party.

Around 11:30 PM several JOs sheepishly sidled up to me. It seems they had stepped through the ceiling while snooping around our attic for "dirt" on the new skipper. Not a big deal; I knew they would pay for the repair. And it did take some guts to face the new CO and fess up.

Sunday was another workday. It started with Captain's mast, an informal hearing that allows a unit commander a good deal of authority and latitude in dealing with violations of the Uniform Code of Military Justice.

Early Monday morning, one of our chief petty officers called me at home. He had a painful knee problem that was made worse by the ladders on a ship, so the medics exempted him from the deployment that was only days away. At the squadron the other chiefs were stoic about it. He had been a major contributor but we would have to get by without him.

Tuesday was a blur. People told me more things and asked me more questions now that I was Checkmate One. Usually I could help, other times just reminded me of the scale of my new job.

At 7:00 Wednesday morning the ready room was full of pilots and RIOs. It was time to get our jets to San Diego. We had kissed our wives and girlfriends and were in the flying mindset. The Ops O, Lieutenant Commander James "Divot" Stauffer, and his team had done a great job planning the cross-country flight and scheduling Air Force tankers to meet us over Oklahoma. This would save time and reduce the risk of breaking down if we landed to refuel.

Wog, the Maintenance Officer, and his crew had logged incredible hours working their butts off. The result: eight jets ready to fly, out of fourteen. Those eight crews started the flight brief, several other crews were told to stick around, and everyone else was told to go home and stay by the phone.

Ninety minutes later, as we started our takeoff roll, my pilot Yank said, "Skipper, be sure to look at the hold short." That's the line just short of the runway where you stop and wait for the OK to take off. As we lifted off the runway, he rolled slightly left so I'd have a good view. There it was, a red-and-white checkerboard strip bordering the hold short line for Oceana runway 5R. He told me that "some of the guys" had a little paint party overnight to make sure Oceana didn't forget the Checkmates while we were deployed. No doubt Captain Checkmate was one of "the guys."

Damn, that was cool!

Ten minutes later we ran into heavy clouds as we climbed out over southern Virginia. Everyone followed the lost-sight plan; when planes in the clouds lose sight of each other, each maintains a different heading and altitude so they don't collide in the murk. When we broke out into clear air at high altitude, I could see eight Tomcats with contrails gleaming in the morning sun. *My* Tomcat squadron.

Damn, that looked *really* cool!

Yank and I talked a little during the free time above the eastern United States. A RIO in one of the other jets had a LANTIRN pod and was describing the incredible resolution he was getting, looking at farmhouses and cars on highways from five miles over their heads. Little did the folks down there suspect they were being watched by peeping Tomcats.

It was a majestic morning, suitable for the start of a big adventure.

After a couple of hours we split up into two flights of four jets, took separation, and descended to join our tankers. By this time aerial refueling was a familiar task, and soon we started to climb back to altitude.

Suddenly my Master Caution light winked on, and a loud whine screeched from the air conditioner. Yank said, "Skipper, I've got a Bleed Duct light. I'm going Air Source—Off."

In a flash we switched to boldface emergency procedure mode. We had a problem with our ECS—our air conditioner. In the F-14 this was far worse than a comfort issue: the NATOPS manual says such leaks "can cause unsurvivable damage," and several recent incidents had caught the Tomcat community's attention. Mine included.

We were probably dealing with a failed ECS turbine, which could cause a fire. So we had to get the jet on the ground right now. Luckily I knew this part of the country from frequent cross-country flights long ago, when I had often hit Cannon AFB for a gas-and-go.

I called our controller. "Forth Worth Center, Navy november golf one-one-four. Declaring an emergency, estimating twenty miles north of Panhandle." That's a navigation point the controller would know. "Proceeding Cannon Air Force Base. Requesting eight thousand."

Yank and I stepped through the procedures and talked up a game plan. I kept the controller in the loop. With a declared emergency we would have a lot of latitude, but it was better if we were all on the same page.

On our squadron frequency, Yank called to the fourth F-14 in the formation. "Sato, come with us." We wanted a wingman in case we lost our radios, or to mark our position if we had to eject. I was thankful that we were over sparsely populated farmland.

Twenty minutes crawled by, and finally both Tomcats were on the ground at Cannon. I climbed out, laid a hand on the plane's skin where the ECS turbine was located, and—*Ow!*—jerked it away before it fried. We'd been close to disaster.

When things settled down, Sato and Fez climbed back aboard their Tomcat to leave. I smacked my forehead; I've got to be in San Diego! I trotted over to their jet and, with sign language, told them we needed to swap RIOs. Sorry, Fez.

Sato—Lieutenant Brady Bartosh—and I landed at NAS North Island around 4:00 that afternoon. Where the CO is, that's where the squadron is, so Divot sent a report that VF-211 was now in San Diego.

We had launched three more jets after the first eight, but that was only enough to break even. I'd left a jet in New Mexico. Another jet was at Scott AFB near St. Louis with a minor issue, and a third jet had an inflight fire and was at Joint Reserve Base Ft. Worth (Texas).

Yank and Fez flew to San Diego two days later in a substitute jet, compliments of the RAG. My hot-skinned Tomcat took weeks to repair, and then was reassigned to another squadron. The jet at Scott was repaired by a maintenance crew from an Oceana squadron and flew to San Diego two days later. The jet at Ft. Worth would never fly again, but the pilot and RIO would; a C-130 cargo plane headed for San Diego gave them a lift.

At the end of the day, we had eight jets in San Diego. From the way the morning started, this was no surprise, but considering the fourteen Tomcats we needed for the deployment, it was dismal. And I'd been Checkmate One for a grand total of five days.

If you think things could only get better, you're in for a surprise. But if you think anything could defeat the Checkmates, you're in for a revelation.

CHAPTER 25

CLAWING OUR WAY BACK

The USS *Nimitz* cruised off San Diego for a couple of beautiful sunny days while the air wing flew aboard. Everyone was anxious to turn west and really get the deployment started. When it ended, we would all be bona fide circumnavigators; we were about to sail around the world. Norfolk, here she comes, the long way, for an overhaul.

Activity aboard the carrier was busy but routine. Not so for VF-211! Getting all fourteen of our Tomcats aboard was a frantic masterpiece of planning and a cliffhanger right up to the last one hooking the arresting cable. Checkmate maintenance personnel at Oceana sweated it out to the absolutely last minute to launch everything they could, then scrambled aboard transport aircraft for San Diego. The Fighter Wing One staff had activated contingency plans so three other squadrons could either help fix our Tomcats or deliver one of theirs. At the last possible hour a final Tomcat took off from NAS North Island. The crew immediately declared an emergency due to an ECS problem and "diverted" to land aboard the carrier. Minutes later the giant ship turned west and headed into the Pacific. Whew! That was close.

This was my first deployment on a nuclear carrier, and man, was it nice! On previous deployments, the older carriers sometimes showcased their limitations—the air conditioning didn't work right, or the fresh water was rationed. On the *Nimitz* the a/c was cold and you had all the fresh water you wanted. The nuclear power was great, but the flavored espresso in the wardroom was irresistible.

On previous deployments we had to balance the carrier's progress with the prevailing wind to decide whether we could fly. With the incredible flexibility of nuclear power, plus a schedule that gave us two weeks to get to Yokosuka, Japan, we flew most days of the transit; for me, ten flights.

The carrier's track took us well north of Hawaii, into the vast Pacific where there were no simple options to divert if anyone had a problem. The missions were simple at first, mainly day and night quals, and I flew with a variety of pilots, from JOs to lieutenant commanders (O-4s). A squadron skipper gets to pick who he flies with, so out of the crowd I chose my primary pilot for the deployment.

My choice was Lieutenant Command Shawn "Twist" Oliver, who had completed one F-14 squadron tour, then served as a RAG instructor, and was back for his second squadron tour. He knew the Tomcat inside out. Calm, confident, capable—perfect.

For my backup pilot, I chose another O-4, Mark "Mach" Singletary. Mach had been a lieutenant in VF-1 when I was in VF-2. He was then a RIO, but had since completed the pilot transition program and had already flown as a pilot in VF-51. So he had a good level of Tomcat experience—in both cockpits.

You may be surprised to hear that one of our pilots was Major Doug "Norton" Carney, USAF, an F-15C pilot who was on an exchange tour. With his blue-suiter background and subtle sense of humor, Norton was a great addition to the squadron.

After years of having little say in who I flew with,

I enjoyed being able to select my regular pilot. I chose an experienced pilot for both tactical and practical reasons, still compensating for my years out of the cockpit. On this deployment I made it a goal to fly with all our pilots. They were a very strong group, JO pilots as well as RIOs. We would soon fly over hostile territory, and I would have flown with any of them.

Everyone settled in for the six-month journey ahead. Three of our Tomcats flaunted the markings of other squadrons, so Maintenance quickly painted them in the Checkmates scheme. Maintenance also had their hands full getting our jets ready for our upcoming commitment to OSW, Operation Southern Watch. The admiral wanted ten F-14s ready to rock and roll when we arrived in the Persian Gulf. Sounds reasonable, but remember, our jets were in rough shape to start with, and most of them were veterans of the 569 bulkhead tear-down. We had our hands full.

We all knew OSW involved combat-coded flights to enforce a no-fly zone in support of a United Nations resolution. It was a real-world, front-page mission, so the pressure was on to get our Tomcats in top condition.

When I wasn't flying, I haunted the workcenters. I remembered, from being a junior officer in VF-24 fifteen years before, that squadron members wanted to know what we were doing next. So I tried to keep them informed. We had an all-squadron meeting called Quarters about once a month, but it disrupted the schedule and was a formal event that didn't allow conversation. The vast majority of our people were hard-working sailors with deep commitment to the squadron. They needed more than Quarters.

Sailors always showed me respect, but I also tried to break down barriers to communication, and felt I succeeded based on certain exchanges. Once several of them asked me why personnel who had been in VF-24 got special privileges. They gave me examples, and one said the favoritism must be officially sanctioned, because the VF-24 check-mark logo had been added to VF-211's tail markings. I told him that was not the intent, that it was a simple tribute to our former sister squadron. Dozens of VF-24 officers and enlisted had come to VF-211 when their squadron was disbanded, a common practice throughout the Tomcat community.

We used to say, "A bitching sailor is a happy sailor." Mostly they bitched about stuff like long hours, or pressure to get things done, which were part of being in an F-14 squadron. But the tail design being hijacked was something I could fix. Within minutes I told the Maintenance Officer to get the VF-24 check mark off our tails. In my opinion, they looked better without it.

On visits like this I was sometimes accompanied by the command master chief, YNCM Ellen Mustain. The "YNCM" meant she had spent most of her career as a yeoman with administrative duties, and was now a very senior E-9. The Navy had established the command master chief position in 1995, and the full-time job was to be the senior enlisted person tasked with improving communication, morale, discipline, and unit effectiveness.

Later in the deployment, Master Chief Mustain was with me in the ready room when I met informally with a group of African American sailors to hear their race-based concerns. They spoke with candor and respect, and I responded where I could. But mostly I listened and learned.

As CO I kept in mind something I learned as XO. The Navy ran occasional "command climate" surveys, and the anonymous comments were candid. Most of our people were satisfied and understood the environment, but one person complained that "the higher ups" didn't know who he was when they would see him walking around the ship. So I made a point of at least recognizing the faces of all three-hundred-plus of my Checkmates.

A skipper has to have an executive officer, a sort of vice-president who goes by the letters XO. So when I became CO, I gained an XO. He was Coconut, a pilot who had flown in East Coast squadrons and earned an excellent rep. It would be an understatement to say his style was different from mine, but that difference would be valuable in the months ahead. There was only one problem: He'd had a painful injury that chose this moment to flare up. Two weeks after the deployment started, he returned to Oceana for treatment.

To fill in for Coconut, I designated Lieutenant Commander Brian "Billy" Kocher. I'd served with Billy in VF-2 when he was a lieutenant. He had already completed his department head assignment in VF-211 and was supporting the admiral's staff, and they let him return to the squadron because we needed him. He had a lot of tactical experience, knew the squadron well, and soon proved capable as acting XO.

Remember my hinting darkly that things could still get worse? Hang on.

The next personnel problem was the loss of three more officers, in addition to my XO: an administrative matter, cancer, and an eye problem. Fighter Wing sent us only one replacement, but they sent a good one. Commander Jack "Jaws" Marshall was a RIO who had completed two squadron tours and was well-known around Oceana. He jumped in with both feet and made a big difference.

Now the airplane problems. Maintenance was busting a gut to keep ahead of them and get back up to speed with sound practices—trying, in other words, to finally get well from the demands of work-ups. And then one night one of our pilots made a hard landing. He was coming down to correct for a high approach—what we call a "high ball"—and the deck was coming up. *Wham!* It was a tribute to the F-14's brawny build that everything survived intact, but when I walked out to the flight deck, that airplane looked "broke." A tire had blown, the plane skewed sideways, and the flaps and slats were still deployed for landing. The jet was hard-down, and Maintenance had another big job on their to-do list.

Maintenance rose to such challenges by working hard, for long hours. The crews in most shops worked an average of thirteen hours per day for at least the first month of the deployment, and I'm sure those were just the hours they documented.

Something had to give. We asked the sortie planners to reduce our daily flying during the transit to the Persian Gulf. This was a difficult request; we asked it but we didn't want it. Aviators want to fly and staffs want to maximize training, and we were approaching the real-world mission of OSW. But we got the cutbacks, and they did help.

There were lighter moments, too, and humans to find them when the going gets rough. One day at lunch some VF-211 JOs were chatting with Dr. Juli Gould, a lieutenant, one of the flight surgeons assigned to the air wing, a specialist at the intersection of flying and health. They told her about the hard landing, and how the aircraft would need some serious disassembly to inspect for damage. Like the 569 bulkhead inspections, this would be a labor-intensive process, made more challenging because they were in the tight confines of a carrier and had to coordinate maintenance with other squadrons.

Doc Juli pulled a brilliant idea out of the sky: "I think we can use a colonoscope to examine the areas!" A senior medical officer performed the inspection, with Checkmate maintenance experts coaching him on what to look for, and together they announced that the patient was uninjured; the structure was sound.

To examine a Tomcat, he should have been a veterinarian. Sorry.

Most of what's in the past few pages happened in the first few weeks of the deployment and challenged the squadron on many levels—operational, personnel, morale. It was my job to get the glitches fixed, and yet my boss, the CAG, hardly knew me. CAG was Captain Vaughn, son of a WWII Navy fighter pilot. He was born in a small town in Texas and talked like he'd just left it, but he had proven himself a very capable strike fighter pilot and leader. CAG was well informed on issues in every one of his squadrons, so he knew what the Checkmates were facing.

One evening in the second week, he wanted to chat, so I went to his office. We talked for two full hours, and it was probably the most intense one-on-one conversation I've ever had. I think he was assessing whether I was up to the task, and based on his continued support I think I passed the interview. Life didn't suddenly become easy, but I felt CAG was in my corner.

When the *Nimitz* pulled into Yokosuka (ignore the u; say yo-KO-ska) on September 21, I needed some fun. It had been less than two years since Laura and I lived in Japan, just a few miles from this base, and all of our Japanese friends and neighbors were still around. One neighbor picked me up at the base's main gate and took me to their house, where others were gathered for an informal party. The beer and sake conspired to give me a hangover the next day, but it sure was a fun evening.

Some 20,000 Japanese visited the *Nimitz* during the port call. It was only a three-day stop, and five days later we dropped anchor at Hong Kong. Once again, it was a welcome break, made more enjoyable because Laura flew over. Some Japanese friends also flew in and we showed them around that spectacular city.

Hong Kong was also a chance to see Checkmate pilots and RIOs on liberty, as The American Club generously allowed officers from visiting ships to use their tennis courts, restaurants, and other facilities. Thirty people showed up for the Checkmates dinner, a lively evening.

After four days the *Nimitz* again weighed anchor and headed south, her crew anticipating a short transit and a few days in Singapore. Many wives flew there to continue their visits.

Meanwhile, 5,000 miles away, they did not get the memo about our port visit plans. The Iraqi Air Force was making a mockery of the Southern No-Fly Zone, apparently testing the coalition's resolve. Fighters would cross the line and then retreat before they could be shot at. So the Secretary of Defense ordered the *Nimitz* Battle Group to bypass Singapore and head directly to the Persian Gulf.

We had heard this might happen, so it didn't come as a complete surprise. Several of our battle group people had taken leave and traveled to Singapore, so we sent helicopters to pick them up at the US Embassy. The embassy also forwarded messages to wives awaiting us in their hotels…including mine. At least our Japanese friends had continued on to Singapore, so Laura had company.

It took us a little more than a week to get to the Persian Gulf. I had four flights, all with JOs. We wanted everyone to fly and be current. Our next operations would be in hostile airspace.

INTEL BRIEF: OPERATION SOUTHERN WATCH

If you think back to the end of Operation Desert Storm in February 1991, you may recall that the war had a limited objective: get Iraq out of Kuwait. Once Iraq started its withdrawal, the coalition negotiated a cease-fire with Iraq. It was very neat in terms of "war," but it left a substantial portion of Iraqi military forces intact, and they were soon used against rebellious groups within their own country. In response, the United States, United Kingdom, France, and Saudi Arabia began Operation Southern Watch (OSW) in August 1992. Although OSW was not a United Nations (UN) operation, its stated purpose was to ensure Iraq complied with a UN resolution. A similar effort was in place in northern Iraq, known first as Operation Provide Comfort, later Operation Northern Watch.

OSW was implemented by declaring a no-fly zone over a large portion of southern Iraq. Main elements included:

- Surveillance: Critical to effective enforcement, normally provided by a US Air Force E-3 AWACS aircraft, but could be provided by Navy E-2 Hawkeyes if necessary. In addition to radar surveillance of the no-fly zone, they provided command and control that was essential to keeping these complex ops on track.
- Counter-air: An armed response was essential, in the form of coalition fighters on patrol within the zone, ready at a moment's notice to attack Iraqi aircraft that flew into the airspace.
- Interdiction, known to us as SFAM: In addition to aerial enforcement, strike and electronic warfare aircraft on patrol carried a variety of air-to-ground weapons to respond immediately to any Iraqi attempt to shoot down a coalition aircraft. Several Iraqi surface-to-air missile (SAM) and gun sites remained intact on the ground under the no-fly zone. These flights usually performed a simulated strike, so we called them strike familiarization—SFAM.
- Other missions related to OSW: Refueling—the airborne armada was supported by Air Force KC-10s, Royal Air Force VC10s, and air wing S-3s. Reconnaissance—USAF U-2s performed reconnaissance from 70,000 feet while TARPS F-14s took photos from more familiar altitudes. Forward Air Controller (Airborne)—required incredible skill and crew coordination; would direct bombing attacks on enemy forces in close contact with friendlies.

An event launched from the ship included some or all of the above mission elements. F-14s flew counter-air, interdiction, and TARPS. Due to realities such as flying over hostile territory, OSW flights were designated as combat operations. Missions flown in support were recorded in green ink in aviators' logbooks—a significant distinction. Based on lessons from Desert Storm and the fact that we were not in a shooting war, OSW aircraft were not permitted to fly below an altitude of 20,000 feet except for TARPS, which were allowed to operate at 15,000 feet.

While it may sound like a tenuous arrangement, OSW was effective in severely limiting Iraqi military air activities. It was an adequate solution short of full combat. By the time the *Nimitz* Battle Group arrived on station, however, there had been a series of incidents that flashed into combat, however brief. These included:

- December 1992: USAF F-16 shot down an Iraqi MiG-25 that violated the Southern No-Fly Zone.
- January 1993: One hundred coalition aircraft, including aircraft from USS *Kitty Hawk* (CV-63), performed a punitive strike on Iraqi radar and missile sites; several days later a USAF F-16 shot down a MiG-23.
- June 1993: Cruise missiles launched from two US Navy ships as punishment for the assassination attempt on former President George H. W. Bush.
- August 1996: Operation Desert Strike, a series of cruise missile attacks launched by Navy ships and USAF B-52 bombers; the B-52s were escorted by F-14s from USS *Carl Vinson* (CVN-70).
- As mentioned in the text, Iraqi fighters occasionally violated the no-fly zone for reasons we could only guess, possibly testing our reaction time or resolve.

This list shows only actions that preceded the *Nimitz*/Air Wing 9 deployment in 1997–98. Our training during workups for the deployment was specific preparation to support OSW and participate in strikes if ordered.

With the variety of missions we could perform, VF-211 configured our F-14s in three ways for OSW:

- Fighter-bomber: These F-14s could be used for either counter-air or SFAM. The typical weapons load was two cluster bombs; one AIM-54, AIM-7, and AIM-9; and a full load of bullets in the gun. We carried a LANTIRN pod on most flights. The weapons load was occasionally changed, such as laser-guided bombs (LGBs) instead of the cluster bombs.
- Super-bomber: Similar to the preceding, but with four weapons rails on the belly, which allowed us to carry four bombs. We rarely loaded four bombs because that would reduce the fuel we could bring back and land with, but if a strike seemed likely we would set up several super-bombers.
- TARPS: Configured for reconnaissance using the large TARPS pod, these jets also carried a jamming pod and AIM-7s and AIM-9s for self-defense. We could download the TARPS pods and use them for counter-air missions, but TARPS aircraft were not LANTIRN-capable, so we didn't use them for interdiction.

Checkmate Maintenance had to work closely with CAG and *Nimitz* personnel to ensure we had the right aircraft on the roof (flight deck) for the day's missions. If we had eight "up" jets, we usually had five fighter-bombers and three TARPS jets on the roof. Later in the deployment we had ten up jets, but the *Nimitz'* flight deck crew usually limited us to eight Tomcats on the roof.

CHAPTER 26

GREEN INK

Warm breeze, distant lights, flight deck packed with silent aircraft—what a beautiful night. It was October 12, 1997 and I just stood a few minutes and took it all in. Nothing spectacular, but it brought to mind something that seemed very risky the last time I was in this part of the world: an aircraft carrier transiting the Strait of Hormuz. When Sax and I flew in this airspace in May 1989 it was a big deal. Then came Operations Desert Shield and Desert Storm, and US carriers were sailing into the Persian Gulf all the time—but I'd never done it until now.

Ship and squadron personnel spent the next day getting ready to fly. Maintainers ran system checks and worked off "gripes," those problems reported by the guys in the cockpits. Ordies staged and loaded weapons for OSW. Aircrews planned flights. We weren't going to war, but we would be logging flights in green ink, the code for combat flights.

I visited workcenters and chatted with sailors. Checkmate maintenance was making progress, and at times during the previous few weeks we had ten up Tomcats, an impressive accomplishment considering our fly-aboard. But once we reached the Persian Gulf, we were averaging only eight up Tomcats. We needed more, so the pressure was on our maintenance people.

I couldn't get rid of the premonition that shots would be fired on the first day. I knew it was unlikely, but I recalled how Iraqi fighter jets kept playing a deadly game of "Chicken." They would sneak into the southern no-fly zone, then bug out when coalition fighters approached. The AIM-120 AMRAAM carried by F-15s and F-16s, as well as the F/A-18s on the *Nimitz*, was a very capable missile, but the F-14's Phoenix had longer range in general. I thought we might catch them by surprise.

Twist and I joined pilots and NFOs from eleven aircraft for the first OSW event briefing. It was midnight, but there was plenty of energy in the room. This is what we'd trained for. Many had literally been here before—flying in OSW during *Nimitz'* previous deployment—or had even been in combat in Desert Storm. 9/11 and its military aftermath were in the unimaginable future, but Desert Storm veterans were everywhere.

The flight lead covered a lot of information—mission flow and timing, callsigns and roles, communications, refueling, rules of engagement, and other high-level specifics. My mission was counter-air, but I paid attention to the whole brief to get the big picture. At 3 AM we would launch from the central Persian Gulf, fly northwest, contact AWACS as we approached Kuwait, and proceed to our assigned station over southern Iraq. Coordination would be crucial, but the detailed plan seemed solid.

The brief ended, and each element went to their own ready room to fine-tune their role. VF-211 would launch two Tomcats, with Twist and I as wingman in one of them. The three F/A-18 Hornet squadrons and VF-211 took turns flying SFAM and counter-air, and this time it was the Hornets' turn at SFAM.

As I listened to the briefings, jotting notes and studying my kneeboard cards, I heard an intimidating array of new terms, controlling agencies, and procedures. I hung in there and after a few flights I was comfortable with this level of complexity.

Then it was time for the familiar ritual of getting into flight gear, with one notable addition. We'd be flying over hostile territory, so everyone carried a sidearm. The Navy had upgraded to 9mm automatics, and we'd been trained on a shooting range. I stowed my pistol in my flight gear, walked to the outside catwalk, and then up the short ladder to the flight deck.

It was 2:20 AM, but clock time was irrelevant as I navigated the familiar hazards under the yellow floodlights. Think back to an earlier chapter and you will be where my brain was—the uncanny quiet, the smell of the steam, the enthusiastic greeting from the plane captain, then pre-flighting the jet by flashlight, climbing the ladder, and strapping in. Then the Air Boss booming over the 1MC, "On the flight deck, aircrews are manning for the oh-three-hundred launch…."

Every aircraft system had to work to launch on an OSW flight, so I was relieved as our jet started up and everything checked good. Planes began launching, afterburners adding light and sound to the spectacle of night carrier ops.

Our turn. Twist and I were flung into the sky. We climbed, joined our flight lead, and headed northwest while I worked through several check-ins and frequency changes. As we flew toward Kuwait, the nearly full moon was so bright that I could shoot a few photos of our flight lead.

My growing comfort evaporated when my radar suddenly failed. I should have reported that our aircraft was down, but it was too late after launch because the spare F-14 would have already shut down. Besides, I didn't want the enormous negative publicity that would come with an aircraft failure on our first OSW mission. So Twist and I agreed to keep this to ourselves while I did what I could to troubleshoot.

The AWG-9 was designed in the 1960s, hardly the golden age of user-friendliness. I had to enter a series of numbers that queried the computer, then use my 1986-vintage pocket guide to decipher the octal code, then click the power off and back on. On click two, our radar woke up and we were back in business.

The moon settled below the horizon and we continued the mission in darkness, flying 23,000 feet above Iraq, on station within an assigned box. I was keyed up, and it was no problem managing my radar and scanning my cockpit. On schedule, we flew south to refuel from a KC-10. A pair of Hornets, the other part of the counter-air element, took over as primary lookouts. We tanked and returned to station for a few more orbits before it was time to RTB.

We headed southeast over Kuwait, checked out with the agencies we had checked in with, and finished with the holding, approach, and arrested landing—all familiar but no less demanding. 2.5 hours went into my logbook, the first green ink (combat flight) of my career.

Climbing down from the jet around sunrise, Twist observed, "Well, Skipper, your first OSW mission is complete. No excitement, but it went well." I decided my premonition about a shot being fired was wrong.

It wasn't. The ready room was full of flyers and excitement, with Sully the SDO in the middle of the hubbub, looking half sheepish and half amused. Yank shouted everyone down. "Let me tell it! Skipper, Sully fired a bullet from a gun! When Norton got out of the spare, he handed his gun to Sully. Sully removed the magazine and was going to put it in the safe and Norton asked if he was going to clear the chamber. Sully insisted it was clear. Norton reminded him we were supposed to visually inspect the chamber. Sully said, 'I'm a red-blooded American male. I have an innate knowledge of firearms. It's clear.' He pointed the gun at the deck and squeezed the trigger—and fired a round!"

Sully had made a mistake, but there was no real damage. The bullet had holed the plywood platform that raised the duty desk, but it hadn't penetrated the steel deck below. No one else knew about the incident, but I said I would have to tell CAG later. When I did, all he said was, "Skipper, you've got bigger things to worry about."

Sully, however, did not get off that easy. He was awarded a new callsign: SYFI. It didn't stand for science fiction. It stood for "Sully You F***ing Idiot!"

During the first few weeks of OSW, several Air Force A-10 pilots visited the *Nimitz*. They were part of the USAF presence that remained after the Gulf War, based at airfields in friendly countries, and one of their missions would be to escort the rescue helicopters if any aviators ended up on the ground in Iraq. They spoke to the squadrons that flew over Iraq—Hornets, Prowlers, and us. Their confidence was impressive. If anyone needed to be rescued, these were the can-do guys.

About half of my OSW flights were SFAM, with realistic targets—bridges, fuel storage areas, power-plants, headquarters buildings in cities. We would attack with LGBs that home in on the laser spot from our LANTIRN pod, so we'd have to identify the target and direct the pod to track it. Lat/long coordinates helped, but it was important to verify the target, so we trained to find it with video from the pod.

Lieutenant Denis "Itchy" Tri showed me how. He was a first-tour RIO and a tactical expert, and he knew a great way to do it. Pointing to a TARPS photo of a city, he said, "Skipper, this building is your target. Notice it's two blocks north of this major road, which runs east-west."

I'm making this up, so don't look at a street map of Iraqi cities to find this target.

"That main street has a traffic circle here," he continued, "and a half-mile to the west it crosses this river at this bridge. You guys will be approaching from the southeast, so this is the second bridge you'll see. That's how you find the target: second bridge, go east past the traffic circle, and two blocks north."

It was an orderly way to use the information and tools available, and it worked like a charm.

On October 23 I was notified that I would plan and lead an SFAM mission. This would be my fourth OSW

flight, so I was comfortable with how they worked. It would be my seventh flight as a strike leader under instruction. The series stretched back seven months to the Fallon det.

I was notified around noon on the 23rd, with a target time the next afternoon. The package would be two Tomcats and two Hornets as bombers, with a Prowler escorting us and two other Hornets as counter-air.

Strike planning was usually done by a team, and I got a lot of help from Lieutenant Jeff "Spotan" D'Alatri, Lex, and a Hornet pilot, as well as Mach, who would be my pilot for this one. It took us four hours to develop the plan—route of flight, timing, comms, etc.—and make the kneeboard cards.

The morning of the 24th I put the key info on the ready room whiteboard. Aircrews arrived, and after the brief we split up into elements, so Mach and I could brief the interdiction aircraft in more detail. A quick snack, then into our gear, then out into the 100°F heat that was typical of a flight deck in the Persian Gulf. All deck personnel wore water backpacks to stay hydrated. We were lucky it wasn't summer.

The day was clear and aircraft start was smooth. I was ahead of the jet as I entered a handful of navigation points into the INS and then checked-in all of the event aircraft. After launch, we headed for the tanker.

We flew over Kuwait, crossed into Iraq, and checked in with AWACS. Suddenly a contact popped up on my radar! It was in Iraq at low altitude, heading south, and approaching launch range for a Phoenix. I tried to sound calm as I reported it to AWACS, but they quickly replied that it was a UN flight. Well, it was exciting for a moment. Okay, back to our SFAM mission.

The orange-brown terrain below offered little visual amusement. When we reached the "initial point," I turned on my mission recorder and started searching for the target on LANTIRN. The technique Itchy had shown me worked well, so I locked the LANTIRN on the target and it started calculating release information for the bomb we were simulating. Then Mach said,

"Simulated bombs away" and our element made a hard left turn to exit the area.

Though I'd not had much training with the LANTIRN system, using it was straightforward…as long as no one was actually shooting at me. I battled complacency by reminding myself we were over hostile territory, and by keeping up a good visual scan behind and below our formation. No one there.

We plugged the KC-10 for a safety cushion and returned to the ship. Late lunch, event debrief, review of my mission tape. We took the debriefs seriously. A few days before, Itchy had pointed out that I didn't have a switch in the correct position, which showed up as a symbol on the tape. This time, I was happy to go through the tape and not find any errors. It was a good flight.

One more instruction flight, and I won my designation as an air wing combat strike leader. I didn't get a patch, just a sense of satisfaction.

CHAPTER 27

SNAPSHOTS FROM THE TIP OF THE SPEAR

We'd left Hong Kong on October 2, 1997, and the weeks at sea had stretched into November. Now we were flying OSW missions—five to seven days straight, then two or three no-fly days to catch up on things like maintenance, paperwork, and sleep. The sense of purpose kept everyone working hard, and our up-aircraft record gradually improved.

Sure, there were bumps in the road. But we were going flat-out, so call them speed bumps. In late October, one of my officers handed me a two-page letter detailing his profound concerns with shoddy maintenance and lax aircrew. He felt we were on course for a serious mishap. I didn't agree, but wanted to hear from my lieutenant commanders, so I quickly arranged an informal meeting. They didn't share his dire outlook, either. But I took his concerns seriously and reassured him privately that I would make sure nobody took shortcuts and everybody followed procedures. I did as I promised, and we continued to fly as planned.

On November 4, Iraqi President Saddam Hussein threatened to shoot down a U-2 spy plane that flew regular runs above Iraq in support of UN weapons inspections. Aboard the *Nimitz* we made sure we had a strong counter-air package over Iraq while the U-2 was flying. And, worst case scenario, we ramped up our preparations for a retaliatory strike. We identified priority targets, reviewed strike plans, configured a few super-bomber Tomcats, and loaded 2,000-pound LGBs on Tomcats and Hornets. I went around to every workcenter and told them, "I need your best effort" for the next few days, and the response was positive.

The U-2 flew unchallenged, and we returned to normal ops.

A ray of sunshine cheered us all when Mach, our maintenance officer, told me we had ten "up" Tomcats. One of them was the hard-landing patient examined with the colonoscope—two months ago and finally flying again. Ten was our goal to support OSW, so I proudly forwarded Mach's report to CAG Vaughn. "Squadron is doing a tremendous job," he responded. We didn't always stay at ten, but we tried, and successes like this made us feel great.

I didn't fly a lot in November; six OSW flights and four training flights. On OSW missions I would use the LANTIRN pod to get a black-and-white glimpse of life in Iraq. Several of us RIOs noticed something odd down there late at night: groups of cars clustered near bridges and highway cloverleafs. From 23,000 feet we could only guess what was going on—socializing, clandestine romance, black marketing? Despite our peering pods, what happened in Iraq stayed in Iraq.

On a moonless night, I would turn off my cockpit lights on the quiet flight home and look at the countless stars against the black velvet sky. Aviators are never far from amazing scenes.

And squadron commanders were never far from their jobs. One afternoon, after patrolling the hostile skies over Iraq, I stepped inside the ship—and there was Master Chief Mustain blurting out an alarming report. "Skipper, Petty Officer X and Petty Officer Y got into a fight. She was badgering him all day, he told her to stop but she continued, and then he spat on her."

I knew both of them as good workers in one of our most important workcenters. They were in their late 20s, and of equal rank (E-4), but one was an African American female, the other an Islamic male. This could get complicated.

Master Chief Mustain continued. "We've already had XOI (executive officer inquiry) and the XO referred them to Captain's Mast. The Legal Officer has everything set up, so we can start as soon as you are ready."

Sailing ship captains held such hearings at the foot of the mainmast, hence the name. I held mine in the ready room, which we cleared of personnel not directly involved. I stood behind the podium where I had notes on procedures, while everyone else stood along the aisle—in this case, the two accused and their superior.

I listened to both sides and made my decision. Some cases were simple: A sailor misses his watch and admits he overslept, I levy a fair punishment, and we all move on. In this case, both admitted some guilt, but I judged spitting on someone to be the greater offense and it received the greater punishment. Both sailors saw they had crossed the line, accepted the consequences, and we all moved on. The squadron needed them.

By mid-November we'd been at sea more than forty-five days, and no port visit was planned for the next five. You know what that meant: Beer Day! We planned it for November 16.

Alas, the real world intruded. At 4 AM on the 16th my phone rang. A Texas drawl said, "Skipper, this is CAG. I need all COs in Strike Planning at 4:30. This looks like it could be for real."

I hopped out of bed, made myself presentable, and joined the other squadron commanders in the strike planning area. Saddam had again threatened to shoot down a U-2. We knew the drill: review and refine strike plans, load bombs on jets. More officers joined us and we spent the day planning and preparing. We assigned targets and launch times, and that evening in the ready room I chose the crews that would fly the initial strikes.

Did you notice that this incident gets a paragraph and not a chapter? Right. False alarm.

But not wasted time and effort. These fire drills added excitement and reminded us how close we were to going into action. Saddam's threats and *Nimitz'* presence were in the daily papers and the nightly news, so this was a national-interest mission. But we didn't need these trappings to keep our focus on the mission. I saw extremely professional performance every day—careful preparation, disciplined execution, thorough debriefs, the standards not only for Checkmate aircrews, but for the entire air wing.

Still, we were humans and we needed a break. On November 19 we enjoyed our three-day-deferred Beer Day along with a flight deck picnic of cheeseburgers cooked on giant grills. All who wanted beer got two; mine were Foster's. Around this time our first port visit was announced: we would spend a week in Jebel Ali starting the next week.

A few days later I flew an OSW mission that should have been a short one. We were on station only briefly, but as we approached the ship, we were told that the recovery would be delayed by bad weather. Heavy rains and shifting winds made landings impossible, and limited space in the Persian Gulf did not allow the ship to find clear air. Holding was tricky in the thick clouds, and some aircraft were beginning to ice up.

My pilot and I felt comfortable with our decent fuel state. The Tomcat could get the most out of 1,000 pounds of gas, especially compared to the Hornet. After fifteen minutes the first Hornets started asking about tanking and were told it was not available.

Things headed downhill quickly. I broke out my pocket checklist and told my pilot I was reviewing the bingo profile. Every flight brief included information on the nearest divert field, and ours was not far away, about 150 miles. But we were warned that if we landed there we might stay awhile if they lacked equipment to support our jets. It wouldn't be like diverting to NAS North Island, refueling, and making the next recovery.

I told my pilot, "I've got a twenty-dollar bill in my pocket, and the ship is leaving soon for Jebel Ali. We could be stuck at the divert for a week." He was in the same financial situation. That settled it; we would avoid a bingo if possible.

As we orbited in thick clouds, the Air Ops crew on the ship was doing everything they could to keep everyone informed and monitor fuel states. They were well aware of the bingo fuel for each aircraft; it was updated for every launch and written on status boards so controllers could help monitor fuel. If I reported that we reached the number, we would be ordered to the divert field. So I had to think ahead. We'd be holding for some time and I had to have a realistic reduction at each report. So I concocted an alternate fuel plan to report to the controllers.

The Hornet with the lowest fuel state was rescued when the ship diverted an S-3 tanker to him. Two other Hornets quickly admitted they were low too, and got their share of the precious go juice.

Meanwhile, the rest of us held our anxiety inside our cockpits and hoped things would work out. My jet slipped below the published bingo fuel, but the NATOPS said that number included a cushion of 2,000 pounds, so we had that to play with.

Still in a holding pattern, we were fast approaching our no-kidding decision point, a fuel level that would leave us with only a few hundred pounds after a bingo divert. Then—sigh of relief!—the ship started to call us down. We were the second jet to leave holding. We followed the controller's instructions for heading and altitude, proceeding through solid clouds. With my pilot focused 100 percent on pea-soup flying, I kept updating my fuel numbers, and also my navigation to our divert field, just in case.

Instead of the usual zip-lip approach, the LSOs were on the radio. In mounting dismay, we heard the Hornet ahead of us getting a wave-off. This was not looking good.

Then, calm and informative, "One-zero-zero, it looks like we can take you. Ship just found a clearing."

We were flying level at 1,200 feet above the ocean, still in heavy clouds, with our gear and flaps down. Three miles behind the ship, we were told to begin our descent. At two miles we popped out of the clouds to one of the most incredible sights I've ever seen. Isolated storms crowded the area, but the *Nimitz* had broken out into clear air and calm seas, her wet flight deck a silver sheen reflecting the canopy of sky.

We continued our approach as my pilot flew what may be the most solid pass I have ever seen. We'd started on a precision approach, so the ship's radar controller made the next call. "One zero-zero, three-quarter mile, call the ball."

I replied, "One-zero-zero, Tomcat ball, state three point six." That was the fuel I *wished* we had.

"Roger ball, Tomcat, lookin' good," the LSO replied. That was the last call they made. I calmly mentioned our airspeed over the ICS, but my pilot was flying a remarkably smooth pass. He had to; if we'd boltered we would have very few options.

The sharp tug of the arresting cable was an incredible comfort. We'd made it! Our gamble paid off. Suddenly everything was back to normal. Climbing out of the jet, I casually cussed the lousy weather to our PC, and he said it was a nice break from the heat.

Later I saw him again on the hangar deck. "Wow, skipper," he said, "100 took a lot of gas when we fueled it."

"Really?" And that was it.

Two days later, the *Nimitz* pulled into Jebel Ali, an enormous port facility about twenty miles south of Dubai. We'd been instructed on safe conduct ashore, with emphasis on not becoming terrorist targets. No large gatherings, no squadron admins. Only a few years after the Gulf War, we were still learning the new environment. This was not Hong Kong.

On top of that, I had to make a painful announcement. Maintenance personnel would work 12 on/12 off during the port visit. We still had too much work to do. Even so, everyone seemed happy just to pull into port.

We'd sent several officers ashore the day before the ship arrived, and they got a message to the ready room that they had found a nice hotel and everyone should stop by for lunch. I was going to Dubai to get away for a few days, so I stopped by.

It was great to see a lot of Checkmate officers in civilian clothes, enjoying the royal food-and-drink service by the pool. Hey, there was Coconut, rejoining us for the deployment.

A couple of JOs told me they had scored a suite here, because the hotel had just opened and was underbooked. So they set up an admin, and while they were fooling around in it the night before, they broke a painting and a lamp. They had already paid the manager, who said the hotel was happy to have them and not concerned about the minor damage.

I heard the words, but what I really heard was "admin," which was prohibited by the rules. Despite the assurances that all was well, I flamesprayed them. I thought about our many hours and months of hard work to improve VF-211's standing in the air wing, and imagined it thrown away. I just couldn't help it, I went off. After a few minutes of venting, I stopped talking, there were a few moments of silence, and then things got back to normal.

A few nights later I realized that all rules were not enforced. No large gatherings? Four squadrons had all-officer dinners in one restaurant. Later, half of the air wing aviators gathered at a club where they played the global hit "Tubthumping" every hour to the wild approval of the crowd. When I walked in several Hornet pilots saw me and said, "Good, we won't get in trouble because you're here!" So I wasn't the only one who actually listened to the in-port restrictions. Soon I was well outranked, so I didn't worry about it, either.

I wish I could take back the butt-chewing by the pool, and I hope the Checkmates who were there have forgotten it. They didn't hold it against me, and we got together for drinks several times during the port visit. That camaraderie was one of the best parts of being in a squadron.

Later I was wandering the market in Dubai, when I ran into a group of chief petty officers. It was the same with them, the camaraderie, the esprit that holds a unit together. It was good to see them getting out.

On the last day of the port visit, a good percentage of officers spent the afternoon aboard the ship, planning OSW flights for the next day.

When we returned to sea, the carrier USS *George Washington* (CVN-73) had joined us in the Persian Gulf, adding fifty strike fighters to American power in the region.

We were halfway through the deployment.

"Play 'Tubthumping' again!"

CHAPTER 28

TRIUMPHANT RETURN

"We are still operating fourteen aircraft!"

I almost slammed the phone on the table. I had used the satellite link to call the Navy's enlisted detailing office to ask for help with manning. They reminded me of the decision to reduce the number of Tomcats in each squadron from fourteen to ten. To adjust manning to support fewer aircraft, they were transferring our sailors on schedule—but they weren't replacing them. Fourteen Tomcats but people to handle only ten—in a word, we were shorthanded. There's another word for it, but it's unprintable.

The Fighting Checkmate Maintenance Department had been working long hours, and their efforts were paying dividends by the middle of the deployment. On most days in December 1997 we reported ten up jets, finally meeting expectations. In December we flew one-third more sorties than in November—257 compared to 187. But maintaining fourteen Tomcats was an uphill battle.

And the hill was getting steeper. At their maximum, our enlisted ranks were filled to only 90 percent of the Navy's allowance, which was common in those days. Around the time the deployment began, we'd welcomed eight new senior enlisted personnel, but six of them had no F-14 experience. Several key technicians from other squadrons had volunteered to help us out for a few months, but by mid-deployment their time was up and they returned to their squadrons.

I told the enlisted detailer my tale of woe, but the phone call was a waste of time.

So we had to do it by the sweat of our own brows.

It was never easy, but the man-hours became more reasonable. Our maintenance man-hours per flight hour, a standard measure of maintenance effort, steadily fell by almost half, from 67.0 in October to 36.2 in January.

As for flying, VF-211 also flew TARPS reconnaissance missions in addition to SFAM and counter-air. We flew a total of forty-five TARPS missions during OSW, and I bagged three of those. One was in early December, a flight over Iraq to update intel. I flew with Lieutenant Mark "Tank" Tankersley, a first-tour JO who gave up nothing to his counterparts in either talent or enthusiasm.

TARPS cameras shot wide strips of film, and a new data-link sent images back to the ship in near-real time. We were assigned to photograph eleven targets in and around Basra—a rail yard, suspected SAM sites, and other facilities that would be struck if a shooting war started. We plotted them on a detailed navigation chart, then factored in sun angle and special features of each target. We plotted it with the fewest turns possible, like that brainteaser with nine dots you're supposed to connect with the fewest lines. We soon had a plan.

We were aware of the regular OSW package, but we were on our own: one TARPS jet and one F-14 escort. Tank and I carried four missiles plus the pod, but the escort would have the lead against any air-to-air threat, and would watch for SAMs while we focused on getting the photos.

We launched on a clear and sunny afternoon, topped off from a KC-10, and began the mission. We flew at 15,000 feet; the photos would be better, and so was our view of the dense, dusty city below. We kept our speed around 400 knots for better maneuvering.

We lined up according to plan and started taking pictures. Imagine shooting snapshots on a high-speed, high-g roller coaster ride. That was us. Heading southeast, I turned the cameras on as we passed over the first target in level flight, then turned them off. Tank threw the stick hard left to crank into a 60-degree turn, and goosed the throttle to keep our speed up. He rolled us level for forty seconds over the next target. Cameras on...cameras off. Hard turn right for 35 degrees. We talked a lot while our wingman jigged and dodged to stay in position. We also used hand-held GPS units, so we didn't worry about a potential failure of the INS like back in the old days.

All OSW missions demanded skill and discipline, but TARPS was the most dynamic. If you could have fun while looking down gun barrels, this might be a way to do it.

We shot the targets, checked out of Iraqi airspace, and returned to the *Nimitz* to find Tomcats all over the sky. VF-211 had contributed four Tomcats to the OSW package, so those plus our two made a total of six holding overhead, waiting for the next launch to finish so we could recover. New procedures let either F-14s or F/A-18s land first, and the daytime visual pattern required sound judgment and careful lookout. Screw up, and you would be debriefed immediately after landing. Checkmate aircrews stepped up and broke the deck like the seasoned pros they were.

The previous VF-211 deployment, 1995-96, included the Christmas holidays and the Grinch was painted on the tail of one jet to mark the occasion. Everybody got a kick out of it, and this year people wanted to do it again. Well, I wanted something more positive than the Grinch, so I asked for suggestions. Mach sketched Brutus, the tough guy in our logo, dressed as Santa Claus. The sailors who painted our jets portrayed the zany Santa Brutus hybrid on the tail of NG-101, and he looked better than I expected.

We flew an OSW mission on December 25 and I made sure I was scheduled, but not in 101 because I wanted to get a photo of "Santa Brutus" over Iraq on Christmas Day. Later we enjoyed roast turkey for a special Christmas dinner. Being away from home on holidays was one of the harder parts of being in the Navy, but we made the best of it.

The *Nimitz* returned to Jebel Ali on December 27 for a five-day stay, on January 10 for four days, and January 30 for four days. Same old port, but we all appreciated the breaks. And there was an important difference on these visits: Checkmate Maintenance no longer had to work 12-on/12-off in port.

Between port visits we kept up the same pace of OSW support and no-fly days. Several times the air wing flew with Marine Corps, Air Force, and allied aircraft in the "strike of the month." It was like an OSW support mission, but with ten times the aircraft, launched from many different locations. These were large and complex operations where positioning and timing were critical, yet we flew them in radio silence. Radio frequencies were assigned, and as events progressed I would switch to a new frequency, but no one said anything. Dead silence. It was eerie and impressive at the same time.

I saw some other aircraft on radar, and looked them up on my big-picture kneeboard card. "Okay," I told Mach, "those specks at left 10 o'clock should be eight F-16s." A minute later we crossed under them. Sure enough, F-16s. We flew our route in formation, and when the last aircraft in each formation was off target they made a brief transmission.

Different aircraft, different services, even different countries, yet it all ticked away like clockwork. That's how well trained we were. Afterwards we gathered for a thorough debrief. VF-211 was the only squadron with 100 percent target acquisition and video to prove it.

I love the F-14 Tomcat. So did all its pilots, RIOs, and maintainers. So do you, if you're reading this book. But on a carrier at sea in 1998 the F-14 was no sentimental favorite. It was the biggest fighter on the ship, so it took up more space. It was also the oldest, so it needed more maintenance than the newer F/A-18 Hornets, and sometimes more hassle to do it. If you had to spread the wings to fix something, you'd have to clear a space on both sides to spread them. And if you moved it, don't step in those puddles of fuel and hydraulic fluid it left on the deck. For the young, hard-working *Nimitz* crew, our F-14s and our squadron were high maintenance. On the hangar deck, Tomcats were parked together in the aft portion and it was known as Jurassic Park.

By late January, however, the strike planners—many of them Hornet pilots—noticed the tremendous progress we'd made. So they gave us a chance to show off, by scheduling an all-Tomcat OSW package. Well, we still launched a Prowler, Hawkeye, and Viking—but no Hornets. Six VF-211 Tomcats covered the counter-air and interdiction roles. Besides enjoying the sight of all those Tomcats, I was honored by the tribute. (Can someone hand me a tissue? Thanks.)

In early February 1998, President Clinton gave Saddam a "bottom line" to stop hindering weapons inspectors. I don't recall any excitement on the *Nimitz*; we just kept flying as we had been. But one never knew when a shooting war would start.

And one never knew when the risks in aviation would claim another life. The air wing aboard the *George Washington* was flying the same as us, and we often saw them on a tanker, or during turnover of OSW patrols. During routine ops one night, two Hornets from the *George Washington* collided and one of the pilots was killed. It was a costly reminder of the risks inherent in Naval Aviation.

The *Nimitz* left the Persian Gulf on schedule the next day, and headed for home. There was scant discussion of making a port visit on the way. We guessed the decision-makers just wanted us home from deployment within six months.

Once we left the Persian Gulf, the air wing staff collected all Navy pistols and bullets. Then I got a phone call: VF-211 was short one bullet, so would I ask everyone to check the pockets of their flight suits. CAG Vaughn had left in December to retire after a distinguished career, and I guess he forgot to mention our bullet-in-the-ready-room incident. I told the short version of the story, left out the part about SYFI, and said I'd told CAG. There was no amusement on the other end of the line.

We transited the Suez Canal—my first time, so it was pretty interesting—and then sped through the Mediterranean and Atlantic. Checkmate Maintenance worked 24/7 to have all fourteen jets up for the fly-off. In one now-or-never whirlwind of determination, they did it. All fourteen up!

This was going to be great—a roaring flyover at Oceana, fourteen Tomcats strutting ashore in a victory parade to show how far we'd come in those six months.

Well, it almost happened. The ship stopped briefly at Naval Station Mayport, Florida, to pick up dependents for a three-day cruise to Norfolk, and like all other squadrons we were required to leave two jets on the ship for the air show. We solemnly promised to fly two jets back to the ship immediately after our flyover, but no. Leave two Tomcats, the homecoming fly-off would be "only" twelve.

The morning of the fly-off, February 26, was a blur of excitement. We briefed most of the details the night before, and then had a final review and update that morning. Pilots and RIOs were paired up by seniority, but CO and XO almost never flew together so I flew with Gigs, our second-most senior pilot after the XO. *Nimitz* flight deck personnel did a great job starting and launching twelve Tomcats.

Gigs and I were the lead and we orbited near the ship while everyone joined up. We did a majestic fly-by of the ship before climbing and contacting US air traffic controllers. Even in those pre-9/11 days there were detailed procedures for aircraft entering US airspace, and we didn't want to embarrass ourselves today.

The formation loosened up for pilot comfort until we approached Oceana. Gigs was very smooth with stick and throttles the whole time, which let everyone close in for a tight formation. He signaled the others, then swept the wings back as we approached the field.

Looking out at the eleven sleek Tomcats around me, I imagined jumping from one to the next; they were almost that close. But I didn't have the mental bandwidth to daydream further; I was totally occupied with coordination and the happy reunion ahead.

We blazed over the field in a triumphal display of airpower, broke into three divisions, and took turns coming into the break. Minutes later I was wrapped around my beautiful Laura as twenty-three fellow Checkmates dutifully followed their skipper's example with their own loved ones.

Soon we were swept up to our familiar ready room, which the wives had decorated for this moment. They served up custom-brewed beer, regardless of whose yardarm the sun would be over, at only 10 AM. The ready room was jumping, with a full-throttle party for fly-off pilots, RIOs, wives, girlfriends, and any family members brave enough to join that exuberant melee. I finally began to realize that I was home from deployment.

The father of one of our RIOs was there because he'd been an Air Force fighter pilot and wanted to see his son and the squadron. He brought along a family friend. *Hey*, I thought, *I know that guy. He's "Hawk" Smith, a legend around Miramar.* Hawk was a former Topgun skipper who had also commanded VF-213. I introduced myself. Hawk said he had never seen such a spirited fly-in celebration, and he could tell VF-211 was a great squadron.

After all we had been through, Hawk's words meant a lot to me, and talking with him was the perfect end to a challenging deployment.

A few days later, when our two air show jets flew home, several of us met them at the ready room and delivered the beers reserved for them. On March 1, I went to the Norfolk Naval Station to welcome home the USS *Nimitz* and about 280 Fighting Checkmates who had not flown off.

Like every deployment, the homecoming meant more than just a party. It meant we could take a little time to recharge our batteries before the cycle started again.

CHAPTER 29

I STAND RELIEVED

It was a great feeling to be the commanding officer, with the authority to give some time off to a deserving squadron. Soon enough, though, we got back to work on things like post-cruise inspections, transferring aircraft, and of course, flying.

My own flying re-started modestly, with seven flights in March. In April I logged four, along with a vacation to France—with Laura, of course. Then the pace picked up with a squadron det to Key West in May.

Around this time I looked ahead at the calendar and talked with Coconut about the change of command. He didn't know it—nobody did—but I had deliberated, consulted, ruminated, and finally decided to retire after twenty years of service, which would be next year in the summer of 1999. VF-211's next deployment was set for January 2000, nearly two years away.

Putting it all together, we planned the change of command for August 1998, three months away. With thumbs-up from CAG and Fighter Wing ONE, I notified Twist, the Admin officer. If you've ever faced a major milestone, you know the feeling of relief to simply have it scheduled. The change of command ceremony would lift a lot of weight off my shoulders, and selecting a date moved it one step closer to reality.

So now I had three months left as CO of an F-14 squadron. Three very busy months. After the Key West det, we sent a six-plane det for two weeks of ship training for the USS *Kitty Hawk* off the California coast. We launched some AIM-54 test shots one day in June (I really wanted to shoot another Phoenix, but let the JOs have these). We escorted a Tomahawk cruise missile

during a test flight. We did a lot of things. The recent deployment was a memory and we were operating at full speed.

Every flight was a chance for me to practice screening out distractions of not only command but also my uncertain future. I didn't want to be the CO who checked out of his job early, and I didn't want to jeopardize our safety by slacking off on my cockpit duties.

I still enjoyed visiting the workcenters around the squadron and chatting with the sailors I had come to respect. I also enjoyed stopping by the Oceana O-club for a beer with other squadron COs and XOs, many of whom I had known since we were JOs. In a rare flash of philosophizing, I noted that we were now the senior guys in the club.

One afternoon I joined the Checkmate JOs at the O-club to kick off a double bachelor party for two upcoming weddings. Sam Adams was the life of the party, but I ordered a Michelob. Mindful of the new emphasis on not driving under the influence, I drained it and headed home. The JOs were headed for low earth orbit, but they'd hired a bus to take them barhopping. Smart move.

Laura and I were watching TV at home around 10:30 that night when I noticed lights going past our house. We lived on a quiet street with little traffic, and something about the lights got my spider-sense tingling, so I went out on the front porch to investigate—just in time to see the party bus pull up to the house. They'd passed it and made a u-turn, and now fifteen JOs were pouring out.

"Hi, Skipper!"

I had just enough time to yell in to Laura, "It's the squadron!" as they rushed into the house. Gab, one of the big ones, actually picked me up over his shoulders. I just asked him not to drop me.

Like a plague of locusts on a field of sweet corn, they ate and drank everything in the house. But Laura liked these guys as much as I did, so we let them pillage while they told us as much as they could remember about their colorful evening.

There would be a lot to miss once I left squadron life.

The change of command was finally set for Friday, August 14, a few days before my fortieth birthday. I scheduled my last flight for the Monday of that week—August 10. Lieutenant Commander Robert "Lex" Luthy, the Ops O, asked me what I wanted to do on the flight, and I said I wanted a 2v2, which would be some tactics and maneuvering but wouldn't use too many aircraft and crews.

In mid-August the squadron was focused on air-to-ground training. Our aircraft acted like old Tomcats; they got finicky. Gigs, the Maintenance O, had to break the bad news the afternoon of my final flight. "Skipper, we don't have four jets available for your final flight. If you really want a 2v2, we will keep working on it and probably be ready tomorrow or Wednesday. Or you can go flying now. Your jet is available," referring to Nickel 101. Aircrews rarely flew the jet with their name painted on it, but it would be a nice touch for my final flight.

"I'll take it."

The flight was on the schedule so I told Twist, "Let's go."

"What do you want to do, Skipper?" he asked.

"Let's just get airborne, go out to the area and do some acro, and then come back."

"Sounds good to me."

Once more I put on the flight gear, read the aircraft logbook in Maintenance Control, and walked the flight line in the warm afternoon sun. Once more I greeted the plane captain and performed a thorough pre-flight—the jet doesn't care if it's your last flight. Once more I strapped in, lowered that enormous canopy, and started up.

I had dreamed of flying Navy jets since I was 10 years old, and was lucky to have done it for most of the past nineteen years, but I wasn't thinking of any of this. I was focused on my crew duties. You don't want to mess up on your last flight.

Oceana Tower cleared us for takeoff, and in full afterburner we blasted out over the Atlantic for a little joyriding. Call it maneuvering training for Twist. He asked if there was anything special I wanted to do and I said no. We just flew for the sheer joy of flying.

While Twist and I chased clouds, there was a lot going on back at the squadron. JOs were filling buckets and rechargeable fire extinguishers with water for the traditional wetting down after a final flight. For airline flyers, they spray the plane. For us, they douse the flyer.

Someone iced down a few bottles of champagne in a cooler. Our thoughtful SDO called Laura and told her when to come over, and they escorted her to the flight line.

I knew "something" would happen, so in my helmet bag I had a pair of sneakers. Instead of coming down the ladder, I planned to run down the back of the jet and escape. Whether it worked or not, at least I would be game.

Twist taxied us to the VF-211 line and into our parking space, in front of an audience of maybe twenty people. Some held buckets, others hefted extinguishers, and all wore devilish grins.

"Looks like they're ready for you!" Twist chuckled. Ah, but I was ready for them. I had already changed out of my boots and into the sneakers, which is not easy in flight gear in a cockpit. I briefed Twist on my escape plan: As soon as we shut down, I would open the canopy and scamper down the back of the jet. I asked him to set the horizontal stabs to help me get to the ground.

My evasive maneuver failed—hadn't I learned anything in those nineteen years? The crowd scrambled to the rear of the jet and started soaking me as soon as I touched the ground. Someone reached over and pulled the beads to inflate my survival vest, another common send-off. Laura gave me a big kiss, I drank my fill of champagne, and we posed for a priceless group photo. The tennis shoes looked dorky, so they completed the image with the inflated vest and soaked CO. Who could forget a moment like that?

Or like this? I was honored at a superb dinner with the squadron's chief petty officers. A common saying is, "Chiefs are the backbone of the Navy," and this group certainly proved they were the backbone of VF-211. Laura and I were moved by their tribute and enjoyed a memorable evening with the chiefs and their spouses and significant others.

We had a fun evening with the officers and spouses, too, a way of saying farewell to the group with whom I had shared so much. We also had a final all-hands quarters. It was easy to sincerely praise the Checkmates who had worked so hard and done so much. You'll find my remarks in the Appendix.

I scheduled the change of command ceremony for VF-211 at 2:11 PM, but I wonder how many noticed the double entendre. By 2:05 people were glancing at their watches and wondering why we were late.

The ceremony was like most, but for me it was special. My speech went longer than Coconut wanted, but that was my prerogative. I was happy to brag about the Fighting Checkmates and all that they had done. And, of course, Captain Checkmate swooped through in the nick of time to save the day from being too formal.

At the appointed part of the ceremony, I read my orders, Coconut read his orders, and CAG stood up and said the magic words to make Coconut the new CO of VF-211.

My response was, "I stand relieved."

It was now Coconut's squadron, and attention shifted to his speech. I sat down and relaxed, smiled at Laura, and only half listened to the rest of the ceremony. I was just enjoying the feeling, the memories, the prospects ahead for Laura and me.

My Tomcat days were over.

EPILOGUE

A year to go. But go where?

I had told CAG and my detailer about my retirement plans, and said not to sweat getting me a cushy job for my final year of Navy service. Later it occurred to me that the Navy could have assigned me to Diego Garcia or some other remote dot in the ocean.

Fortunately, they didn't. I was assigned to the USS *George Washington*, the carrier that arrived in the Persian Gulf when I was there on the *Nimitz*. Home from its deployment, the *George Washington* now rested in Norfolk, an easy commute for me.

I was the carrier's new Assistant Air Department Officer. An Air Department Officer is the Air Boss I've mentioned in these pages, and his assistant is the Mini Boss. That was me. As the Mini Boss, I got to make that fabled announcement several times: "On the flight deck, aircrews are manning for the 1300 launch…."

A few weeks after I left the Checkmates, Laura and I went to the Fighter Fling, the annual formal on the East Coast. VF-211 was awarded the Mutha Trophy for being the most colorful squadron. It was an accolade most deserved, and we enjoyed hanging out with the winners the whole evening. The Checkmates deployed again in Tomcats in 2000, and in 2004 began the transition to the F/A-18F Super Hornet, which caused a redesignation to VFA-211.

Once my retirement was approved, the ship realized that they needed a Mini Boss who would train in that job and then step up to Air Boss. They brought in a pilot who had just finished commanding an F/A-18 squadron, and I stayed aboard as the "Micro Boss."

I talked to several other commanders on the ship about retirement. I was the only one leaving. My contemporaries remained enthusiastic about serving. One told me, "I love it when we get underway, when we pass the breakwater and cruise into the open ocean." And I could tell he really meant it. That was good for the country, the Navy, and for me. I needn't worry about who would do the job after I left.

With the *George Washington* still in post-deployment mode, the pace was slow. I used my newfound spare time to job search and prep for retirement. I sent out hundreds of resumes and went on several job-search trips, but ended up as a project manager at a small information technology company owned by a former neighbor. The resumes made great reading, but my personal network got me the job.

One slow afternoon, I opened my logbooks and totaled my flight time. To my amusement, I'd logged 2,499.7 flight hours. If I had told Twist, "Let's burn a little more gas," I would have reached 2,500. But who would believe an even number like that? I also finished with 688 traps, 249 of them at night—no further comment.

My twenty years, two months, and twenty-three days in the US Navy were an adventure. They included seven years, three months, and two days at sea—a little more than one third. When I was a 10-year-old dreaming of flying Navy fighters, I had no idea what it would really be like. The experience exceeded anything I could have imagined. When I think back on it all, many adjectives come to mind, and most of them are words you would expect from reading this book. But the unexpected word that keeps popping up is "rewarding."

And if any 10-year-old boy or girl ever asks me for career advice, two words will pop up.

Fly Navy!

APPENDIX

Final Remarks to VF-211 at Quarters, Aug 6, 1998

When a CO leaves a squadron at the end of his (or her) command tour, he has multiple opportunities to address various portions of the squadron: the chief petty officers, the officers, and the audience at the change of command ceremony, which includes family members and interested parties from other squadrons. These remarks were from my last address to the Fighting Checkmates, all ranks, when it was just us. Presented here without modification, with all caps in places to remind myself to emphasize certain things.

(Opening, ad-libbed: I haven't gotten around to the shops as much as I intended lately… Let me give you some perspective. Comparisons between squadrons are always going to happen. How does VF-211 do? We have two CPO-selectees; some air wing and Tomcat squadrons had only one, or none. We also had thirty-one people selected for advancement off the March exam cycle, which is more than any squadron I've heard about. So your hard work is paying off.)

I've been Commanding Officer of the Fighting Checkmates for a year, beginning days before the deployment. That was a great time to become CO.

Can you imagine the thoughts back here in Oceana when we sped past Singapore and headed into the Gulf early? Everyone with red blood in their arteries wanted to be on NIMITZ. Before we arrived, Iraq had been violating the UN-mandated no-fly zone regularly. Making a mockery of the international community's attempt to deal with a problem in a peaceful way. We showed up ready to shoot Phoenix at max range! But the Iraqis quit breaking the rules, so we couldn't shoot.

Then we got ready to launch strikes. Remember when I went around to every shop and said, "I need your best effort for the next week"? I thought we'd be making headlines. You responded impressively. We provided the admiral with TEN TOMCATS ready for combat ops.

And even though we didn't drop bombs or launch anything more than some chaff, IF WE HAD NOT BEEN THERE AND READY, things would be different. We flew practice missions over Iraq, provided real-world defense for U-2s and other friendly assets, and collected TARPS INTEL. But our PRESENCE and FORCE in support of United States policy earned our pay.

I was thinking about this on cruise—why are you in the Navy? When I ask, many of you may say "to get money for college." But there are other ways to do that. You were lured by the promise of adventure, camaraderie, travel, professionalism, or some of the other things associated with the Navy. I think one reason is "to make a difference."

YOU will probably not be THE PERSON who drops the bomb or pulls the trigger to depose our enemy. But you make that possible. You are part of an organization composed of heroes and patriots:

- People who we can rely on to pick up fire hoses and extinguish a small blaze caused by one cruise missile that gets through, after we shot down six others;

- People who can load missiles and bombs in a hurry so Tomcats can return to support a Marine landing force that is achieving a breakthrough;
- People who destroy enemy aircraft on the way into a target, then select air-to-ground and shwack the target;
- People who perform demanding jobs on a daily basis when we are NOT in combat, so we can do these things when we are.

And it's not just combat. I have heard leaders in other countries and other militaries who KNOW that the US Navy is critical to stability. That's important because stability allows the "global economy" to keep working.

Since we returned, we tried to take some post-cruise leave and have some slow time. It wasn't quite as much as I wanted, but that's the way it goes. Since returning from cruise

- We built three Tomcats . . . then transferred them.
- We sent six jets to KITTY HAWK, to help our pilots stay current, and help the HAWK.
- We provided a week's worth of sorties so Topgun could train its class.

- We've shot eight Phoenix and several Sidewinders.
- We have flown over seven hundred flights, an average of twenty-three sorties per week!

Some of this effort helps us stay "ready." Some of it helps others. But this effort is what makes the US Navy important.

(pause)

This Navy is not CNO, MCPON, and some admirals. It doesn't run on regulations and skippers telling people what to do. It runs ONLY on the combined efforts of 300,000 sailors who always do their jobs to the best of their ability. You have shown that you are as good as any who ever served our country. I have been very proud to say I am CO of VF-211. Stay safe, stay focused on your mission, and thank you for a memorable year.

★

Note: The abbreviations and lingo were familiar to my audience, the men and women of VF-211. Most have been explained elsewhere in this book. The CNO (Chief of Naval Operations) and MCPON (Master Chief Petty Officer of the Navy) were senior leaders, officer and enlisted, respectively.

GLOSSARY

Note: These definitions refer to how these terms were used in the author's experience in US Navy aviation operations in the 1980s and 1990s.

1v1: One versus one maneuvering training (dogfighting). A good building block for crews to learn the performance of their aircraft and how to evaluate other aircraft.

A-4 Skyhawk: Developed in the mid-1950s, the A-4 was a simple, versatile aircraft operated by the US Navy, Marine Corps, and more than a half-dozen foreign forces. Used by the Navy's Blue Angels from 1974 to 1986, as well as Topgun and other adversary squadrons. Built by Douglas, later McDonnell Douglas. As of 2020, A-4s are still used by several foreign countries as well as commercial adversary service providers in the United States. The letter A in the designation indicates its mission is attack, which is air-to-ground.

A-6 Intruder: Sophisticated, two-seat air-to-ground attack jet used by US Navy (until 1997) and Marine Corps (until 1993). Built by Grumman.

AAM: All aircrew meeting.

ACM: Air combat maneuvering, a general term for close-in air-to-air combat training with adversary aircraft. Basically, dogfighting. It could involve one friendly fighter against one enemy, known as a one-versus-one or 1v1, or multiple aircraft on each side, such two-versus-three or 2v3. Friendly fighters are always listed before the v.

AFB: Air Force Base.

Afterburner, or burner: Assembly that injects and ignites pure fuel in a metal tube that extends aft of the basic engine. Most fighters have them. Increases thrust by fifty percent or more, but fuel consumption goes up ten times or more. The F-14's afterburners had five stages or zones, so Zone 5 was max burner.

AIM-7 Sparrow: Medium-range air-to-air missile carried by many types of aircraft. Guided by radar, it is twelve feet long, weighs five hundred pounds, and has a maximum range of roughly thirty miles. Largely replaced by the newer and more capable AIM-120 AMRAAM.

AIM-9 Sidewinder: Short- to medium-range air-to-air missile carried by many types of aircraft. Seeks the infrared (heat) of the target's exhaust, it is roughly nine feet long and weighs less than two hundred pounds. Primarily for short range, it can fly more than ten miles under certain conditions. Widely used, with updated versions still in service.

AIM-54 Phoenix: Long-range air-to-air missile, carried only by F-14s. Guided by radar, it was thirteen feet long, weighed 1,000 lbs., and had a maximum range of one hundred miles. No longer in use in the United States.

Air Boss: Unofficial name for the Air Department Officer on an aircraft carrier. Runs the six-hundred-person Air Department and is responsible for operations on the flight deck and in the air around the carrier.

Air-to-air: Weapons and missions that attack other aircraft in flight.

Air-to-ground: Weapons and missions that attack targets on the ground.

Air wing: Collective term for the squadrons on an aircraft carrier. In the 1980s and 1990s these typically included two fighter squadrons (air-to-air), three attack squadrons (air-to-ground), one electronic warfare squadron, one anti-submarine warfare squadron, one airborne early warning squadron, one helicopter squadron, and sometimes a small number of additional aircraft. The total number of aircraft aboard was more than seventy.

Angle of attack: The angle at which an aircraft's wings meet the air stream. Despite the word "attack," the term is not related to weapons, and applies to all aircraft.

AOCS: Aviation Officer Candidate School, formerly a training program for college graduates who wanted to enter Naval Aviation and had not gone through the Reserve Officer Training Corps (ROTC) program. In 2007 AOCS was combined with the Navy's regular Officer Candidate School (OCS).

AOM: All officers meeting. See AAM.

Arresting cable: The multi-strand steel cable on an aircraft carrier that is caught by the aircraft tailhook to bring aircraft to a stop. Diameter varies from one to almost one and a half inches. For decades US carriers had four arresting cables, but newer carriers have only three. Also known as a cross deck pendant.

Attack aircraft: An aircraft with the primary mission of attacking ground targets. Designated by the letter A, such as A-6.

Attitude: An aircraft's orientation. For example, nose-high attitude refers to an aircraft flying with its nose above the horizon.

Auto-dog: Soft ice cream.

AWG-9: The F-14A Tomcat's radar and weapons control system (WCS).

Bag: Aviator slang for the Nomex flight suit.

Bagging traps: Slang for making repeated landings on an aircraft carrier.

Ball: Short name for the optical landing system (OLS) on an aircraft carrier that pilots use as a reference for carrier landings. Also called a meatball.

Bandit: An aircraft identified as enemy. This is a refinement of the general category of bogey, which is an unknown radar contact that may be friend or foe.

Bearing: The direction to an object or target in degrees, with reference to north on the compass. When the direction was measured from own aircraft nose (e.g., "20 degrees left") we used the term "azimuth."

Bingo: Condition when aircraft fuel reaches a level where the aircraft should stop performing its mission, whether training or combat, and return to base or head for aerial refueling.

BN: Bombardier/Navigator, the Naval Flight Officer in an A-6 Intruder.

Bogey: A radar contact. "Bogey" indicates an unknown aircraft and "bandit" indicates an enemy.

Boldface: Steps in emergency procedures that had to be memorized verbatim and performed in the event of a specific emergency. The F-14A NATOPS manual (1995 edition) listed corrective actions for nearly one hundred specific emergencies. Of these, seventeen emergencies with a total of sixty-nine "boldface" steps that had to be committed to memory. The boldface test required verbatim responses, 100 percent correct.

Bolter: When an aircraft has its hook down for a carrier landing, but doesn't catch an arresting cable. Pilots always add full power at touchdown on the carrier deck, so if a bolter occurs the plane is set up to go around.

Bomb: A weapon used against a ground target. May be unpowered and unguided, but guided bombs ("smart bombs") have become more common. Some bombs have a small rocket engine to allow them to be dropped/launched at a distance from the target.

Bouncing: Slang for field carrier landing practice (see FCLP).

Bow: The front of a ship.

Break: A maximum-performance turn in response to

a threatening aircraft or missile. Also used to help tactical aircraft return to an airfield or carrier faster, as they would fly back at high speed and then perform a break turn overhead, slowing quickly to landing speed. Due to aerodynamics (induced drag associated with lift), a break turn caused the aircraft to rapidly lose speed.

Brief/debrief: The brief is a session where the upcoming flight is described. The debrief is held after the flight to discuss the mission, crew performance, and other topics.

Bulkhead: Navy term for a wall on a ship, or a major partition inside an aircraft.

C-2 Greyhound: Cargo aircraft that can land and take off from aircraft carriers. Built by what is now Northrop Grumman, in service since 1966. The letter C in the designation indicates its mission is cargo. As of 2020, the C-2 is being phased out and replaced by a cargo version of the V-22 Osprey.

CAG: Informal term for the commander of the air wing, a Navy captain (O-6). Originated when the air wing was known as the air group; hence the acronym for "commander, air group." When the air group was changed to the air wing (1963), the CAG term did not change.

Callsign: An aviator's nom de guerre, used because aviators didn't want to use real names on the radio, and because there could be multiple people with the same name. In practice, callsigns basically replaced given names.

Canopy: The clear bubble above an aircraft cockpit, usually a strong plastic on modern tactical aircraft.

CAP: Combat air patrol, a mission in which a fighter crew patrols assigned airspace using radar, visual lookout, or other sensors. In the author's experience, fighters were sometimes assigned "CAP" missions when a carrier operated in the open ocean, even though there was no combat. These flights often became simple training flights involving fighter(s) on other CAP stations.

Catapult, or cat: The device that launches aircraft from carriers, capable of accelerating a 60,000-pound-plus fighter from zero to 150 mph in about two seconds (in concert with the fighter's engines). US carriers have four catapults. For decades, US carriers used steam catapults, but starting with USS Gerald R. Ford (CVN-78) an electromagnetic catapult has been deployed.

CH-46 Sea Knight: A versatile twin-engine helicopter that was used by the US Navy and Marine Corps starting in 1964. Built by what was then Boeing Vertol. Retired from Navy service in 2004 and the Marine Corps in 2015.

Checklist: A standard list of procedures for various critical phases of a flight. In 1995, the F-14A takeoff checklist had eighteen steps, and the landing checklist had ten.

Chock: Object that can be placed above and/or behind a parked aircraft's tires to keep them from rolling. Made of wood, hard rubber, plastic, or metal.

Clearance Delivery: The air traffic control agency that coordinates an aircraft flight plan with other agencies for the safe and orderly start of a flight.

Closing speed: The combined speed of two aircraft approaching each other. If one aircraft is going 200 knots and another is flying toward it at 400 knots, their closing speed is 600 knots.

CO: Commanding officer. The senior officer of a squadron, could be either a pilot or NFO. Has a callsign from earlier days, but when not flying was called CO or Skipper by those in the squadron.

Cockpit: The area in an aircraft where the pilot sits, along with flight crew in multi-crew aircraft.

Comm: Communications.

Control surfaces: Collective term for the stabilizers, rudders, and other movable devices on an aircraft that control its flight and cause it to maneuver.

Control wipeout: Moving the control stick or yoke to its limits, front and rear and side to side, to ensure the control surfaces move correctly and freely.

CQ: Carrier qualification, the rigorous process of training and certifying aviators for landing on aircraft carriers. Often shortened to carqual.

Cross country: Slang for a training flight to an airfield that is outside the normal operating area.

Cruise: Sometimes a euphemism for a deployment.

DDD: Detail data display, a four-inch scope at F-14 RIO's eye level that displayed raw radar. Unlike the radar stereotypes in in movies, it showed black blips on a green background.

Debrief: See brief.

Departure Control: Air traffic control agency responsible for aircraft that leave the immediate area of the airfield (where the tower is responsible) and before they switch to the en route air traffic control system.

Deployment: An extended period of real-world operations away from home station during which aircraft carriers demonstrate US national interests and exercise with friendly nations, or engage in combat operations. Navy deployments in the 1970s and early 1980s were seven and a half months. In the mid-1980s, typical deployments were shortened to six months. This lasted until early in the twenty-first century, when the demands of combat in several locations increased deployment length.

Detachment, or det: When a unit or part of a unit leaves home station for a short period of time, typically one week to one month but sometimes longer. A det can refer to the entire operation itself or the portion of the unit that performs it.

Division: Navy term for four aircraft operating together; also known as a four-ship. Also an organizational level within the Maintenance department referring to people performing similar tasks, such as the Av/Weps division consisting of the Avionics branch and Weapons branch.

Dogfight: Slang for aggressive close-in maneuvering by opposing aircraft. See ACM.

Drag, thrust, gravity, and lift: The four forces affecting an aircraft in flight. Thrust comes from the engine (jet, propeller, rocket). Drag is the opposite of thrust; it is the resistance of the air against an object pushing through it. Lift is generated by airflow over the wings and any other airfoil surfaces. Gravity, familiar to all humans, is the opposite of lift.

E-2 Hawkeye: An important command-and-control and airborne radar aircraft with a distinctive circular radar dome (radome) above the fuselage. Crew of five, consisting of two pilots in the cockpit and three NFOs in the fuselage. Built by what is now Northrop Grumman. As of 2020, the E-2 is in service with the US Navy and several foreign forces.

EA-6B Prowler: Electronic warfare and attack jet based on the A-6 Intruder, with a crew of one pilot and three NFOs. Built by what is now Northrop Grumman, retired from the US Navy in 2015, from the US Marine Corps in 2018. Replaced by the EA-18 Growler variant of the F/A-18 Super Hornet.

Ejection seat: A seat that can rapidly carry aircrews out of an aircraft in case of an emergency, usually rocket powered and equipped with a parachute. Has evolved into a very complex and capable system.

Engagement: General term for one or more aircraft attacking other aircraft. Similar to a dogfight.

Enlisted personnel: The largest component of a military force, who comprise the ranks performing warfare-specialized or technical tasks. Enlisted personnel may have college degrees, but a degree is generally not required.

EP-3: Sophisticated electronic reconnaissance aircraft derived from the P-3 Orion anti-submarine and maritime surveillance aircraft. Normal crew of twenty or more, with a large variety of sensors, and no weapons. Land-based, not aircraft carrier-capable. Built by Lockheed. As of 2020, operational in the US Navy and Japan Maritime Self Defense Force.

F-4 Phantom II: A versatile jet fighter used by the US Navy, Marine Corps, and Air Force as well as eleven foreign forces. Entered service in 1960. Performed many roles, including counter-air, strike, reconnaissance, and more. Retired from US service, but as of 2020 is still in use overseas. Built by McDonnell Douglas, and McDonnell had a tradition of giving occult names to fighters.

F-5 Tiger II: Developed by Northrop in the 1960s as a lightweight strike fighter for US allies. The F-5E and F-5F (single-seat and two-seat versions, respectively) were developed in the 1970s and had significant improvements over earlier models. Used as adversaries by the US Navy, Marine Corps, and Air Force. As of 2020, still used as operational fighters overseas, and by the Navy and Marine Corps as adversary aircraft.

F-14 Tomcat: A large, sophisticated, maneuverable fighter developed in the late 1960s that served in U.S. Navy fighter squadrons from 1974 through 2006. Manufactured by Grumman Aerospace, which had a tradition of naming fighters after cats. Missions included MiG sweep, escorting attack aircraft, interceptor, reconnaissance, and (later), attack. Had greater maneuverability and better cockpit visibility than its predecessors. Also had one of the longest-range weapons systems ever deployed on a fighter. As of 2020, F-14s are in service with Iran, the only other country to operate them.

Variants: The F-14A was the original production version, with TF30 engines and the AWG-9 radar. The F-14B was equipped with more powerful F110 engines, and was originally known as the F-14A+. The F-14D had the more powerful F110 engines and a new radar, the APG-71.

F/A-18 Hornet: Versatile strike fighter developed in the 1970s to replace the A-7 and F-4. The design applied advances in aerodynamics, materials, electronics, and powerplants to create a highly maneuverable and effective aircraft. As of 2020, the original Hornet has been retired from US Navy service and the larger Super Hornet is the Navy's front-line strike fighter. Versions used by the US Navy and Marine Corps and at least seven foreign forces. Flown by the US Navy's famous Blue Angels flight demonstration team.

FACIT: Informal term for a flight with no scheduled training objectives. Acronym for f**k around and call it training.

FAST: Fleet Air Superiority Training, a one-week program run by the Navy Fighter Weapons School to give F-14 and E-2 Hawkeye aircrews specialized training in defending an aircraft carrier from a raid by bombers, cruise missiles, and/or jammers. FAST consisted of Topgun-level lectures and complex scenarios in simulators. Has been discontinued.

FCLP: Field carrier landing practice, which is training at an airfield to land on an aircraft carrier.

Fight's on: The radio call to begin a training intercept or dogfight.

Fighter aircraft: An aircraft with the primary mission of attacking and destroying other aircraft in the air. Designated by the letter F, such as F-14.

Flight hours: Normally the length of time from takeoff to landing or engine shut-down, recorded in hours and tenths. Used for aircrew logbooks as well as scheduling aircraft maintenance.

Flight suit: An aviator's coverall, usually made of flame-resistant Nomex fabric.

Flightline: The area of an airfield between hangars and runways, where aircraft are parked. Also called the ramp.

Formation: A well-defined group of two or more aircraft. Each type of aircraft has reference points that pilots watch to stay exactly in position and to keep the formation consistent. In tactical formations, the aircraft fly much farther apart.

Foul deck: Temporary condition of an aircraft carrier landing area when it is not ready for an aircraft to land. The most common cause is that an aircraft that just landed is still taxiing out of the landing area, but can also be caused by personnel or vehicles.

Fuel ladder: A simple diagram that showed time and fuel state, to help aircrews manage fuel according to expected aircraft carrier recovery time. See the Intel Brief on this.

Furball: Aviator slang for a dogfight where friendly fighters are engaged with enemy aircraft.

Fuselage: The body of an aircraft.

G: The force of gravity, used in flying to indicate the increased forces on an aircraft and crew in a turn or pull-up. A plane (or any vehicle) traveling straight and level at a constant speed experiences 1 g, Earth's gravity. Making a tight turn at high speed can increase the force to 6 g or more, making everything feel like it weighs six times as much: your head, your helmet, your arm.

Gas and go: Slang for a short refueling stop, usually on a cross-country flight en route to the destination.

GPS: The Global Positioning System, an extremely accurate means of determining an object's position using specialized equipment that processes signals from satellites.

Gravity: See Drag.

Ground Control: The controlling agency that directs traffic on the flightline at an airfield, taxiing to or from the runway.

G-suit: An inflatable garment worn tight around the lower abdomen and legs that automatically inflates to squeeze the lower portion of the body when the aircraft is pulling g's. This reduces pooling of blood, keeping more of it in the upper body and supplying blood to the brain. It really works.

Helo Dunker: A training device carrying several people that descends into a pool, to provide training in underwater egress from a helicopter after a crash.

Helo: Slang for a helicopter.

Hold short: A location near a runway where aircraft pause while waiting for clearance onto the runway. Can also be a command, telling an aircraft to go to the location and wait.

Hop: Slang for a flight.

Horizontal stabilizer: The small wing-like objects that extend from the tail area of an aircraft.

ICS: Intercom system, which allowed the F-14 pilot and RIO to communicate via the microphones built in to their oxygen masks and headphone speakers in their helmets. Virtually all multi-person aircraft have ICS.

INS: Inertial navigation system, which determines aircraft location based on precise measurements of gyroscopes within the aircraft. Could provide accurate position information, but the INS used in the F-14A could fail without notice.

Intercept: A series of maneuvers by a fighter that brings it into position to identify, escort, or destroy another aircraft.

John Wayne: To do something the hard way or continue doing a task when an automatic system isn't available.

KC-10: An aerial refueling tanker operated by the US Air Force, developed by McDonnell Douglas from their DC-10 airliner. Could also carry cargo and passengers. Its maximum fuel load of more than 350,000 pounds was significantly greater than that of the KC-135. In service as of 2020.

KC-135: An aerial refueling tanker operated by the US Air Force. Built by Boeing, developed in conjunction with the 707 airliner. Like the KC-10, could also carry cargo and passengers. In service since 1956, it remains in service in 2020.

Kneeboard: Rigid metal or plastic plate that is strapped to an aircrew's leg to hold cards and allow writing during the flight.

Knock it off: Standard radio call to end an engagement.

Knots: Nautical miles per hour, a measure of speed. A nautical mile is 6,076 feet, which is about one-sixth longer than a statute mile, so speed in knots is roughly 1 1/6 times faster than the miles per hour most people are used to. Here are some common speeds converted to mph:

150 knots = 172 mph
300 knots = 345 mph
450 knots = 520 mph
600 knots = 690 mph
1,000 knots = 1,150 mph

Landing gear: The struts, wheels, tires, brakes, and associated parts that support the weight of an aircraft on the ground. Carrier-capable aircraft must have stout landing gear to withstand repeated carrier landings.

Lead or flight lead: The pilot who is in control of a group of aircraft. In a tactical situation, the lead can change quickly.

Leave: Military term for vacation.

Lift: See Drag.

LSO: Landing Signal Officer, a specially trained pilot who monitors carrier landings for safety and operating efficiency.

Mach: Ratio of aircraft speed to the speed of sound. Pronounced "mock." An aircraft going Mach 1 is flying at the speed of sound; Mach 2 is twice the speed of sound. The speed of sound varies based on temperature, altitude, and other conditions, but is approximately 660 knots or 770 mph at sea level.

Max conserve: Throttle setting that gave the longest flying time, without consideration for speed or distance. In the F-14A this resulted in an airspeed of 225 knots. Commonly used for peacetime patrol missions, when the aircrew might conserve fuel to use for ACM at the end of the flight.

Max trap: The maximum weight at which a carrier-capable aircraft can perform an arrested landing (trap). It is based on the aircraft's structure as well as the arresting gear's mechanical ability. See the Intel Brief on Fuel Ladder.

Meatball: See Ball

Merge: Merge plot, the condition when two or more radar targets are very close to each other, when their radar blips have merged on the display. If a controller calls "merge plot" and the fighter does not have sight of the other aircraft, the fighter is likely in a defensive situation.

MiG: Acronym for Mikoyan-Gurevich, a leading builder of fighter aircraft in the Soviet Union and Russia, named after the two founding designers.

Military power: The maximum power level of a jet engine without engaging afterburner.

Missile: General term for a flying object that has a guidance system and a powerplant—often a rocket engine. Missiles are made for air-to-air, air-to-ground, surface-to-air, and other applications.

MISSILEX: Missile exercise. Launching missile(s) at targets for training.

NAS: Naval air station.

NATOPS: Naval Air Training and Operating Procedures. A system of manuals and procedures that greatly increased Naval Aviation safety.

NFO: Naval Flight Officer, a US Navy or Marine Corps aircrew member who is not a pilot. NFOs are referred to by different terms for different aircraft, such as the F-14's Radar Intercept Officer (RIO) and A-6's Bombardier/Navigator (BN). Most Navy aircraft do not have duplicate flight controls for NFOs. NFOs wear gold wings on their uniform similar to pilot wings, except pilot wings have one anchor in the middle, and NFO wings have two crossed anchors.

Nomex: A flame-resistant material used to make flight suits and other articles of clothing. A trademarked name. Flight suits are not flameproof or heatproof, but provide some protection in the event of a flash fire.

Officers club (or O-club): A structure on a military base for use by commissioned officers that includes a restaurant, bar, and often recreational facilities such as a swimming pool. Some Navy bases and air stations also have enlisted clubs and chiefs clubs (for chief petty officers); others have all-ranks clubs.

PC: Plane captain, usually an enlisted person who is responsible for an aircraft. In the US Navy, PCs are usually fairly new to a squadron, but they have broad responsibilities for routine inspection and servicing of aircraft, and preparing them for flight.

Phonetic alphabet: The use of a word to represent each letter to ensure clarity of communication over a radio. The US military phonetic alphabet is: Alfa, Bravo, Charlie, Delta, Echo, Foxtrot, Golf, Hotel,

India, Juliett, Kilo, Lima, Mike, November, Oscar, Papa, Quebec, Romeo, Sierra, Tango, Uniform, Victor, Whiskey, X-Ray, Yankee, Zulu. The pronunciation of numbers is similar to common pronunciation except for "Niner."

Plane captain: see PC.

POW: Prisoner of war.

Preflight/postflight: Preflight is an orderly inspection of an aircraft to ensure that important systems are ready for flight. The official preflight inspection of an F-14A Tomcat with no weapons had more than one hundred items. Postflight is a walk-around inspection after completion of a flight.

Qual: Short for qualification or qualified, depending on context.

Radar lock: The condition of a radar system when it is automatically tracking a target. Usually involves the antenna pointing at the target and adjusting itself to continue pointing. This results in the most accurate information, but the radar cannot see other targets when it is locked. The F-14's AWG-9 and modern radars can also provide accurate information about multiple targets without being locked onto only one, sometimes known as track-while-scan.

RAG: Slang for squadrons that trained aviators in specific types of aircraft. It came from replacement air group, a term that was officially replaced in 1963 by fleet replacement squadron, but the RAG nickname stuck. There are RAGs for the F/A-18, E-2, and other types—at least one RAG for every major type of aircraft the Navy flies. The F-14 had two RAGs: VF-124 at NAS Miramar and VF-101 at NAS Oceana.

Ready room: The room on an aircraft carrier or in a hangar on an air base from which a squadron manages its operations. The SDO sits in the ready room. The hub of a squadron.

RIO: Radar intercept officer, a category of Naval Flight Officer who was the second crewman in the F-14 Tomcat. Almost always spoken as "rio," as in Rio Grande. For crew coordination purposes, RIOs were primarily responsible for communication and navigation, as well as operating the F-14 radar. RIOs in the F-14 did not have flight controls (throttles, control stick, and rudder pedals). In most current fighters, the second crewman is called a weapon systems officer (WSO).

Roger: Radio or ICS reply indicating that a statement is received and understood. Does not necessarily mean that you will follow an instruction; that is "wilco," for will comply.

ROTC: Reserve Officer Training Corps.

RTB: Return to base.

Runway: The long, level surface at an airfield used for takeoffs and landings. Usually made of concrete.

S-3 Viking: Carrier-based anti-submarine and maritime surveillance aircraft, with a crew of four. Also used as an aerial refueling tanker. Built by Lockheed. Retired from fleet service in 2009.

SA: Situational awareness, a broad term encompassing aircrew knowledge of many factors, from minimum essentials such as their own fuel state and weapons load, to more complex subjects such as the requirements of their mission and the number and location of threatening enemy aircraft.

SDO: Squadron duty officer, the junior officer responsible for making the squadron operate effectively and safely during his watch. In a Navy fighter squadron, the SDO was usually a lieutenant or lieutenant (junior grade) who was assigned for twenty-four hours and sat behind the duty desk in the ready room while aircraft were flying.

Section: Navy term for two aircraft operating together.

SERE: Survival, evasion, resistance, and escape; a training course.

Simulator, or sim: A ground-based training device that may be a simple cockpit or a complete, accurate replication of an aircraft.

Skipper: Common term for the commanding officer of a squadron. Though it may sound casual, it is a term of respect.

Soviet Union: A political entity, a federation of fifteen republics that spanned Europe and Asia. Dissolved in 1991.

Speed brakes: Movable panels that are normally recessed, but can be extended to increase drag and thus slow an aircraft.

Squadron: An organization that operates aircraft. In the Navy, a squadron included maintenance and administrative personnel in addition to aircrews. Squadron size varied by type: in the 1980s, F-14 squadrons had twelve aircraft, S-3 squadrons had ten aircraft, and E-2 squadrons had four to six aircraft. F-14 squadrons were briefly equipped with fourteen aircraft, then reduced to ten. In my experience we never called it a squad.

Stall: Condition that occurs when a wing increases its angle too much, the air no longer flows smoothly over it, and the wing loses lift. Can be dangerous if it occurs near the ground or if the pilot does not apply the proper controls in response to the stall.

State: Fuel state, the amount of fuel aboard an aircraft, often given in thousands and hundreds of pounds. For example, "state eight point six" indicates 8,600 pounds of fuel. Can also be reported as "state tiger," which indicates enough fuel and weapons to perform a mission.

Strike fighter: An aircraft that performs air-to-air and air-to-ground missions well. In addition to fundamentals such as aircraft and weapon system design, aircrew training and weapons load are important considerations.

Subsonic/supersonic: Subsonic aircraft cannot safely exceed Mach 1, the speed of sound (see Mach). Supersonic aircraft are designed to operate at speeds above Mach 1.

Suitcase: To have an accurate understanding of the situation; to display great SA.

TACAN: Tactical air navigation, a system that uses stations at known ground locations or on ships, and an aircraft-mounted indicator that shows direction and distance to the station.

TACTS: Tactical Aircrew Combat Training System. Also known as ACMI—Air Combat Maneuvering Instrumentation. A system of ground receiving stations, transmitters in aircraft, processors and displays that provides an accurate, high-quality depiction of aircraft. Useful for real-time observation but especially for debriefs.

Tail: The rear of an airplane. An imprecise term that may refer to the vertical stabilizers or horizontal stabilizers.

Tailhook: A strong hook at the end of a steel tube used to catch a cable to bring an aircraft to a rapid stop. On an F-14 the assembly was more than seven feet long. Many military aircraft have arresting hooks for emergency use, but those on Navy carrier-based aircraft were designed, like the airplanes themselves, for the stress of repeated arrested landings.

Tally-ho: Radio transmission indicating the aircrew has sight of an enemy aircraft.

Target drone: An unmanned flying vehicle used for missile exercises. Some are only slightly larger than the air-to-air missiles that intercept them, while others are conversions of full-size aircraft originally flown by aircrews.

TCS: Television camera set, a magnified TV camera, mounted under the F-14's nose, which could be slaved to the radar. Useful for visual identification of targets.

Throttle: The lever in a cockpit that controls engine speed. Mounted on the left instrument panel in most tactical aircraft.

Thrust: See Drag.

TID: Tactical information display, a round display screen, nine inches in diameter, in the F-14's rear cockpit. Symbols showed radar targets and other situation information.

Topgun: Unofficial name for the Navy Fighter Weapons School, which was established in 1969 to provide "post-graduate" training for combat aircrews. Currently located in Fallon, Nevada, under the Naval Aviation Warfighting Development Center.

Touch and go: A brief touchdown on a runway or aircraft carrier, when the aircraft does not intend to stop. Instead of applying the brakes or using the tailhook, the pilot adds power at touchdown and flies away again.

Tour: Time served at a specific squadron, ship, or other assignment. In the Navy, many tours are three years, although they can vary greatly.

Tower: The air traffic control facility that controls flying traffic in the vicinity of an airfield.

Trap: Slang for an arrested landing.

Vertical stabilizer: The fin that extends from the top of the rear fuselage and provides yaw stability (left-and-right) on an aircraft in flight.

VC10: An aerial refueling tanker operated by the UK Royal Air Force. Developed from the VC10 airliner (introduced in 1964), retired from the RAF in 2013. Distinctive for the location of four engines at the rear of the fuselage.

Wave-off: Command for a pilot to abort an approach, add power and climb, when an intended landing should not be made. A wave-off usually indicates an unexpected situation, such as an aircraft or vehicle that was expected to be clear is still in the landing area or on the runway.

Waypoint: A specific location along a route, usually expressed in latitude and longitude but may be described as a visually significant object.

Wilco: Will comply. See Roger.

Windscreen: The fixed forward part of the canopy.

Wingman: The second aircraft in a two-plane formation. Often supports the first aircraft, which is the lead.

XO: Executive officer. The second-ranking officer in a squadron, under the CO, could be either a pilot or an NFO. In Navy squadrons, became the CO when the current CO detached for his next duty or if he was lost. Had a callsign from his earlier days, but was always called XO by those in the squadron.

Zone 5: Maximum afterburner in the F-14A. Minimum afterburner was Zone 1.

ACKNOWLEDGMENTS

You may have gathered that this is my third book, and writing it has actually been the most enjoyable. In a moment I'll tell you why. But first, let me say thank you to the many people who have provided information or other assistance along the way. I've grouped them by squadron and in alphabetical order.

Squadronmates from VF-2: Paul Akerlund, Dave Chandler, Jack and Tish Fields, Bob Ingham, Rick Jordan, Brian Kocher, Tony Moore, Jeff Mullen, Tom Page, Michelle Sherwood Quillin, Jim Russell, Jeff Ruth, Jon Schreiber, Marv Serhan.

VF-211 squadronmates: Brady Bartosh, Doug Carney, Jeff D'Alatri, Robert Luthy, Shawn Oliver, Pat Porter, Dave Schreiner, Mark Singletary, Mark Tankersley.

Others who assisted: Thomas Baranek, William Barto, Ken Camut, David F. Brown, Doug Denneny, Dorian Dogaru, John Greco, Mark Hasara, Steve Jacobsmeyer, Haagen Klaus, Alfredo Maglione, Peter Mersky, the Naval History and Heritage Command, Christian Nentwig, Bill Paisley, Martin and Terri Pring, Zeno Rausa, Jim Ray, Luke Ridenhour, David Root, Tom Twomey, R. Kevin Williams, and Lance Yhost.

There was a time when I wasn't sure I would write this book. Then, through one of those fortunate events that make our lives interesting, I met David Robinson, a former Navy pilot (Douglas JD-1) and retired editor at National Geographic books. I know him as TOD—see the Intel Brief on Callsigns—and quickly realized that he is a person you'd want in your party if you were stranded on a desert island: He has an endless sense of humor that matches his intelligence. These qualities and his way with words make him a great editor and great person to work with. I knew that with his assistance I could create the book I wanted. So, thank you, TOD and your charming wife, Ritsuko, for all you have contributed.

Thanks also to Jay Cassell, my editor at Skyhorse, and the whole team at Skyhorse—you are a pleasure to work with.

Most important, I would like to thank my lovely wife, Laura, for her many contributions and unfailing support.

This assistance is greatly appreciated. Any errors or omissions are solely the responsibility of the author.